In Afghanistan's Shadow

In Afghanistan's Shadow:
Baluch Nationalism and Soviet Temptations
Selig S. Harrison

Carnegie Endowment for International Peace ℤ

New York   Washington, D.C.

Credits

Photographs by David Burnett/Contact (pp. xii, 6, 13, 14, 32-bottom, 70), Abbas/Gamma (pp. 92, 114-top), Paireault/Gamma (p. 152), and the Mall Studios, London (p. 63). Photographs on p. 98 are courtesy of S. Sgt. Fred W. Karnes, USA. Other photographs were obtained or taken by the author. The maps (following p. 84) were prepared by Frank and Clare Ford of the Ford Studios, Arlington, VA.

ISBN 0-87003-029-9; 0-87003-030-2 (paper)

Library of Congress catalog card number: 81-67142

Printed in the United States of America

Contents

Maps follow page 84

Foreword

In November 1977, the Carnegie Endowment selected the Afghanistan-Pakistan-Iran region as one of the danger zones on the international scene that would receive special emphasis in its Program for Journalists. Less than six months later, a Communist coup took place in Kabul, and in December 1979, Russian forces crossed the Oxus River frontier, touching off a new phase of tension in Soviet-American relations that is still continuing.

The Carnegie Journalists Program, established in 1974, attempts to anticipate "near-horizon" problems and trends that could lead to international conflict or to large-scale human suffering. By presenting independent, on-the-spot, factual reporting and analysis of such situations in their early stages, it hopes to focus attention by government and public-opinion leaders in the countries studied, as well as in the United States and the larger international community, while there is still time for ameliorative action. The findings of this program are made available in a variety of ways, ranging from magazine articles, op-ed essays, and books to radio and TV appearances, lectures, and academic seminars.

The Endowment gave the task of monitoring emergent developments in South and Southwest Asia to a widely recognized specialist, Selig S. Harrison, who has covered the area for more than three decades. Writing from Afghanistan in mid-1978, he was one of the first analysts to warn that the civil war then developing between the new Communist regime and Pakistan-based Islamic resistance groups could lead to Soviet military intervention. He sharply underlined the independent, national-communist character of the revolutionary regime in Kabul as a critical factor that could help to provoke such intervention. At the same time, looking further ahead, he emphasized that Moscow might be tempted to use its foothold in Afghanistan to fan the fires of separatism in the politically vulnerable Baluch areas of neighboring Pakistan and Iran. His 1978 *Foreign Policy* article, "After the Afghan Coup: Nightmare in Baluchistan," called attention to the explosive potential of the movement to create an independent Greater Baluchistan that would stretch for some 900 miles along the Arabian Sea up to the Strait of Hormuz.

Against the background of a deepening struggle in Afghanistan and steadily growing American involvement in Pakistan and the Persian Gulf area, Harrison presents in this book a wealth of new findings that amplify and update his earlier warnings concerning the volatility of the Baluch issue. He shows that separatist sentiment has been steadily growing in Baluchistan in recent years, reveals hitherto unpublished information concerning the character of the nationalist and Communist movements in Baluchistan, and introduces us to their leaders through extensive interviews. While it contains introductory historical chapters, the book focuses primarily on the major economic and political conflicts between the Baluch and the Pakistani and Iranian central governments and on possible ways of neutralizing separatism through constitutional adjustments. In the absence of a greater readiness for compromise on the part of Islamabad and Teheran, the book suggests, the likelihood of Soviet manipulation of Baluch nationalism will increase.

Yet Harrison offers surprising evidence indicating that Moscow is ambivalent with respect to the desirability of supporting Baluch independence. On the one hand, he contends that Baluchistan could become the focal point of a superpower confrontation if the Afghan struggle should escalate, since it is the "Baluch card" that Moscow would be most likely to play in retaliation for U.S. assistance to the Afghan resistance or for expanding U.S. military links with Pakistan. On the other, he concludes that "the Soviet approach to the Baluch issue is likely to be influenced to a significant extent by the nature of the evolving American role in Pakistan and Iran. There is still a chance to avert a superpower confrontation over Baluchistan through restraint on both sides; and by the same token, there is a growing danger that pre-emptive moves by one side or the other could set in motion an uncontrollable chain reaction of challenge and response."

This book is part of a larger continuing project in which Harrison is examining the reasons for Soviet involvement in Afghanistan, possible ways in which the situation there might develop, the impact of the Afghan crisis on surrounding countries—notably Pakistan, India, and Iran—and the policy choices confronting these countries as well as the United States, the Soviet Union, and the international community.

In its methodology, this book exemplifies the distinctive character of the Carnegie Journalists Program, which consciously seeks to combine the investigative techniques of the responsible foreign correspondent with the detachment and analytical discipline of academic research work. Thus, Harrison has relied primarily on interviews in order to open up a subject that has received almost no attention in academic, journalistic, or other writings in the West except for a handful of anthropological studies and hastily contrived journalistic accounts assembled after a few days in

Baluchistan. On a series of field trips between 1977 and 1981, he has talked with some 340 primary sources, principally Baluch leaders of all persuasions, many of them underground in Baluchistan itself and others living in exile in Europe and the Persian Gulf; political figures, officials, and scholars in Islamabad, Kabul, Teheran, and Moscow; and participants in the 1973–1977 Baluch insurgency in Pakistan, including Pakistani military officers and Baluch guerrilla leaders now hiding out in base camps in southern Afghanistan. Many of his Baluch sources have cooperated on the understanding that their anonymity would be preserved in order to avoid prosecution on treason charges. However, in most cases, Harrison has named names. He has buttressed his firsthand findings with a review of documentary material and nationalist literature in Baluchi, Urdu, Persian, and English, much of it never before obtained by foreign observers.

Harrison, one of the first Senior Associates to be appointed to the Journalists Program, brings to his work at the Endowment a rich background in scholarly journalism, with a broad stream of articles and books on Asia to his credit. His academic work has included research and teaching assignments at Harvard, Columbia, the Brookings Institution, and the Johns Hopkins School of Advanced International Studies. As a journalist, he has been a foreign correspondent in many Asian posts over a thirty-year period, has served as the *Washington Post* bureau chief in New Delhi and Tokyo, and is a former managing editor of the *New Republic*. Drawing on his background in East Asia, he conducted a pioneering study for the Endowment of the political implications of China's offshore oil development, culminating in his 1977 Endowment book *China, Oil and Asia: Conflict Ahead?* In his present work, he builds on his six years as a resident correspondent in South and Southwest Asia.

As always, Endowment sponsorship of this book implies a belief only in the importance of the subject and the credentials of the author. The views expressed are those of the author. Comments or inquiries on this and other work of the Endowment are welcome and may be addressed to the Carnegie Endowment for International Peace, 11 Dupont Circle, NW, Washington, DC, 20036, or 30 Rockefeller Plaza, New York, New York 10112.

Thomas L. Hughes
President
Carnegie Endowment for International Peace

Acknowledgments

I should like to express my appreciation to the many individuals and governments whose cooperation has made this work possible. Since more than three hundred people were interviewed, most of them on the understanding that their names would not be revealed, it is not possible to single out many of those who have been most helpful. However, I should like to record my gratitude to General Mohammed Zia Ul-Haq, President of Pakistan; Iqbal Butt, former Director-General of External Publicity in Islamabad, and his successor, Khalid Ali; Lt. Gen. Rahimuddin Khan, Governor of Pakistani Baluchistan; Lt. Gen. Arbab Jahanseb, former army commanding general in Pakistani Baluchistan; and Jafar Nadim, former Undersecretary of State in the Iranian Foreign Ministry. Others in high places, now deceased, who were particularly helpful were President Zulfiqar Ali Bhutto of Pakistan, presidents Mohammed Daud and Hafizullah Amin of Afghanistan, and Premier Amir Abbas Hoveida of Iran.

For valuable guidance in the difficult early stages of my research I would like to thank Maj. Gen. M. G. Jilani (ret.) of the Pakistan Army, Lawrence Lifschultz of the *Far Eastern Economic Review*, and K. B. Nizamani, editor of *Nedae Baluchistan*. For their help in anthropological and linguistic studies relating to the Baluch, I remain grateful to Joseph Elfenbein, Richard Frye, Stephen Pastner, Philip Salzman, and Brian Spooner. Yuri Gankovsky of the Institute of Oriental Studies in Moscow gave me a valuable elaboration of his own writings on the Baluch and enabled me to meet with other relevant Soviet specialists.

Among the many Baluch of many persuasions in Pakistan and Iran who have assisted me, a special word of appreciation is due to Ghaus Bux Bizenjo; Akbar Bukti; Aslam Gichki; Sikander Jamali; Mir Ahmed Yar Khan Baluch, the late Khan of Kalat; Mahmud Aziz Kurd; Akber Y. Mustikhan; Khair Bux Marri; Sher Mohammed Marri; Sher Baz Mazari; Ataullah Mengal; and Malik M. Towghi.

Extensive translations from eight languages, made possible by the Carnegie Endowment, have greatly enriched this work. I would like to thank the following for their translations: Iran B. Jewett (Urdu and Persian); Iftikhar Ahmad and Mujahid Iqbal (Urdu); Hamid Sultan

Baloch and Malik M. Towghi (Baluchi); Ali K. El-Amin (Arabic); Ruhul Ameen Yousufzai (Pushtu); George Liber, Jerome Ochs, and Irwin Selnick (Russian); Jeffrey Thickman (German); and Thomas Gora (French).

I am grateful to many colleagues at the Carnegie Endowment for their generous support and continuing encouragement, especially Thomas L. Hughes, President, and Larry L. Fabian, Secretary. I relied heavily on Susan C. Fisher, Manager of Publications, and her predecessor, Diane B. Bendahmane; Richard H. Moss, Staff Editor, who edited the book with care and insight; the research staff of the Endowment library; and Evelyn Morris, Anne Chong, and Margaret Byron, who transcribed and typed the manuscript at various stages of its evolution.

S.S.H.
April 1981

After Afghanistan

1

Visiting Pakistan on a troubleshooting mission for President John F. Kennedy in 1962, Henry Kissinger, then a Harvard professor, impatiently brushed aside a local journalist who asked him to comment on the insurgency then beginning to surface in the restless province of Baluchistan. "I wouldn't recognize the Baluchistan problem," Kissinger snapped, "if it hit me in the face."[1]

Until recently, Baluchistan has been all but unknown to the outside world, an obscure, exotic place of interest primarily to ethnographers and venturesome explorers. Since the Soviet occupation of neighboring Afghanistan, however, it has suddenly been discovered by Western policymakers. Warning of the historic Russian drive for warm-water ports, American officials now point to Baluchistan as one of the most likely future Soviet targets in Southwest Asia. President Jimmy Carter was deliberately vague in his pledge to defend the "Persian Gulf region," but his national security adviser, Zbigniew Brzezinski, specifically underlined the applicability of the "Carter doctrine" to Baluchistan as part of a broader U.S. commitment to Pakistan.[2] Similarly, the Reagan administration has based its policy of expanded military links with Islamabad primarily on the premise that Baluchistan's security is crucial to the security of the adjacent Persian Gulf.

A glance at the map (see Figure 1) quickly explains why strategically located Baluchistan and the five million[3] Baluch* tribesmen who live there could easily become the focal point of superpower conflict. Stretching across a vast expanse of western Pakistan and eastern Iran**—an area slightly larger than France—the Baluch homeland commands more than 900 miles of the Arabian Sea coastline, including the northern shores of the Strait of Hormuz, through which oil tankers bound for the

---

* "Baluch" is the correct form to use in describing or referring to the ethnic group. "Baluchi" refers specifically to the language.

** The overwhelming majority of Baluch live in Pakistan (3.65 million) and Iran (one million); an estimated 90,000 are native to the border areas of southern Afghanistan. Another 335,000 Baluch have migrated to the Arab sheikhdoms of the Persian Gulf. The Soviet census lists 13,000 Baluch in Turkmenistan, and some 5,000 live in East Africa.

West and Japan must pass on their way out of the Persian Gulf. Soviet control of the Baluch coast would not only give Moscow a powerful new springboard for spreading its political influence throughout the Middle East and Southwest Asia, but would also radically alter the military balance in the region. Coupled with continued Soviet access to military facilities in South Yemen, Soviet use of naval and air bases at Gwadar, Pasni, and other Baluch ports would make it difficult, if not impossible, for the United States to defend the Strait of Hormuz in a conventional war, given the limited and conditional character of projected U.S. military facilities in Oman, Somalia, and Kenya.

In the most common scenario envisaged by those who foresee further Soviet expansion, Moscow simply sends its troops and tanks across Baluchistan to the Persian Gulf, a distance of less than 350 miles, annexing the Baluch area directly to a Soviet-controlled Greater Afghanistan. But this worst-case scenario completely ignores the role of the Baluch themselves and thus grossly oversimplifies the nature of the Baluchistan issue. On the one hand, it obscures the complex political difficulties that Moscow would confront in attempting to control the Baluch through conquest. On the other, it underrates the danger that Moscow might pursue its objectives more flexibly through a combination of political and military means, perhaps using allied Baluch groups as proxies.

While not ruling out the possibility of a naked Soviet military thrust, Pakistani and Iranian leaders are more concerned that Moscow might help Baluch nationalist factions to pursue their long-standing goal of an autonomous or independent Baluchistan through guerrilla warfare. In that scenario, Moscow would give the Baluch sophisticated weaponry, technical advisers, logistical support, and funds, but would seek to avoid the risks and costs of direct aggression. Alternatively, Moscow might attempt to achieve its purposes without supporting a Baluch insurgency, using the threat of such support to pressure Pakistan or Iran, or both, into granting the use of Arabian Sea ports for military purposes.

Whether or not Moscow decides to play its "Baluch card," the Baluch nationalist movement has achieved a momentum of its own and is likely to have an increasingly significant impact on the course of events in Southwest Asia. This book seeks to fill a vacuum in knowledge about the Baluch movement and to underline its importance as a little-recognized but critical factor in a region where ethnic conflict tends to dominate political life. Baluch nationalism is among the most intractable of the seven significant separatist challenges that threaten the integrity of multiethnic Pakistan and Iran. In Pakistan, the dominant Punjabis confront serious Pushtun and Sindhi disaffection. In Iran, separatist elements in the Kurdish, Arab, Turkoman, and Azerbaijani areas have waged perennial political and military struggles against Persian* rule. As the Iran-Iraq war showed in 1980, it is not difficult to envisage situations in which regional powers, acting on their own initiative, might support Baluch separatism as part of their larger efforts to manipulate ethnic differences in pursuit of local ambitions. For example, if Baghdad is unable to bring Teheran to its knees, there will be a growing possibility of Iraqi moves to set up independent states in the non-Persian areas. Similarly, if Indo-Pakistani tensions are aggravated by superpower rivalry in Afghanistan, as chapter ten elaborates, support for the dismemberment of Pakistan is likely to increase in India.

The origins of the Baluch nationalist movement go back to the forcible incorporation of the Baluch into Iran by Reza Shah Pahlavi in 1928 and, later, into the new state of Pakistan left behind by the British Raj in 1947. The Baluch waged unsuccessful military struggles of varying magnitude to preserve their independence and have been fighting intermittently ever since to throw off Pakistani and Iranian domination. In Iran, the Shah's iron repression kept the Baluch largely under control (with the exception of a brief, Iraqi-supported insurgency) until the Khomeini revolution in 1979 led to a weakening of the central authority and an outpouring of long-suppressed nationalist feeling. In Pakistan, by contrast, Baluch insurgents have waged an on-again, off-again guerrilla struggle ever since the departure of the British, culminating in the mid-1970s in a brutal confrontation with 80,000 or more Pakistani troops in which some 55,000 Baluch were involved at various stages of the fighting. At the height of the fighting, in late 1974, U.S.-supplied Iranian combat helicopters, some manned by Iranian pilots, joined the Pakistan Air Force in raids on Baluch camps. The Baluch, lacking any substantial foreign help, were armed only with bolt-action rifles and homemade grenades.[4]

Significantly, when they started their poorly prepared insurgency in 1973, the Pakistani Baluch were fighting not for independence but rather for regional autonomy within a radically restructured, confederal Pakistani constitutional framework. By the time the shooting subsided in 1977, however, separatist feeling had greatly intensified. The wanton use of superior firepower by the Pakistani and Iranian forces, especially the indiscriminate air attacks on Baluch villages, left a legacy of bitter and

---

* The Farsi-speaking Persian ethnic group has traditionally dominated multiethnic Iran, which also consists of Baluch, Kurds, Arabs, Turkomans, Azerbaijanis, and tribes such as the Bakhtiaris and Lurs.

enduring hatred. Since nearly all Baluch felt the impact of Pakistani repression, the Baluch populace is now politicized to an unprecedented degree. In mid-1980, I found a pervasive mood of expectancy among the Baluch, a widespread desire to vindicate Baluch martial honor, and a readiness to renew the struggle when and if circumstances appear to be favorable.

There is still a chance to avert renewed conflict through negotiations, but the communication gap is rapidly widening between the Baluch and Pakistani and Iranian leaders. To the dominant Punjabis in Pakistan, who make up 58 percent of the population, it is unthinkable that the Baluch minority of less than 4 percent should have special claims to Baluchistan, which represents 42 percent of the land area of the country. By the same token, in Iran, where the Baluch constitute at most 2 percent of the population, the ruling Persians, who make up 52 percent, angrily reject the proposition that provincial boundaries should be demarcated in accordance with historic ethnic homelands. Both Islamabad and Teheran view the sparsely settled expanses of Baluchistan as a safety valve for surplus population, a source of badly needed raw materials, and an area of vital strategic importance over which the central government should rightfully hold undisputed sway. But for the ideologues of Pakistani and Iranian nationalism, the Baluch and other minorities cannot be permitted to stand in the way of modernization programs addressed to the overall development needs of the impoverished millions living in all parts of their respective countries.

As a report on the Baluch movement and its destabilizing potential, this book is deliberately Baluch-centered. It treats Baluch nationalism as a dynamic, self-contained phenomenon worthy of attention in its own right rather than as a subordinate aspect of the larger problems of Pakistani and Iranian nationalism. Thus, it examines Pakistani and Iranian attitudes relating specifically to the Baluch and their demands, focusing in particular on how these attitudes condition the Baluch movement and affect the prospects for compromise between the Baluch and Islamabad and Teheran. It does not give "equal time" to a consideration of Pakistani and Iranian nationalist perspectives that embrace the gamut of problems confronting Pakistan and Iran as multiethnic states. That broader examination will be part of a subsequent book.

What are the principal grievances underlying Baluch demands for autonomy, and what are the possible elements of an accommodation between the Baluch and Islamabad and Teheran? How strong is the Baluch nationalist movement in organizational terms? Does it have enough discipline and unity to wage a meaningful struggle for independence, assuming that it receives significant foreign military help? Who are its leaders? Does Moscow have a significant Communist political base in Baluchistan, or would it have to depend on alliances with non-Communist Baluch nationalists to legitimize a Soviet-sponsored independent state?

In order to assess the potential of Baluch nationalism as a flash point for intraregional tensions and superpower rivalry in Southwest Asia, it is not enough to focus on the political and economic conflicts of the recent past or even, as some have done, to search for the roots of Baluch attitudes in the stormy encounters of the Baluch with British colonial armies.[5] It is first necessary to understand how the Baluch view the larger panorama of their embattled earlier history. This report turns next, accordingly, to an exploration of the deeply ingrained historical memories that underlie Baluch nationalism, memories of a tempestuous struggle for survival stretching back more than 2,000 years. Chapter three presents a brief account of the controversial circumstances surrounding the annexation of Baluchistan to Pakistan and the early struggles of the Baluch nationalist movement there, culminating in the 1973–1977 insurgency. Chapters four and five offer a close-up look at the principal nationalist leaders and a survey of the major contemporary nationalist groups.

The special problems of the nationalist movement in Iran receive separate treatment in chapter six, setting the stage for an examination of émigré Baluch groups in the Arab states across the Persian Gulf from Iran and their links with Sunni Arab leaders seeking to destabilize the Shiite-dominated Teheran regime. Chapter seven assesses Communist strength in Baluchistan, pointing up the handicaps faced by the Baluch Communists in past years as a result of Soviet unwillingness to support Baluch independence. After an examination of Pakistani and Iranian attitudes toward Baluch demands, focusing in particular on economic issues, chapters eight and nine seek to assess the economic viability of an independent Baluchistan and weigh the possibilities for political accommodations between the Baluch and Islamabad and Teheran, taking into account the overall political prospects in the two countries. Finally, chapter ten discusses the impact of Baluch nationalism on Soviet and American policy options in Afghanistan, Pakistan, Iran, India, and the Persian Gulf.

Baluchistan lifestyle, 1981

Myths and Memories

2

If it were not for the strategic location of Baluchistan and the rich potential of oil, uranium, and other resources described in chapter nine, it would be difficult to imagine anyone fighting over this bleak, desolate, and forbidding land. Most observers compare it to the moon, but a team of U.S. Geological Survey experts on assignment in Iranian Baluchistan insisted that it was the closest thing on earth to Mars. Date groves do survive in scattered oases, and the southeastern corner of Baluch territory encompasses the rich agricultural pockets of Las Bela and Kachhi. Forests of juniper also flourish in some of the northeastern mountain ranges near the Afghan border. But for most of its 207,000 square miles, Baluchistan alternates abruptly between stark mountains and arid expanses of semidesert wasteland.

Rocky brown scrub country stretches for hundreds of miles, punctuated only by isolated formations of white or coral limestone that jut up in lurid volcanic shapes. Then suddenly, the desert gives way to precipitous peaks. Knife-backed ridges hem in tight little valleys where low stands of dwarf palm, thorny shrubs, and rough grass struggle for survival. For the uninitiated, getting from one of these valleys to the next on foot can be a precarious business: there are few passes, and many of them are not negotiable even by local donkeys accustomed to the jagged terrain. Except for mountain goats, ibex, and panthers, the Baluch have always had the barren ranges to themselves and have learned the hard way how to find safe footing and where to hide. "The lofty heights are our comrades," goes a sixteenth-century war ballad, "the pathless gorges our friends."[1]

Savage extremes of climate make mountains and plains alike almost unbearable for outsiders. In winter, the temperature often drops to −40° F. In summer, it soars to 130° F. in the shade in the more exposed areas. Rainfall is erratic, seldom exceeding five inches a year, and programs for water conservation are still insignificant, making water a scarce commodity. Few of the rivers in Baluchistan follow fixed courses. In August and September, thunderstorms and dust storms strike unpredictably and violently, often followed by torrential rains and flash floods. The lack of adequate and predictable water supplies has shaped the seminomadic lifestyle characteristic of most Baluch. Instead of relying solely on either nomadic pastoralism or on settled agriculture, most Baluch practice a mixture of the two in order to survive.

The focal points of tribal life are widely dispersed settlements of small agricultural plots, located in valleys where broad, ill-defined river-beds have been hollowed out by floods and on the northern plateaus where the rainfall is greatest. As many as ten families may have shares in a single plot. To the extent that the rains permit, the tribesmen grow such crops as wheat, millet, barley, onions, and peppers, in addition to tending their animals. But survival requires frequent migration to escape extremes of weather, replenish water supplies, and find fresh grazing lands for the flocks. The traveler through Baluchistan sees frequent evidence of this continual migration in the sporadic clusters of black goatskin tents that dot the landscape.

Goats and sheep are the mainstay of the tribal economy and are carefully herded to protect them from wolves and leopards. The favorite feast of the Baluch is *sajji*, a roast leg of lamb cooked on spits between shimmering beds of hot rocks often piled as high as five feet. The Baluch also keep donkeys, cows, and camels, but they are left to fend for themselves. The cows often stray far afield but generally stay near water; the donkeys tend to graze near the nomad camps. By contrast, camels need less water and pasturage, and some of the most bedraggled camels in the world can be seen wandering aimlessly throughout Baluchistan. There is a Baluch saying that if you see a cow, you have found water; if you see a donkey, you have found a camp; and if you see a camel, you are lost.

In many parts of Baluchistan, tribes living near date-growing oases trade their butter, milk, and grain for dates during the late summer and early autumn. The Baluch also eat a variety of wild plants, notably the heart of the hardy dwarf palm, which grows even in dry riverbeds. The leaves of the dwarf palm can be made into tents and produce a tough fiber used for rope shoes, mats, spoons, and even water pipes. Baluch women learn at an early age how to use this fiber, how to weave woolen rugs and garments, how to manipulate goatskin water bags on their backs over long distances, and how to cook in the open while the wind whistles. As in other pastoral Muslim societies, the Baluch keep their women veiled and practice arranged marriages. In the unabashedly male-centered Baluch ethos, women play a conspicuously subservient role in everyday life but are exalted in legends and folklore, which revolve around romantic triangles and martial struggles over insults to tribal honor generally involving victimized women.

The Baluch, who are Sunni Muslims of the Hanafi rite, are notably casual about religious observances. Religious leaders play a relatively marginal role in Baluch society, except in Iranian Baluchistan, where *maulavis* and *dervishes* have grown in importance in recent years. It is the tribal power structure that counts in Baluch rural society. Each of the seventeen major tribal groupings in Baluchistan is headed by a *sardar* (chieftain), and there are some 400 tribal subgroupings headed by lesser chieftains.

Out of the total Baluch population of some 5 million, nearly 1.5 million have migrated in search of work to Pakistani and Iranian cities outside Baluchistan or to the Persian Gulf. Of the remainder living in Pakistani and Iranian Baluchistan, more than 70 percent live a semi-nomadic life in rural areas. The poverty of this rural life is apparent in the fact that in Pakistani Baluchistan alone, only 3.3 million acres are cultivated out of a total acreage of some 85 million. Only 800,000 of these cultivated acres are irrigated, and most of the irrigated land is centered in the Las Bela and Kachhi areas, where non-Baluch settlers, encouraged by Islamabad, compete for the limited land available.

Some of the better-watered valleys support limited agriculture and have begun to attract light industry in recent decades. As chapter nine will elaborate, the potential for economic expansion in Baluchistan appears to be considerable, given the extent of underground water and mineral resources revealed by the limited surveys so far undertaken. But there are relatively few population centers for an area so vast in size. Pakistani Baluchistan has one town, Sibi, with a population of some 25,000, and twelve towns with populations of 7,500 or more.* Among these, the fishing ports at Gwadar, Pasni, and Ormara are often cited as possible targets of Soviet ambitions for a warm-water port on the Arabian Sea. The only city, Quetta, with a population of 122,000, sits on the border of the neighboring Pushtun tribal belt and has a more or less equal ethnic mix of Baluch, Pushtuns, and Punjabi settlers. Iranian Baluchistan has four towns with 10,000 inhabitants or more—Khash, Iranshahr, Sarawan, and Chah Bahar—as well as a multiethnic city of 75,000, Zahedan, which includes as many Sistanis and Persians as it does Baluch (see Figure 2).

As development activity has slowly increased over the years, leading to a gradual proliferation of educational facilities, there has been a steady

---

* Bhang, Dadar, Fort Sandeman, Gwadar, Kalat, Khuzdar, Mach, Mastung, Nushki, Ormara, Pasni, and Turbat. The urban-rural breakdowns in the 1961 and 1972 Pakistan censuses show an increase in the urban population of Baluchistan province from 228,468 to 399,583. The 1972 figures show 189,002 in Quetta district, 74,431 in Makran district, and 33,791 in Sibi district. ("Population [Urban/Rural by Sex, Division and District], 1961/1972," Table provided by the Information Ministry, Government of Pakistan, 16 March 1981.)

influx to urban centers. It is in these restive urban areas of Baluchistan and among Baluch migrants in Karachi and the Persian Gulf that literacy—and political consciousness—have been growing most rapidly. Most estimates suggest a literacy rate among the Baluch of 6 to 9 percent. Assuming a total Baluch population of five million, such estimates point to a literate Baluch population of 300,000 to 450,000, which is substantially higher than projections of census statistics would indicate.[2] Taking into account census projections and the available rough estimates of high school and college graduates, a credible estimate would be in the neighborhood of 250,000. This literate population provides the most volatile raw material for the organized Baluch nationalist movement. But the strength of Baluch nationalism, as we shall see, comes from the growing politicization of the countryside as a result of the 1973–1977 insurgency and the widespread acceptance of a common nationalist leadership cutting across the rural and urban areas of Pakistani Baluchistan and, more tenuously, Iranian Baluchistan as well.

Who Are the Baluch?

To the neighboring Pushtun tribes, who live in fertile riverine valleys, Baluchistan is "the dump where Allah shot the rubbish of creation."[3] But for the Baluch, their sense of identity is closely linked to the austere land where they have lived for at least a thousand years. According to the *Daptar Sha'ar* (Chronicle of Genealogies), an ancient ballad popular among all seventeen major Baluch tribes, the Baluch and the Kurds were kindred branches of a tribe that migrated eastward from Aleppo, in what is now Syria, shortly before the time of Christ in search of fresh pasturelands and water sources. One school of Baluch nationalist historians attempts to link this tribe ethnically with the Semitic Chaldean rulers of Babylon,[4] another with the early Arabs,[5] still others with Aryan tribes originally from Asia Minor.[6] In any case, there is agreement among these historians that the Kurds headed toward Iraq, Turkey, and northwest Persia, while the Baluch moved into the coastal areas along the southern shores of the Caspian Sea, later migrating into what are now Iranian Baluchistan and Pakistani Baluchistan between the sixth and fourteenth centuries.[7]

Western historians dismiss the *Daptar Sha'ar* as nothing more than myth and legend, totally unsubstantiated by verifiable evidence, and it remains for future scholars to probe into the murky origins of the Baluch. These legends are cited here not because they have serious historiographic value but because they are widely believed and are thus politically important today. For the most part, Aleppo is a unifying symbol of a common identity in the historical memories shared by all Baluch. In recent years, however, Arab attempts to attribute Arab ethnic origins to the Baluch have become a divisive factor in the nationalist movement (see chapter six).

Whatever the authenticity of the Aleppo legends, scholars in Baluchistan and in the West generally agree that the Baluch were living along the southern shores of the Caspian at the time of Christ. This consensus is based largely on linguistic evidence showing that the Baluchi language is descended from a lost language linked with the Parthian or Median civilizations, which flourished in the Caspian and adjacent areas in the pre-Christian era.[8] As one of the oldest living languages, Baluchi is a subject of endless fascination and controversy for linguists. It is classified as a member of the Iranian group of the Indo-European language family, which includes Farsi (Persian), Pushtu, Baluchi, and Kurdish. Baluchi is closely related to only one of the members of the Iranian group, Kurdish. In its modern form, it has incorporated borrowings from Persian, Sindhi, Arabic, and other languages, nonetheless retaining striking peculiarities that can be traced back to its pre-Christian origins. Until 150 years ago, the Baluch, like most nomadic societies, did not have a recorded literature. Initially, Baluch savants used the Persian and Urdu scripts to render Baluchi in written form. In recent decades, Baluch nationalist intellectuals have evolved a Baluchi script known as Nastaliq, a variant of the Arabic script.

Ethnically, the Baluch are no longer homogeneous, since the original nucleus that migrated from the Caspian has absorbed a variety of disparate groups along the way. Among these "new" Baluch were displaced tribes from Central Asia, driven southward by the Turkish and Mongol invasions from the tenth through the thirteenth centuries, and fugitive Arab factions defeated in intra-Arab warfare. Nevertheless, in cultural terms, the Baluch have been remarkably successful in preserving a distinctive identity in the face of continual pressures from strong cultures in neighboring areas. Despite the isolation of the scattered pastoral communities in Baluchistan, the Baluchi language and a relatively uniform Baluch folklore tradition and value system have provided a common denominator for the diverse Baluch tribal groupings scattered over the vast area from the Indus River in the east to the Iranian province of Kerman in the west.* To a great extent, it is the vitality of this ancient cultural heritage that explains the tenacity of the present demand for the political recognition of Baluch identity. But the strength of Baluch na-

---

* See chapter nine for a discussion of Brahui, a language spoken by certain Baluch tribes, which is increasingly converging with Baluchi.

tionalism is also rooted in proud historical memories of determined resistance against the would-be conquerors who perennially attempted, without success, to annex all or part of Baluchistan to their adjacent empires.

Reliving their past endlessly in books, magazines, and folk ballads, the Baluch accentuate the positive. They revel in the gory details of ancient battles against Persians, Turks, Arabs, Tartars, Hindus, and other adversaries, focusing on how valiantly their generals fought rather than on whether the Baluch won or lost. They point to the heroes who struggled to throw off the yoke of more powerful oppressors and minimize the role of the quislings who sold out the Baluch cause. Above all, they seek to magnify the achievements of their more successful rulers, contending that the Baluch were on the verge of consolidating political unity when the British arrived on the scene and applied their policy of divide and rule. This claim is difficult to sustain with much certainty on the basis of the available evidence. Nevertheless, the Baluch did make several significant attempts to draw together politically, and their failure to establish an enduring polity in past centuries does not prove that they would fail under the very different circumstances prevailing today. As Baluch writers argue, given the technologies of modern transportation and communication, the contemporary Baluch nationalist has new opportunities for cementing Baluch political unity that were not open to his forebears.

The Search for Political Identity

In order to validate their demands today, Baluch nationalists focus on the unification efforts made by three Baluch monarchs who ruled during the three centuries preceding the British Raj. The first nation-builder cited in Baluch historical accounts is Mir Chakar Rind,* who in the fifteenth century established a short-lived tribal confederacy reaching from the Makran coast to the present-day Marri tribal area south of Quetta. Mir Chakar ruled from his capital at Sibi from 1487 until his death in 1511, but his kingdom was destroyed by a civil war between the two leading Baluch tribal federations, the Rinds and the Lasharis. Baluch nationalist writers extol Mir Chakar for making the first serious effort to unify the Baluch politically, but reserve their highest encomiums for his brilliance as a general who personified Baluch martial virtues.

There is considerable confusion surrounding the later years of Mir

---

* *Mir* is an honorific title in the Muslim world, applied especially, but not exclusively, to descendants of the Prophet Mohammed.

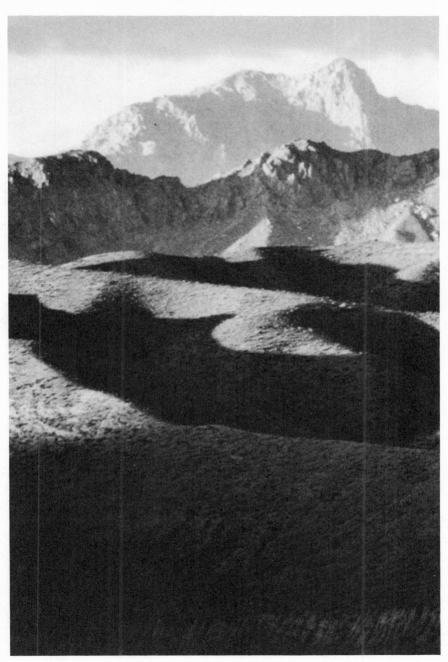

"The pathless gorges, our friends"

A Baluch nomad encampment in Pakistan

Chakar's reign, especially the circumstances of his abandonment of his capital at Sibi. While some historical evidence suggests that he was defeated by the Lasharis, most Baluch nationalists are reluctant to concede that Mir Chakar was forced to leave Sibi in defeat and argue instead that he pulled up stakes in order to go on to still greater triumphs by leading a Baluch invasion of northern India. Whatever the circumstances of his departure from Sibi, it is clear that he did lead a sizable army into the Punjab, achieving "complete possession" of Multan and other areas of the south Punjab during the early sixteenth century.[9] The British historian M. Longworth Dames writes that Mir Chakar's military successes "seem to have led to something like a national migration."[10] Mir Khuda Bux Marri stresses that Mir Chakar led an army of 40,000 men into the Punjab, pointing out that Babur, founder of the Moghul Empire, conquered India with only 12,000 soldiers. With an army of 40,000, he speculates, Mir Chakar must have had some 200,000 to 300,000 followers on the march, including family members.[11]

Although never able to subdue the Lasharis, Mir Chakar is hailed in nationalist accounts as a Baluch Attila, and the exploits of his army during the Rind-Lashari war are idealized as "the Iliad of the Baluch race."[12] Similarly, his march into the Punjab, where he died, is proudly remembered, even though he failed to lay the foundations for enduring control over the areas that he conquered. The Baluch who settled in the Punjab are not closely linked to the mainstream of Baluch life today.

The principal link with their past for most Baluch is the vast body of popular ballads dating back to the days of Mir Chakar. Handed down from generation to generation and first recorded by British scholars, these ballads, sung by professional wandering minstrels, center to a considerable extent on the Rind-Lashari conflict. One of them, for example, glorifies Mir Chakar's role in the battle of Nali, where "forty thousand warriors collect on Mir's call, all descendants of one ancestor, all bedecked with coats of mail and iron armour covering their head, chest and forearms; all armed with bows and arrows, silken scarves, overcoats, red boots on their feet, silver knives, sharp daggers and golden rings on their fingers."[13]

After Mir Chakar's death in 1511, the Moghul Empire, based in Delhi, made several unsuccessful attempts to incorporate the Baluch, who were able to cooperate militarily to preserve their independence. However, the Baluch tribes were unable to restore even a modicum of political unity until the Ahmadzai tribe established the Kalat Confederacy in 1666. Based in the Kalat highlands, southwest of Mir Chakar's former capital, the new confederacy gradually encompassed an area even larger than Mir Chakar's domain. During the early eighteenth century, Abdullah Khan, the fourth Khan of Kalat,* claimed the allegiance of Baluch tribes scattered from Kandahar (now in southeastern Afghanistan) across the Makran area to Bandar Abbas (now in Iran). In the southeast, his jurisdiction included the Dera Ghazi Khan district on the edge of the Punjab. Recent indications of possible uranium deposits in Dera Ghazi Khan have led Baluch historians to emphasize that it fell within the Kalat Confederacy under Mir Abdullah and most of his successors.

Although the boundaries of Abdullah Khan's confederacy were far-flung, he was forced to pay tribute to Iranian monarchs in order to forestall their incursions in the distant western border areas of his realm. Moreover, he did little to knit the areas under his military control into a unified state. That task was left to the sixth Khan of Kalat, the dynamic Nasir Khan, who ruled for more than half a century, beginning in 1741. Nasir Khan's most notable achievement was the creation of a unified Baluch army of some 25,000 men and 1,000 camels, an impressive force by eighteenth-century Southwest Asian standards. For the first time in their history, most of the major Baluch tribes were rallied under the banner of an agreed system of military organization and recruitment.

Administratively, Nasir Khan came closer to establishing a centralized bureaucratic apparatus covering all of Baluchistan than any other Baluch ruler before or since. He had a *wazir* (prime minister), who supervised all internal administration and foreign affairs matters, and a *vakil*, whose responsibility it was to collect revenue from crown lands as well as tribute from loosely affiliated principalities or chiefdoms. There were two legislative councils, loosely described as a "Baluch parliament" by the late Khan of Kalat, consisting of a lower chamber chosen by the tribes and an upper chamber of elders serving in an advisory capacity. Members of the lower house, or their representatives, remained in Kalat at all times. The Khan built a network of roads, lined with new *caravanserais* (inns accommodating caravans), and was famed for constructing elaborate mosques.[14] There is some confusion among historians, however, as to whether he had a systematic basis for revenue collection. In political science terms, Nina Swidler writes, the Khanate of Kalat fell midway between the conventional categories of the kin-based tribe headed by an autocratic chief, with no larger political affiliation, and the centralized bureaucratic state. In her view, the khanate was never able to exact revenue from the tribes or to administer uniform tax levies on the caravan trade passing through Kalat. While the tribes did provide reliable military support, she states, the khanate relied for its financial

---

* A title of Turkish origin, *khan* is loosely applied to local chieftains or princes of varying importance.

support on irrigated crown lands in the Sarawan district commandeered at an early stage of the dynasty.[15] Challenging this view, the Khan of Kalat spoke of the collection of a traditional Islamic tax by the Kalat government dating back to the Nasir Khan period.[16] Nationalist historian Mohammed Khan Baluch states that Baluch legends attribute a treasury of four million rupees to Nasir Khan in his heyday.[17] Other sources suggest that land taxes were required from certain outlying areas that did not have a troop quota.

Nasir Khan paid tribute during the first several years of his reign to the powerful Persian emperor Nadir Shah, who had conquered the warring tribes of adjacent Afghanistan and had helped him to win the Kalat throne in the face of rival claims to the succession. Nasir Khan repudiated this tributary status following Nadir Shah's assassination in 1747 and the subsequent decline of centralized power in Iran. However, when Ahmad Shah Durrani stepped into the resulting vacuum and established the new kingdom of Afghanistan, Nasir Khan was forced to acknowledge Afghan suzerainty for eleven years, a fact cited by Afghan nationalists today to justify the idea of a Greater Afghanistan, incorporating Baluchistan. Once he had firmly established his army, Nasir Khan took on the Afghans militarily, fighting Ahmad Shah Durrani's forces to a standoff in 1758. Thereafter, Kalat enjoyed sovereign status until the arrival of the British, though it remained a military ally of Afghanistan.

At the height of his power, Nasir Khan renewed Kalat's claims of sovereignty over the Iranian Baluch areas and sent occasional expeditionary forces to his western borderlands. Nevertheless, it should be emphasized that the freewheeling Iranian Baluch tribes were for all practical purposes a law unto themselves. Separated by geography from the main body of the Baluch tribes to the east and themselves divided into several distinctive regional subgroupings, the Iranian Baluch have been on the fringes of Baluch political life throughout history and continue to be so today. Taking the self-contained character of Iranian Baluch life into account, this book treats the contemporary Baluch nationalist movements in Pakistan and Iran in separate chapters.

While they consistently rebuffed Persian and Afghan incursions, the Iranian Baluch were never able to produce a unified political or military grouping of their own, even for a brief period. Certain strong chieftains were able to establish localized confederacies, notably Dost Mohammed, who was beginning to extend his sway over southeastern Iran when Reza Shah Pahlavi subdued his forces in 1928, using air power and artillery for the first time in Iran.[18] Dost Mohammed's son, Mir Amin, former mayor of the Iranian Baluch town of Sarawan, said in a 1978 interview that his father had envisaged the creation of an independent Baluch state along the Makran coast. This state would have embraced not only the coastal areas of Baluchistan that became part of Iran, he recalled, but would also have reached into what is now Pakistani Baluchistan as far as Pasni (see Figure 2). However, at the time of Reza Shah's conquest, Dost Mohammed had in fact achieved only a shaky control over roughly one-third of the Iranian Baluch areas and had signally failed to create unifying bureaucratic or military machinery comparable to that developed by Nasir Khan.

For Baluch nationalists today, Nasir Khan's achievements remain an all-important symbol, providing some semblance of historical precedent for the concept of a unified Baluch political identity. Nationalist authors invariably cite a tribute to Nasir Khan by a British observer, Sir Henry Pottinger, who termed him "a most extraordinary combination of all the virtues attached to soldier, statesman or prince" and reported after a tour through Baluchistan that "the most distant districts were always as alert in obeying his orders as those near at hand."[19] "Forward March," the "national anthem" sung at Baluch political gatherings, invokes the name of Nasir Khan, enjoining all Baluch to

> March on, march on!
> This living slavery
> Is forbidden to the Faithful.
> Slavery is for the heathen,
> From his pen Nasir said it.
>
> March on, march on!
> With pride in your motherland,
> With devotion in body and soul,
> Come out of slavery.
> March on, march on![20]

Another patriotic song often sung in student meetings and other nationalist gatherings concludes that

> Pleasant as the homeland of another may be,
> Populous and affluent and great of name,
> Streams of honey may run there.
> But for Nasir
> The "dry wood of the homeland" is better
>   than all the world.[21]

Why did the unity built by Nasir Khan collapse during the decades after his death in 1805? Was it, as most available evidence would suggest, simply because his successors succumbed to the centrifugal pulls of tribal strife?

The issue is confused in that his passing from the scene coincided with the beginnings of the "Great Game" between Britain and Russia in Afghanistan and British adoption of the "Forward Policy," designed to push the jurisdiction of the Raj to the Afghan frontier. When the British concluded that Afghanistan should become a buffer state to shield their Indian empire from Russia, Baluchistan, as a key area flanking Afghanistan, immediately acquired a new strategic significance. Determined to establish direct control over the access routes to Afghanistan, the British fought bloody battles with the Baluch for more than forty years. By 1876, they were able to subdue Kalat and obtain formal treaty rights to station troops there in return for handsome subsidies and guarantees of tribal autonomy. Playing off rival chiefs against each other during the closing decades of the century, Britain systematically proceeded to divide the Baluch area into seven parts. In the far west, the Goldsmid line gave roughly one-fourth to Persia in 1871; in the north, the Durand line assigned a small strip to Afghanistan in 1894; and in British India, the Baluch areas were divided into a centrally administered enclave (known as British Baluchistan) guarding a key mountain pass, a truncated remnant of the Kalat Confederacy, and three smaller puppet principalities.

A leading contemporary Baluch nationalist, Ghaus Bux Bizenjo, former governor of Pakistani Baluchistan, argued in a 1978 interview that Nasir Khan's successors would have consolidated an enduring polity if it had not been for the deliberate manipulation of the internal divisions in Baluch society by the British Raj. In Bizenjo's view, the Baluch failed to sustain their nationhood primarily because they happened to live in an area of vital military importance to the British. It was historical accident, he explained, that gave the Afghans the opportunity for independent statehood denied to the Baluch. Just as it served the interests of the British to foster a unified Afghanistan as a buffer state, so it was necessary, conversely, for Britain to divide the Baluch in order to make the frontiers of the Raj contiguous with Afghanistan and to assure unimpeded military dominance in the frontier region.

Nasir Khan's Kalat Confederacy might have emerged in a buffer state role instead, Bizenjo contended, if the Russians had moved south sooner than they did and if they had swallowed up Afghanistan before Britain embarked on its Forward Policy. "Remember," he said, alluding to the founding of Kalat in 1666, "we Baluch had created a state eighty years before Afghanistan was established."

Suggesting a more elemental explanation for the failure of the Baluch to achieve political unity, Brian Spooner, an anthropologist who has studied Iranian Baluchistan, stresses ecological factors. Given its forbidding topography and the fragmentation of its limited pasture lands, Spooner points out, Baluchistan lacks the large-scale nomadic settlements found in many other pastoral societies where grazing areas are more concentrated. The resulting dispersion of Baluch nomads has "made it difficult for tribal leaders to build up large confederacies," especially in the face of peculiarly severe transportation and communication problems.[22]

In ecological terms, Spooner classifies Baluchistan as "a marginal area, in the sense that at a given level of technology it can support fewer people per unit area in poorer circumstances than is the case in surrounding areas." It is generally true of such marginal areas, he concludes, that "their history is a function of the history of neighboring areas, that economic development of them is difficult except as the result of direct interest from an external power, but that unless they are important for communications, mineral deposits or other strategic considerations, such interest is not exerted. The investment required to achieve or maintain political control is not justified."[23]

Applying his analysis to the specific historical experience of Baluchistan, Spooner found only one instance in which an external power had shown much interest in the political unification of Baluchistan during the eight centuries between the Tatar invasion and the advent of the British. That was when the Persian emperor Nadir Shah gave his blessing to the young Nasir Khan, "confirming and legitimizing" a regime that lasted for the next half century. Before the Shah's intervention, the Kalat dynasty had been on the verge of collapse, Spooner maintained, and it began to fall apart once again in the early nineteenth century following Nasir Khan's death.[24]

If one accepts this interpretation of history, it logically follows that the Baluch will find it difficult, on their own, to achieve the unity necessary for a successful independence movement and for the long-term preservation of their sovereignty. By the same token, however, their prospects appear considerably brighter if one assumes even relatively limited intervention by a foreign power or powers. Surveying the Southwest Asian scene in the 1980s, it takes little imagination to envisage contingencies in which one external power or another might conclude that "the investment required to achieve and maintain political control" was fully justified by "communications, mineral deposits or other strategic considerations." Moreover, it should be remembered that the nineteenth and twentieth centuries marked a major watershed for the Baluch, who had never lost their freedom before their conquest by the modern armies of Britain, Iran, and Pakistan. The rise of Baluch nationalism now taking place in response to alien domination has posed qualitatively new questions about the nature of Baluch social and political identity for which answers are not to be found in the historical record.

The Emergence of Baluch Nationalism

3

In both Iran and Pakistan, the contemporary Baluch nationalist movement has been steadily germinating since the subjugation of the Baluch by the Pahlavi dynasty in 1928 and by the Muslim League regime of Mohammed Ali Jinnah in 1947. As chapter six will show, however, the maturation process has been much slower in Iran, where the Pahlavis not only applied their superior military power with devastating effect, but also stifled the growth of an educated, politically conscious Baluch leadership. It is in the more favorable political climate of Pakistani Baluchistan that the nationalist movement has been able to sink its strongest roots.

In Iranian Baluchistan, Persian rulers were able to break the power of Baluch chieftains by first defeating them on the battlefield and then inducing them with carrot-and-stick techniques to act as middlemen for Teheran in dealing with their tribesmen. By contrast, British colonial administrators did not attempt to extend the administrative machinery of the Raj into the Baluch areas, with the exception of British Baluchistan, a narrow strip of territory bordering Afghanistan. So long as tribal leaders did not interfere with British military access to Afghanistan and British strategic control of frontier areas, the *sardars* enjoyed virtually complete control of their tribal affairs and were paid subsidies as well. By reinforcing the power and autonomy of the tribal chieftains, this permissive policy set the stage for subsequent conflict between the Pakistani Baluch and Islamabad.

Since the departure of the British, Pakistani leaders have attempted to reverse the policy of tribal autonomy, emulating the hard-line approach toward the *sardars* successfully applied in Iran. However, unlike the Persian rulers, who deliberately curtailed education in the Baluch areas, Pakistani leaders have fanned the fires of political awareness by providing expanded educational opportunities and other tokens of modernization. In the eyes of Pakistani nation-builders, the goal of a strong, centralized state made it imperative to break down the power of tribal chieftains as part of a larger effort to merge Baluch identity into an all-embracing Pakistani identity. But to most Baluch, tribal identity and Baluch identity are merely different layers of a single psychological whole. Islamabad's assault on the tribal social structure and its commitment to a monolithic Pakistani nationalism constitute a frontal challenge to Baluch values. The result is a simmering guerrilla struggle that has flared up with progressively increasing intensity in 1948, 1958, 1962, and finally with full force in the 1973–1977 insurgency.

The Struggle Against Accession to Pakistan

The incorporation of the Baluch into Pakistan came as a traumatic blow to nationalist leaders who had campaigned clandestinely for an independent Baluchistan during the last decades of the British Raj. The British attempted to suppress nationalist activity and resisted pressures for the introduction of education in the Baluch areas. Nevertheless, several hundred Baluch were permitted to obtain a high school and, in some cases, a college education, most of them from sardar-related families whose good will was valuable to the Raj. Even this limited exposure to education produced an upsurge of political consciousness under the stimulus of the October Revolution in the Soviet Union and the anti-British struggle led by Mohandas K. Gandhi and Jawaharlal Nehru.

During the twenties, recalled Mir Ahmed Yar Khan, the last ruler of Kalat, "most of the educated youth of the day" thought that Soviet objectives were progressive and would serve the Baluch cause by hastening the end of British rule and setting the stage for Baluch independence.[1] This pro-Soviet climate did not result in a significant Communist party, as chapter seven explains, but it accelerated the ferment that led to the emergence of an organized nationalist movement. One of the favorite anticolonial issues of the late twenties was the revival of British efforts to recruit Baluch soldiers into the imperial Indian army. The British had liquidated the Baluch element of the Duke of Connaught's Own Baluchis in 1910 after finding the Baluch difficult to discipline and prone to "the disconcerting habit of departing without notice."[2] When British military authorities decided to try again in 1929, Baluch nationalists, sparked by a small Communist cadre, waged a successful antirecruitment campaign. That movement culminated in an armed mutiny and the dismissal of all Baluch soldiers from what is still called the Baluch Regiment of the Pakistan Army, despite the fact that it has not included Baluch for nearly half a century.[3]

In the early 1930s, Baluch newspapers began to appear, and several underground Baluch political groups were organized, most notably Abdul Aziz Kurd's Anjuman-e-Ittehad-e-Baluchistan (Organization for the Unity of Baluchistan). In August 1933, the group's weekly newspaper, Al-Baloch of Karachi, published a map depicting an independent Greater

Baluchistan that embraced the Baluch areas of Iran as well as Kalat and the other Baluch principalities of Pakistan, British Baluchistan, Dera Ghazi Khan (a Baluch-claimed district in the Punjab), and the province of Sind.[4] By 1935, Kurd, Yusuf Ali Magsi, and other non-Communist nationalists had openly formed the Kalat National party, dedicated to the goal of an "independent, unified Baluchistan" following the departure of the British. As the necessary prelude to independence, the party demanded that the British restore the Baluch principalities of Kharan, Makran, and Las Bela to Kalat (see Figure 2). This party enjoyed the tacit approval of the Kalat ruler, Mir Ahmed Yar Khan, and was initially accorded a measure of freedom by the British before it was outlawed in 1939.

As the prospect of independence from Britain approached, Baluch leaders had to decide whether to seek sovereignty, as advocated by the Kalat National party, accession to Pakistan, or some intermediate status such as a confederal relationship with Pakistan. The Khan of Kalat made clear from the beginning that he sought independence and that he saw himself as heir to the tradition of Baluch nationalism personified by his ancestor Nasir Khan.

The Khan argued that the legal status of Nepal and Kalat was different from that of other princely states in the Indian subcontinent. While the other "native states" dealt with the British Indian government in New Delhi, Nepal and Kalat maintained their treaty relations directly with Whitehall. More important, the 1876 treaty which permitted Britain to occupy Baluchistan pledged that the British "would respect the sovereignty and independence of Kalat."[5]

In a memorandum submitted to the British Cabinet Mission in March 1946, the Khan asserted that the government or governments succeeding the Raj would inherit only the treaty relationships of the colonial government in New Delhi, not those of Whitehall. Once the British withdrew, the memorandum said, Kalat would retain the independence it had enjoyed prior to 1876. Similarly, the Baluch principalities that had been tributaries of Kalat, and which were later "leased" to the British under duress, would revert to Kalat. As a result, the memorandum stated, Kalat

> will become fully sovereign and independent in respect to both internal and external affairs, and will be free to conclude treaties with any other government or state.... The Khan, his government, and his people can never agree to Kalat being included in any form of Indian union. The Khan and his government will, however, always be glad to enter into an alliance with any government which succeeds the British government in India on the basis of the strictest reciprocity.[6]

The Cabinet Mission attempted to finesse the issue with a non-committal statement that left undecided the future of all of the princely states in the subcontinent. When Pakistan was formally established a year later, the issue was still unresolved, with the Khan insisting on his right to full independence and Pakistani leaders demanding unconditional accession. On August 15, 1947, one day after the creation of Pakistan, the Khan declared Kalat's independence, but offered to negotiate a special relationship with Pakistan in the spheres of defense, foreign affairs, and communications. Pakistani leaders summarily rejected this declaration, touching off a nine-month diplomatic tug of war that came to a climax in the forcible annexation of Kalat. The full story of the British role in the tangled maneuvering that resulted in Kalat's annexation has yet to be revealed by historians. But it is clear that Baluch leaders, including the Khan, were bitterly opposed to what happened.

Pakistani historians, who seek to magnify the role of the Muslim League in the annexation of Baluchistan, maintain that the Khan's stand was not representative of Baluch sentiment and point as evidence to a pro-Pakistan assembly of Baluch leaders in Quetta on June 29, 1947. These historians fail to note that the participants had been appointed by the British Raj and that the assembly's recommendations related only to the small area known as British Baluchistan.[7] Moreover, the Pakistani version of the accession debate is discredited by a study of the discussions of the Kalat Assembly on the accession issue and by interviews with a variety of Baluch leaders that confirm the authenticity of the official assembly proceedings.

The fifty-two-member lower house of the Kalat Assembly was chosen in the immediate aftermath of the Khan's declaration of independence. According to Inayatullah Baloch, a nationalist historian, the Khan staged elections in which the Kalat National party won thirty-nine seats, showing that nationalist sentiment clearly outweighed conservative tribal influence.[8] Other sources confirm that elections were held but suggest that they were hastily arranged and were not very broad-based. In any case, the assembly met for a week in early September 1947 and again in mid-December. Although most members clearly desired an alliance with Pakistan, an overwhelming consensus favored independence as a precondition for such a relationship. Speaker after speaker argued that Pakistan had shown malice toward the Baluch by perpetuating the separate status of the three "leased" Baluch principalities detached from Kalat by the British. If a unified Baluch identity had been recognized within the framework of Pakistan, several members said, it might have been possible to consider accession. But Pakistan had shown its true colors. Formalizing the dismemberment of Kalat, the Khan said, was "tantamount to the political castration of the Baluch."[9]

Assembly member Ghaus Bux Bizenjo, then twenty-nine, the principal spokesman for the independence forces, advanced many of the same arguments used by separatists today. On December 14, 1947, Bizenjo declared that

> we have a distinct culture like Afghanistan and Iran, and if the mere fact that we are Muslims requires us to amalgamate with Pakistan, then Afghanistan and Iran should also be amalgamated with Pakistan. They say we Baluch cannot defend ourselves in the atomic age. Well, are Afghanistan, Iran, and even Pakistan capable of defending themselves against the superpowers? If we cannot defend ourselves, a lot of others cannot do so either. They say we must join Pakistan for economic reasons. Yet we have minerals, we have petroleum and we have ports. The question is, what would Pakistan be without us?

Bizenjo made clear that he was prepared for close ties between a sovereign Kalat and Pakistan.

> I do not propose to create hurdles for the newly created state in matters of defense, external affairs, and communications. But we want an honorable relationship and not a humiliating one. We don't want to amalgamate with Pakistan. We cannot become such culprits in the eyes of history that we would take the Baluch into non-Baluch territory. If Pakistan wants to treat us as a sovereign people, we are ready to extend our friendship. But if Pakistan does not do so and forces us to accept this fate, flying in the face of democratic principles, every Baluch will fight for his freedom.[10]

Looking back on his 1947 speech in an interview in 1978, the sixty-year-old Bizenjo stressed that the dominant sentiment in the assembly was for a sovereign Baluch state. "We were opposed to accession, and we were not thinking of a confederation," he said, "but rather of special arrangements embodied in a treaty under which we would mutually conduct our defense, our foreign affairs, and our communications. We envisaged two sovereign countries in a treaty relationship."

The showdown between Kalat and Pakistan came on April 1, 1948, when the Pakistan Army ordered its garrison commander in Baluchistan to march on Kalat and arrest the Khan unless he signed an agreement of accession. The Khan capitulated, but his younger brother, Prince Abdul Karim, who was then governor of the newly annexed Baluch principality of Makran, gathered the arms, ammunition, and treasury funds under his control and declared a revolt against Pakistan. After leading some 700 followers across the border into Afghanistan, Abdul Karim issued a manifesto in the name of the Baluch National Liberation Committee disavowing the unconditional accession agreement signed by the Khan, proclaiming the independence of Kalat, and demanding fresh negotiations with Pakistan. K. B. Nizamani, one of the participants in this minirevolt, recalled in a 1980 interview that Abdul Karim had the tacit approval of the Khan, who saw the move as a last-ditch means of pressuring Pakistan and regaining some of his princely prerogatives. Bizenjo, Gul Khan Nasir, a prominent Baluch nationalist writer, and other leading Baluch political figures were cool to the idea of a military showdown with Pakistan, Nizamani said, fearing that it would be doomed to failure. Abdul Karim, however, embarked on his adventure confident that he would obtain Afghan support. He reasoned that since Afghanistan had objected to the inclusion of the Baluch and Pushtun areas in Pakistan and had even opposed the admission of Pakistan to the United Nations, Kabul could be persuaded to support a military initiative by the Baluch before the new Pakistani state became too well established.

According to the official Pakistani version of the episode, Abdul Karim's forces were "substantially" expanded with Afghan help and then proceeded to launch guerrilla operations against the Pakistan Army in Jhalawan district in late May. Units of General Akbar Khan's Seventh Regiment soon tracked the guerrillas down, forcing Abdul Karim to surrender in mid-June.

According to Nizamani and other Baluch nationalists, however, Abdul Karim came back without Afghan support* and had just begun to wage desultory guerrilla actions when the Khan, threatened with reprisals by Pakistani authorities, persuaded his brother to surrender with assurances of safe conduct and amnesty from the Pakistan Army. Pakistani officers reportedly signed a safe conduct agreement with Abdul Karim's representatives in the Harboi mountains and swore an oath on the Koran to uphold it. However, in this account, Pakistani forces dishonored the agreement by ambushing and arresting the Prince and 102 of his companions on their way to Kalat.

---

* Nationalist historian Inayatullah Baloch states that Afghanistan denied support to Karim because Kabul favored the inclusion of Baluchistan in an Afghan-controlled "Pushtunistan" and was opposed to an independent Baluchistan (Inayatullah Baloch, "The Emergence of Baluch Nationalism," *Pakistan Progressive*, New York, December 1980, p. 22). See my discussion of Pushtun-Baluch tension over the issue of Baluch independence in chapter seven.

The "Broken Treaties"

Abdul Karim's adventure was clearly of little immediate importance because it lacked both unified Baluch political support and Afghan military support. But what did make it significant in the long run was the widespread Baluch belief that Pakistan had betrayed the safe conduct agreement. The Baluch regard this as the first of a series of "broken treaties" which have cast an aura of distrust over relations with Islamabad. Abdul Karim and his followers were all sentenced to long prison terms and became rallying symbols for the nascent nationalist movement.

Nationalist sentiment grew rapidly among the Baluch in response to the aggressive centralizing policies pursued by Pakistani leaders. The hastily contrived Pakistani state that emerged out of the 1947 partition of the subcontinent consisted of a homogeneous, numerically dominant Bengali eastern wing and a heterogeneous western wing divided into ethnically distinct Punjabi, Sindhi, Pushtun, and Baluch regional components. Punjabi leaders, who controlled the military and bureaucratic power structure of the central government, feared that the three minority provinces in the western wing would combine with the Bengalis against them. They decided to consolidate the western wing into a single, unified province that would balance Bengali strength in a projected national governmental structure based on the concept of parity between the two wings. When central authorities began to take concrete steps designed to pave the way for this restructuring of West Pakistan, known as the One Unit plan, Baluch leaders immediately reacted by organizing open opposition in defiance of a ban on political activity. In 1955, Abdul Karim, who had completed his prison term, formed the Ustoman Gal (People's party), which opposed One Unit and demanded the formation of a unified Baluchistan province. The Khan of Kalat supported the concept of a unified Baluch state but wanted it to be under his leadership. Reviving his 1947 demand for independence and for the restoration to Kalat of other Baluch areas taken away by the British, the Khan mobilized widespread demonstrations against the One Unit idea through the tribal chieftains in his former domain.

Against a background of growing restlessness in Baluchistan, the Pakistan Army moved into Kalat on October 6, 1958—one day before martial law was declared throughout Pakistan, setting the stage for the establishment of Ayub Khan's military regime. The army arrested the Khan in his palace, commandeered his ancestral valuables, roughed up civilians who demonstrated in his favor, and detained fifty of his retainers as well as an estimated 300 Baluch political leaders in other towns. The central government charged that Abdul Karim and an uncle of the

Khan had been secretly negotiating with Afghanistan for support of a full-scale Baluch rebellion and had assembled a force of 80,000 tribesmen. However, the only evidence put forward to substantiate these charges was the fact that the Khan's Afghan wife had gone to Kabul for a holiday. The Khan's partisans maintain that these allegations were deliberately planted to provide a pretext for the nationwide imposition of martial law.[11]

The dimensions of this revolt were not as great as depicted in government accounts. Nor were the events of October 6 as bloody as depicted in the Khan's memoirs. Nevertheless, the Khan's arrest, climaxing a decade of steadily accumulating tensions, touched off a chain reaction of violence and counterviolence that has continued in Baluchistan to the present day. Aggressively patrolling the Jhalawan district, the army demanded that tribesmen turn in their weapons at local police stations. This demand outraged the Baluch, who regard the possession of guns as their birthright. The tribesmen refused to comply with this edict, provoking numerous skirmishes in which the army deployed tanks and artillery in towns and remote areas throughout the district. As tribal resistance grew and guerrilla bands began to form, the army blockaded the passes leading from Jhalawan to neighboring Sarawan (see Figure 2). The blockade led to a celebrated battle on October 10, 1958, at a remote mountain village known as Wad. Nauroz Khan, a chief of the Zehri tribe, emerged as the leader of a hastily assembled guerrilla force numbering 750 to 1,000 men.

Aroused by the bombing and confiscation of his house and property, Nauroz Khan, who was then ninety years old, led guerrilla activities against the army in Jhalawan and surrounding districts for more than a year, proclaiming that he would fight on until the Khan was returned to power and the One Unit plan was abandoned. The government responded by bombing villages suspected of harboring guerrillas and by reinforcing army units. Finally, with no end to hostilities in sight, representatives of the army and the guerrillas met in early 1960 to discuss peace terms. According to Pakistani sources, no agreement was reached. But in nationalist accounts, Nauroz Khan and his men agreed to lay down their arms in return for the withdrawal of the One Unit plan and a promise of safe conduct and amnesty. Once again, as in the case of Abdul Karim in 1948, the army representatives sanctified their safe conduct pledge with an oath on the Koran and, once again, they dishonored the pledge. In any event, Nauroz Khan was arrested, and his son and five others were hanged on treason charges in July 1960.

Popular accounts relate that the condemned cried, "Long live Baluchistan!" as they went to the gallows. One of them reputedly tied a copy of the Koran around his neck, shouting that if he were hanged, the Koran must also be hanged, since the government had broken its holy oath. Nauroz Khan's sentence was commuted to life imprisonment, and he died in Kohlu prison in 1964, a martyr to the Baluch cause. Stories of his alleged torture by the army are still a staple commodity of Baluch magazines. On a visit to the Quetta headquarters of the Baluch Students Organization in 1978, I saw a giant montage, covering an entire wall, which showed Nauroz next to scenes of his son's hanging and other atrocities.

The Beginnings of Insurgency

That a relatively small Baluch guerrilla force had been able to pin down well-equipped, numerically superior army regulars greatly disturbed military leaders and prompted them to set up new garrisons at key points in the interior of Baluchistan following the 1960 fighting. Faced with the specter of an expanding and seemingly permanent army presence, a group of politically conscious Baluch began to map plans for an organized guerrilla movement capable of defending Baluch interests. Most of the group were attracted to Marxist-Leninist ideas and wanted to emulate successful leftist guerrilla movements in other countries.

"At first we had a simple objective," Sher Mohammed Marri, the prime mover in this initiative, recalled in a 1978 interview. "We were struggling to save the Baluch nation, which was being crushed by the Pakistani government. We did not define our long-range objectives at that time on the question of independence or autonomy within Pakistan, because we were too busy concentrating on our immediate objective, namely, ousting the Pakistan Army from Baluchistan. We wanted to introduce scientific methods of guerrilla warfare into a struggle that had previously been waged in a disorganized, random manner. We wanted to give the struggle ideological firmness so that it would last from year to year. Until then, the Baluch had fought bravely on a tribal basis when they felt their dignity and honor had been insulted, but they were not organized in such a way that no one would dare to insult them in the first place."

Sher Mohammed, a towering hulk of a man with an oversized turban, a protuberant red moustache, and a long white beard, is a cousin of two leaders of the Bijarani section of the important Marri tribe and a close ally of the powerful *sardar* (chieftain) of the entire tribe, Khair Bux Marri. His father and uncle served prison terms for their anti-British activity, and Sher Mohammed himself served a total of fourteen years in prison, first for organizing a labor party during the preindependence period, despite a British ban on political activity, and later, on two different occasions, for alleged seditious activity against the interests of Pakistan. He played a pioneering role in stimulating grassroots nationalist organizing activity but has never achieved the stature of the three preeminent Baluch nationalist leaders described in the next chapter, Khair Bux Marri, Ghaus Bux Bizenjo, and Ataullah Mengal.

The late president of Pakistan, Zulfiqar Ali Bhutto, charging that Sher Mohammed had links with the Soviet Union, once dubbed him General Sherov. However, while Sher Mohammed calls himself a Marxist-Leninist, his move to create a guerrilla movement in the early 1960s was not supported by the pro-Soviet Communist party of Pakistan. Then as now, the party's line has been that communist forces should strive together to win control of all of Pakistan and that separatist movements in the minority provinces will only serve the interests of feudal and "bourgeois nationalist" elements.

For more than two years, Sher Mohammed and an initial nucleus of twenty ideologically attuned followers quietly laid their plans, seeking to get a network of base camps in place before taking on the army. As the name for their movement, they chose the Baluchi word *parari*, which is used to describe a person or group with grievances that cannot be solved by talk. For their models, Sher Mohammed and his followers looked to the experience of guerrilla struggles in China, Vietnam, Cuba, and Algeria, "but we tried to find a Baluch synthesis rather than to rely on what had happened anywhere else." By July 1963, the Pararis had established twenty-two base camps of varying sizes spread over 45,000 square miles, from the Mengal tribal areas of Jhalawan in the south, where Ali Mohammed Mengal was in command, to the Marri and Bukti areas in the north (see Figure 2). Manned by what they called a "command force" of 400 full-time volunteers, each camp could call on hundreds of loosely organized, part-time reservists.

By design, the Pararis generally attempted to avoid large-scale encounters with the army. Instead, they harassed the Pakistani forces in classic guerrilla fashion by ambushing convoys, bombing trains, sniping at sentries, and raiding military encampments. In retaliation the army staged a series of intermittent offensives marked by free-swinging reprisals and air attacks, which only served to solidify support for the guerrillas. In the first of these offensives, the army bulldozed 13,000 acres of almond trees owned by Sher Mohammed and his relatives in one of the few fertile orchard areas of the Marri region. This action provoked a major battle in December 1964, when 500 Pararis staged a raid on an army camp that resulted in heavy casualties on both sides.

Mir Hazar Ramkhani, chairman of the Revolutionary Command of the Baluch People's Liberation Front

Sher Mohammed Marri, founder of the Parari guerrilla movement (precursor of the Baluch People's Liberation Front)

*Prince Abdul Karim,
leader of the 1948
Baluch insurgency
against accession to
Pakistan*

*Akbar Bukti, former
Governor of Baluchistan
(Pakistan)*

The Pararis claim that their most spectacular success came in a series of clashes with army units in the Gharur area during December 1965. Pakistani forces allegedly suffered almost 200 casualties, a figure belittled by the Pakistani military leaders involved. Numerous witnesses confirm that the Pakistan Air Force staged air strikes during the Gharur fighting, but there is no convincing evidence to support Baluch charges that napalm was used in another battle near Bambore. In any event, stories of atrocities committed by the armed forces circulated widely in Pakistan during the late 1960s. General Tikka Khan, commander of Pakistani forces, was castigated as the Butcher of Baluchistan by anti-government leaders. The fighting in Baluchistan continued sporadically until 1969, when Yahya Khan, who succeeded Ayub Khan in that year, induced the suspicious Pararis to agree to a cease-fire by ordering the withdrawal of the One Unit plan.

Between engagements, the Pararis worked to expand the command force, which had grown to nearly 900 by 1969 and continued to increase in number slowly but steadily after the cease-fire. These full-time volunteers not only conducted military training for reservists, but also operated makeshift medical facilities, schools, and grain-marketing depots, establishing their movement as a virtual parallel government in certain areas. The authority of the guerrillas was largely unchallenged in the Marri area, where they enjoyed the active, albeit covert, support of the tribal *sardar* and received food and other necessities from the Baluch populace. Here, in particular, the Pararis hoped to establish a "liberated" zone or base area, comparable to Mao's Yenan, in the event that the Baluch embarked on a full-scale struggle for independence from Pakistan.

Despite their acceptance of the cease-fire agreement, the Pararis assumed that a renewal of hostilities with Islamabad would prove unavoidable sooner or later. Thus, they decided to keep intact as much of their organizational infrastructure as possible and to continue the training of reservists. Some of their forces in the Mengal areas fell apart once the fighting subsided in 1969, but most of the command force continued to function. When Sher Mohammed came down from the hills after the cease-fire, his young deputy in the Marri areas, Mir Hazar Ramkhani, then thirty-seven, went underground and continued to carry on clandestine organizational activities.

The War Years: 1973–1977

The Parari decision to maintain a state of combat readiness was to prove of some importance three years later, when a new and more serious phase of conflict erupted between the Baluch and Islamabad. Under Mir Hazar's leadership, the Pararis were to play a key role in the Baluch armed struggle against the Bhutto regime, which took power in 1971. The Pararis gradually evolved during the fighting into a well-established movement, now known as the Baluch People's Liberation Front.

The full story of the three-year political struggle between Islamabad and the Baluch leading up to the explosion of hostilities in 1973 does not merit detailed treatment here. On the surface, this Byzantine saga of maneuver and countermaneuver appears to constitute an instructive case study in the problems of federalism in the Pakistani context, since the conflict between Bhutto and Baluch leaders ostensibly centered around significant issues relating to the extent of autonomy to be exercised by local authorities.[12] As later chapters show, however, the specifics of the constitutional controversy between Islamabad and the Baluch were not of decisive importance in themselves. Bhutto's larger political objectives in Pakistan, pressures on Islamabad from the Shah of Iran, Iraqi-Iranian tensions, and Soviet support for Baghdad in its conflict with Teheran were also key factors that contributed to the outbreak of hostilities.

What is germane for our present purposes is that the events leading up to the 1973–1977 insurgency greatly intensified the mutual distrust between the Baluch and Islamabad which had been deepening since 1947. In Pakistani eyes, Yahya Khan had lived up to the cease-fire agreement with the Pararis by abolishing the One Unit concept in 1970, creating a consolidated Baluchistan province, and permitting the Baluch to have their first free elections along with those held in the rest of the country. Bhutto had given a further demonstration of Pakistani good faith, in this perspective, by permitting the Baluch to set up their own provincial government for the first time, based on the 1970 balloting, only to be confronted by a belligerent and uncompromising assertion of provincial prerogatives that was incompatible with the national constitution. In Baluch eyes, however, it was not out of keeping with the constitution's autonomy provisions to oust Punjabi bureaucrats from posts of authority in Baluchistan, to resist Pakistani military and paramilitary intervention in local conflicts, or to harass Punjabi farmers who had taken over the best of the limited arable farmland in the province with Islamabad's backing. Moreover, the Baluch were keenly aware that they had given an unambiguous electoral mandate to the state government headed by Ghaus Bux Bizenjo as governor and Ataullah Mengal as chief minister. The government commanded a 13–7 majority in the Baluchistan Assembly, and its opponents were almost all Pushtuns and other non-Baluch.

When Bhutto suddenly dismissed the Baluch provincial government on February 12, 1973, he did not confine himself to the charge that Bizenjo and Mengal had repeatedly exceeded their constitutional authority. He also gave his action a broader international significance by alleging that they had done so in collusion with Iraq and the Soviet Union as part of a sinister, long-term plot to dismember both Pakistan and Iran. His dismissal of the Baluch leaders was timed to coincide with the sensational disclosure that a cache of 300 Soviet submachine guns and 48,000 rounds of ammunition, allegedly consigned to Baluch leaders, had been uncovered in the Iraqi embassy in Islamabad. The arms were shown to diplomats and journalists and were undoubtedly of Soviet origin, but there was no proof that they were destined for Baluchistan, some 800 miles to the south.

Iraqi officials blamed the incident on antigovernment plotters in the Iraqi intelligence agency who were seeking to embarrass the Saddam Hussein regime.* In any event, Baghdad explained, the weapons were not destined for Pakistani Baluchistan but rather for Iranian Baluchistan, where Iraq was then openly supporting Baluch guerrilla activity in retaliation against the Shah's support of Kurdish rebels (see chapter six). Western intelligence sources have generally accepted the Iraqi explanation, contending that the arms were initially intercepted by Pakistani authorities in Karachi and were later taken north to distant Islamabad in order to maximize the impact of their exposure on the diplomats and foreign journalists, who were concentrated in the capital.

Baluch leaders contended that Bhutto deliberately contrived the "Iraqi arms conspiracy" to provide a pretext for their ouster, aided by dissidents in Baghdad. Some circumstantial evidence supports this claim, but stronger evidence suggests that the key to this still unsolved mystery may lie in the divisions within Baluch ranks in 1972 and 1973 over the tactics to be followed in dealing with Islamabad. Bizenjo, at one extreme, believed that it was possible to work within the system and avoid a costly military confrontation. Sher Mohammed, confident that a new military showdown was approaching, was anxious to get foreign arms for his

---

* The arms cache was allegedly discovered in the residence of Nasir Al-Saud, the Iraqi military attaché in Islamabad and was unveiled to diplomats and journalists there. Al-Saud disappeared from Pakistan three days before the exposure and was later executed, on July 2, 1973, together with Iraqi intelligence chief Nazim Kazzar, in connection with a coup attempt against Saddam Hussein. Antigovernment journalists in Pakistan, who linked the Baghdad coup attempt to the Iranian intelligence agency, SAVAK, said that Al-Saud had collaborated with Iranian and Pakistani intelligence agents in staging the Islamabad arms exposure.

Pararis and appears to have made arrangements for Iraqi arms deliveries on a visit to Baghdad in August 1972. The arms were to have been shared between the Pararis and Iranian Baluch groups. As many informed observers see it, one of the few top-ranking Baluch leaders who knew about this scheme, Akbar Bukti, leader of the Bukti tribe, proved to be a turncoat. By tipping off Bhutto, Bukti unseated his arch rivals, Bizenjo and Mengal—who insist they did not know about the arms—and obtained the governorship for himself. Ironically, Bhutto's dismissal of the Baluch provincial government made his prophecies of a Baluch insurgency self-fulfilling by vindicating Sher Mohammed and forcing Bizenjo, Mengal, and Khair Bux Marri to support a military struggle.

In early April 1973, less than six weeks after the ouster of the provincial government, Baluch guerrillas began to ambush army convoys. Bhutto responded dramatically by flying to Teheran, where he announced after a meeting with the Shah that Iran would provide $200 million in emergency military and financial aid. Then he challenged the Baluch by dispatching four hastily assembled divisions to reinforce the skeleton garrisons in Baluchistan and by jailing Bizenjo, Mengal, and Khair Bux Marri, who was chairman of the governing Baluch political party, the National Awami (People's) party.

To the Baluch, the dismissal of their elected government and the arrest of their leaders on what were regarded as trumped-up treason charges constituted a direct affront. The *Ryvaj,* the traditional code of honor, requires the "true" Baluch to fight, if necessary, to defend his personal and tribal honor, and the overwhelming majority of Baluch tribal leaders regarded Bhutto's action as a deliberate insult to all Baluch, requiring military redress.

Largely unnoticed by the outside world, the struggle between Islamabad and the tribesmen grew in ferocity over the next four years. More than 80,000 Pakistani troops roamed the province at the height of the war. The fighting was more widespread than it had been during the conflicts of the fifties and sixties and touched most of the Baluch population at one time or another. Every area had its legendry of Pakistani villains and Baluch heroes. One unusually dramatic example of Baluch heroism in the face of army excesses occurred in August 1973, soon after the fighting started, and immediately became as well known to Baluch as the Nathan Hale story is to Americans.

Seeking to avenge an ambush in which Pakistani forces had suffered heavy casualties, an army unit stormed into the village of Mali. The soldiers set up an improvised fortress in one corner of the village and then began to ransack huts one by one in search of concealed weapons. Men and women alike were roughly lined up in the village square. Shootouts occurred with those who resisted. Some of the older villagers were beginning to surrender when seventy-two-year-old Mir Luang Khan, elder brother of the Baluch poet and political leader Gul Khan Nasir, hobbled out of his hut on crutches to the center of the square. Shouting that he would die before permitting the troops to violate Baluch honor by intruding on the female members of his family, he picked up his outmoded muzzleloader and started to fire at the soldiers in their forti- fied huts. Soon most of the able-bodied men in the village had joined him in hand-to-hand fighting that lasted for four hours. Army sources con- cede that reinforcements had to be called in before the village could be subdued but deny Baluch eyewitness accounts claiming that fourteen Pakistani soldiers were killed before Mir Luang Khan was shot in the head while hiding with his followers in the village mosque. The Baluch bitterly acknowledge that thirty-five Mali villagers were killed by Pak- istani machine gun and artillery fire, many of them women and children, and compare Mir Luang Khan to Nauroz Khan, the martyred leader of their 1958 uprising.

By July 1974, the guerrillas had been able to cut off most of the main roads linking Baluchistan with surrounding provinces and to disrupt periodically the key Sibi–Harnai rail link, thereby blocking coal ship- ments from Baluch areas to the Punjab. In the Marri area, as we shall see in chapter nine, attacks on drilling and survey operations effectively stymied "imperialist-sponsored" Pakistani oil exploration. Army casu- alties soared as the frequency and effectiveness of ambushes and raids on military encampments increased. "The hostiles were becoming quite bold as the year progressed," recalled the former army commander in Baluchistan, Lt. Gen. Arbab Jahanseb. "They thought they had reached the stage of confrontation with the armed forces in which they would actually be able to drive us out of Baluchistan. They were determined to stop oil exploration. We knew that we had to respond very forcefully or we would simply be unable to bring the situation under control." At this juncture, the Pakistan Air Force was called in. Helicopters were used not only to ferry troops but also to conduct combat operations in mountain- ous areas.

Initially, the Pakistanis employed the relatively clumsy Chinook heli- copters that they had received from the United States under their own military aid program, fitting them with guns for combat use. But in mid-1974, Iran sent thirty U.S.-supplied Huey Cobra helicopters, many of them manned by Iranian pilots. The Huey Cobra was developed during the Vietnam war and had devastating firepower, including a six-barrel, twenty-millimeter automatic cannon with a firing rate of 750 rounds per minute. Until the Huey Cobras arrived, the only way that the

Pakistani forces could block off guerrilla escape routes after an encounter was by concentrating troops at key points on roads and trails. That tactic rarely worked, since the Baluch had much greater knowledge of the terrain. Once the Pakistanis were backed up by six or more gunships, however, special patrols could move in while the helicopters sprayed gunfire into the area ahead of them, slowly herding the guerrillas into ever-shrinking sanctuaries. Even when they sought to hide in previously secure mountain redoubts, the Baluch were often flushed out by the ubiquitous, readily maneuverable Huey Cobras.

The turning point in the war came in a brutal six-day battle at Chamalang in the Marri region (see Figure 2), which helps to explain the continuing intensity of Baluch bitterness toward Pakistan today. Every summer, the Marri nomads converge on the broad pasture lands of the Chamalang valley, one of the few rich grazing areas in all of Baluchistan. In 1974, many of the men stayed in the hills to fight with the guerrillas, but the women, children, and older men streamed down from the mountains with their flocks and set up their black tents in a sprawling, fifty-square-mile area. Chamalang, they thought, would be a haven from the incessant bombing and strafing attacks in the highlands. As the fighting gradually reached a stalemate, however, the army decided to take advantage of this concentration of Marri families as a means of luring the guerrillas down from the hills. The Pakistani officers calculated—correctly—that attacks on the tent villages would compel the guerrillas to come out into the open in defense of their families.

After a series of preliminary skirmishes in surrounding areas, the army launched Operation Chamalang on September 3, 1974, using a combined assault by ground and air forces. Interviews with Pakistani officers and Baluch participants indicate that some 15,000 Marris were massed at Chamalang. Led by the Pararis, guerrilla units formed a huge protective circle around their families and livestock. They fought for three days and nights, braving artillery fire and occasional strafing attacks by F-86 and Mirage fighter planes and Huey Cobras. Finally, when the Baluch ran out of ammunition, they did what they could to regroup and escape. Most of the important Parari units and their commanders managed to get away.

Army accounts claim that 125 guerrillas were killed and 900 captured, and independent estimates suggest that at least 50,000 sheep and 550 camels were captured at Chamalang and auctioned off by the army at bargain prices to non-Baluch in the Punjab. The Baluch minimize their own losses and claim to have killed 446 Pakistani soldiers, but it is clear that their casualties at Chamalang were damaging. They were never able to regain the military initiative in the three ensuing years of savage but increasingly uncoordinated fighting. Government statistics show that the most intensive hostilities in Baluchistan occurred between the start of the insurgency in 1973 and the end of 1975. Of 178 major recorded army encounters with the guerrillas during this period, 84 took place in the Marri area during 1974, with the rest scattered widely over other Baluch areas, especially Khuzdar and Jhalawan (see Figure 2).[13]

Faced with an unrelenting army offensive, Mir Hazar Ramkhani concluded in late 1975 that the best way to keep the Parari movement alive was to operate out of sanctuaries in southern Afghanistan. Leaving behind a skeleton force in Pakistan, he crossed the border with most of his men, their families, and their livestock. They eluded Pakistani sentries by marching stealthily at night in small groups over circuitous mountain routes. The Mohammed Daud regime permitted the Pararis to set up two large encampments and several smaller ones relatively close to the Afghan-Pakistani border (see Figure 2). Officially, they were described as refugee camps to forestall objections from Islamabad. In practice, Mir Hazar's encampments functioned as guerrilla base camps to which his lieutenants in Pakistan and the chieftains of other guerrilla bands regularly came for supplies and strategy meetings. Guerrilla units fighting in the hills periodically came to the Afghan base camps for a period of rest and medical treatment and were replaced by fresh contingents.

After they shifted their headquarters to Afghanistan, the Pararis underwent a significant transformation, as I shall elaborate in chapter five. They adopted an ambitious new program, broadened their membership base, changed their name to the Baluch People's Liberation Front, and began publishing their monthly organ, *Jabal* (Mountain).

When I visited these camps in February 1977, dozens of Baluch guerrillas returning from combat areas described bloody clashes that had just taken place and assured me that the worst of the fighting was yet to come. Later, however, touring Pakistani Baluchistan, it was clear that the degree of popular involvement in guerrilla activity was slowly ebbing. Soon after his ouster of Bhutto in July, General Zia Ul-Haq freed the imprisoned Baluch leaders, Bizenjo, Mengal, and Marri, and eventually reached an uneasy truce with them, temporarily ending the insurgency. Baluch moderates, led by Bizenjo, persuaded other Baluch leaders that it was pointless to continue fighting without adequate weapons, arguing that every effort should be made to test the good faith of the new military regime.

Interviewed in Kabul shortly after the truce started, Mir Hazar was skeptical and bitter, predicting that the agreement would collapse "within four or five years." He warned that "we will never again be caught without the proper weapons. Look what we did with those old guns! We didn't choose the time to fight this time. The fight was thrust upon us. But next time we'll choose the time and the place and we will be properly armed." Then, with a scowl, he asked, "Why doesn't anyone notice our struggle? In the beginning, the Bengalis didn't want independence, but it was forced upon them by Punjabi bullheadedness, and if Pakistan doesn't change its attitude, we'll have no alternative but to go the same way."

Zia made what he regarded as a significant concession to the Baluch in 1978 by releasing an estimated 6,000 prisoners held in controversial prisons at Kohlu and Loralai, where numerous instances of torture were alleged to have occurred. He also declared an amnesty for guerrillas who had gone to Afghanistan, an offer which was declined by the suspicious Pararis but accepted by several smaller groups. However, on substantive issues relating to autonomy for Baluchistan in a restructured Pakistani constitutional system, Zia proved to be as unresponsive to Baluch demands as previous Pakistani leaders had been.

By late 1979, after more than two years of unsuccessful negotiations between the Baluch leaders and Islamabad, Bizenjo and other moderates found it increasingly difficult to make a convincing case for continuing the dialogue with Pakistan. Zia's strict martial law regime, with its ban on political activity, forced most Baluch leaders to remain silent or to operate underground. Resuming political arrests, the police focused initially on the powerful Baluch Students Organization, staging a series of roundups of key leaders that began in 1979 and were still continuing in early 1981. Marri and Mengal, who were increasingly circumspect in public, argued privately that Zia, a Punjabi, was prejudiced against the Baluch and that his plan to replace martial law with an electoral system based on proportional representation would virtually disenfranchise the Baluch and other ethnic minorities.

Ostensibly for medical treatment, Marri and Mengal went into voluntary political exile in Europe in November 1979 and were still there in March 1981, actively seeking foreign support for an independent Baluchistan, while leaving the door open for a resumption of negotiations with Pakistan.

Talking with the Triumvirate

4

The Baluch nationalist movement was radically transformed by five years of guerrilla warfare. Prior to the war, it was little more than a tenuous coalition of a dozen or more feuding tribal leaders patched together intermittently from crisis to crisis. It conspicuously lacked both a significant organizational base and a commonly accepted leadership transcending tribal divisions. Now, as a result of the conflict, the movement is not only becoming better organized but has also started to unite behind three loosely allied leaders who emerged as martyrs during the war years and constitute the unchallenged ruling triumvirate of Baluch politics: Khair Bux Marri, Ghaus Bux Bizenjo, and Ataullah Mengal.

Marri, Bizenjo, and Mengal share a common commitment to the objective of autonomous Baluch-majority states within the Pakistani and Iranian framework or, if this should prove impossible, ultimate independence. In temperament, style, and political philosophy, however, they are strikingly different personalities. Marri, the charismatic, idealistic, Marxist-minded *sardar* of the militant Marri tribe, favors active preparations for a renewed guerrilla struggle. He headed the now outlawed National Awami party in Baluchistan but disdained public office during the short-lived period of provincial self-rule during 1972 and 1973 and advocates a hard line against Islamabad. Bizenjo, once the youthful firebrand who sought to prevent Kalat's accession to Pakistan in 1947, is now the cautious elder statesman who hopes to win autonomy for Baluchistan through negotiations with Pakistani leaders. Bizenjo was Bhutto's choice as governor when the Baluch were given provincial self-rule. As chief minister during the Bizenjo regime, Mengal, *sardar* of the Mengal tribe, also earned a reputation as a parliamentary-minded moderate. He no longer shares Bizenjo's hopes for compromise with Islamabad but is equally chary of Marri's Marxism. It is Mengal, a skillful mediator, who holds the triumvirate together.

To a great extent, the future of Baluch nationalism will be determined by whether these three men can cooperate effectively in future crises, reconciling their differences with respect to the appropriate tactics for the nationalist cause. Until their arrest in 1973, they worked together in the National Awami party, but their organizational activities have diverged since their release from prison in 1977. Marri has covertly encouraged the underground Baluch People's Liberation Front, while Bizenjo promoted the moderate Pakistan National party until Zia banned political activity. This divergence has been reflected in factional alignments in the Baluch Students Organization and in various local nationalist groups. Nevertheless, with Mengal acting as balance wheel, the three leaders have maintained compatible personal relationships and consult each other on major decisions involving contacts with Pakistani leaders and non-Baluch political groups. All three of them are under growing pressure from younger nationalist leaders to forge a closer working unity expressed, organizationally, in some form of coordinating council of nationalist groups committed to an agreed program of action. The first signs of movement toward such unity came in February 1981, when Mengal and Marri cooperated to help create a London-based coalition of Baluch émigré groups, the World Baluch Organization. Nominally dedicated to cultural and social objectives, the new body was expected to facilitate fund-raising among Baluch living abroad in support of Baluch nationalist activity in Pakistan and Iran.

Khair Bux Marri: Marxism and Cockfights

It is not an accident that the *sardar* of the Marri tribe has been the most consistent advocate of a militant Baluch nationalism. Khair Bux II lives in the shadow of his grandfather, Khair Bux the Great, who led Marri resistance against the British in the nineteenth century, and his father, Meherullah Khan Marri, who spearheaded underground anti-British political activity in the decades immediately preceding the 1947 transfer of power. Marris are proud of the key role they have played in past Baluch struggles against foreign rule, too proud in the eyes of some other Baluch tribes who accuse them of having a "master race" complex. As the most numerous Baluch tribe, with a population of some 135,000, historically centered in a strategic, 3,300-square-mile area in the northeast corner of Baluchistan (see Figure 2), the Marris have come to think of themselves as the vanguard of the Baluch cause, especially in the wake of their pivotal role during the 1973–1977 fighting.

In spite of recurring government efforts to undermine his position, Marri has a strong hold on his tribe, which gives him a solid base for his nationalist activity. As Meherullah's eldest son, he was the unchallenged heir to tribal leadership in the patrilineal Marri society. Khair Bux is the seventh leader of the ruling Bahawalan dynasty. An American anthropologist who lived among the Marris for more than a year found a "very striking" attitude of respect for the *sardar* in Marri society "...often approaching awe. It ascribed magical and superhuman qualities to his person and encompassed attitudes which elsewhere in the Middle East are reserved for saints and other holy men."[1]

A slender, stately figure in his early fifties with a lively intellect and a deceptively gentle manner, Marri is a powerful orator and the most influential theoretician of the nationalist movement. However, he has often been indecisive, even naive, in dealing with the nitty-gritty of every-day political activity. He has cosmopolitan intellectual tastes (he reads *Time, Newsweek,* and the *Economist,* as well as Marxist periodicals) and had traveled abroad twice before going into political exile in 1979, visiting both the United States and the Soviet Union. His lifestyle, however, is distinctly Baluch. He makes a point of wearing traditional attire, even in Western countries, and is a fervent devotee of cockfighting, the closest thing to a Baluch national pastime.

Unlike many Third World nationalists who developed an ideological commitment during their college years, Marri was a late starter in politics. Former classmates who knew him as a student at Aitcheson College in Lahore remember him as a happy-go-lucky playboy typical of ruling-class families in preindependence India. Indian Ambassador to Pakistan Shankar Bajpai, who had known Marri well in college, barely recognized him at a diplomatic reception in 1977. Bajpai was astonished to find that the lighthearted youth he remembered had become an intense, intro-verted political crusader who bore the physical and psychological marks of five years in prison, three during the Ayub regime and two at the hands of Bhutto.

Ayub's forcible imposition of One Unit, exemplified by the arrest of *sardars* who opposed the plan and the brutal abandon of General Tikka Khan's military campaign from 1958 to 1960, transformed Marri. "They injured his self-respect," said Mukhtar Hassan, a political analyst for the newspaper *Jasarat.* "It was as simple as that, and he will never forget it." "When Ayub sent the army, Khair Bux was converted from an apolitical young man with no strong ideological leanings to an idealistic, self-educated Marxist who was hungrily searching for answers to the un-expected situation in which he found himself," said Hamida Khurro, a Sind University political scientist who met Khair Bux on a good will mission of Pakistani leaders to the Soviet Union.

Once his political consciousness had been aroused, Marri became the most vocal and unyielding hard-liner in Baluch councils. During the 1960s, his tacit support enabled the Pararis to establish a guerrilla move-ment with a secure network of base camps in Marri territory. In 1968, when Bizenjo and Mengal were ready to accept a compromise with Ayub, Marri balked. Two years later, openly expressing his doubts, he agreed

Khair Bux Marri, former chairman of the governing National Awami Party in Baluchistan (Pakistan)

at the eleventh hour to the more favorable settlement with Yahya that paved the way for elections in Baluchistan.

Marri won one of the Baluch seats in the Pakistan National Assembly and became chairman of the governing National Awami party during the brief period of provincial self-rule in Baluchistan. He continued to suspect Islamabad, however, and quietly helped the Pararis to maintain their guerrilla infrastructure in the hills. In 1973, when Bizenjo signed Bhutto's new constitution, Marri refused, charging that its autonomy provisions were meaningless. Marri's refusal was vindicated, in the opinion of most Baluch, when soon afterward Bhutto summarily dismissed the provincial government and arrested its principal leaders. In 1977, when the Baluch leaders were released by Zia, Marri reluctantly agreed to join with Bizenjo and Mengal in negotiations with Islamabad, but he insisted on major Pakistani concessions as the basis of any settlement. The Baluch should not support the new military regime, he argued, unless Zia agreed to withdraw the Pakistan Army completely from Baluchistan and make adequate compensation payments to the victims of military atrocities. When Zia rejected these terms, Marri was once again vindicated and became firmly established as the most steadfast guardian of Baluch interests.

Pakistani officials make no secret of their belief that Marri is the most "dangerous" of the Baluch leaders, and Marri firmly believes that the Bhutto government tried to poison him during his imprisonment. His evidence is circumstantial and inconclusive, but he continues to be so suspicious that he refused to go to a hospital when he had a hernia operation in early 1978. Instead, he went to the trouble and expense of arranging for a trusted surgeon to perform the operation in his own home in Quetta. "He was concerned that they would somehow manage to have him murdered if he went to a hospital," explained Ataullah Mengal.

Marri's Pakistani critics charge that he is simply a disgruntled feudal baron who has resisted the modernizing programs of Ayub and his successors for selfish reasons. In imposing the One Unit system, Ayub challenged the status of the forty-odd Baluch *sardars* as land-holding tribal chiefs, branding the *sardari* system as incompatible with the objective of integrating the tribal areas into a centralized Pakistani administrative system. Marri argues, however, that he was not fighting Ayub in order to preserve his privileges. As he points out, some *sardars* proved more than willing to surrender the formal trappings of their positions and cooperate with successive Islamabad regimes in return for the continuance of their privileges under a new guise.

Marri, Mengal, and other "progressive" *sardars* disdained such a bargain, charging that Islamabad did not want to modernize the Baluch areas, but only to control them. As evidence, Marri points to the fact that once Ayub found a few *sardars* who would play his game, the land reforms promised as part of the One Unit plan evaporated. In contrast, Marri and Mengal were preparing to implement land reforms of their own when Bhutto ousted the elected Baluch provincial regime in 1973. Marri even abolished many of the oppressive taxes imposed on his tribe by previous chiefs, an action that has endeared him to rank-and-file Baluch.

In addition to a reduced level of the tax revenues normally going to a *sardar* from his tribesmen, Marri receives an income from crown farms and orchards. In the early 1960s, these lands yielded an estimated 50,000 rupees ($10,000) a year. But when Marri gave moral support to the Pararis, Ayub responded by bulldozing fertile orchards and setting fire to some of his other properties. Later, during the 1973–1977 insurgency, while Marri was in prison, the Bhutto regime seized much of his other income-producing farmland, further reducing his revenues. His modest residence in Quetta, where I first interviewed him in August 1978, consists of several small adobe buildings—one of them air-conditioned— grouped around a courtyard. It is a comfortable establishment by Baluch standards but notably spartan in comparison with the opulent homes of pro-Islamabad Baluch businessmen and Punjabi officials elsewhere in the city.

Marri's opposition to the extension of central government development programs to the Marri areas is criticized even by some Baluch. "How can you take the position that there will be no roads and no schools in the Marri area, in this day and age, when you sit in Quetta in an air-conditioned room?" exploded Mahmud Aziz Kurd, a Bizenjo lieutenant. According to Munir Khan, the former chief secretary of Baluchistan, an Islamabad appointee, Marri has betrayed a sentimental desire to preserve tribal mores as well as a thinly veiled fear that development programs would undermine his leadership. In one conversation, Khan said, Marri complained that projected road-building programs would "create difficulties because when you start spending money in this way, a tribal society such as ours will get corrupted. Contractors will come in spreading money about, and people will lose their heads."

Marri himself contended that he has never opposed the modernization of the Marri area but rather what he considers the "exploitative and political character" of central government programs. As an example he cited periodic attempts by Amoco and other foreign companies to drill for oil in the Marri hills with Islamabad's encouragement, recalling with satisfaction that Marri resistance has largely blocked petroleum exploration activity and had even prevented related road-building efforts until recently. "We saw what happened in the Bukti areas, where they have 'developed' the Sui gas, 80 percent of which goes out of Baluchistan to make others rich," Marri said. "Of course we want to do these things, to modernize and to develop in ways and at a speed that we think makes sense under our conditions. We were starting to do this when we were in power. But they don't want us to carry out modernization under our own control. They want to modernize us in their own way, without listening to us." Most of the roads built in Baluchistan, he declared, were "not for our benefit but to make it easier for the military to control us and for the Punjabis to rob us. The issue is not whether to develop, but whether to develop with or without autonomy. Exploitation has now adopted the name of development."

Marri has maintained a calculated public silence since his release from prison in 1977, but he continues to carry on behind-the-scenes political activity. Although he rarely receives journalists and authors, he finally agreed after repeated requests to a "brief" interview on August 1, 1978. His manner was disarmingly modest and unpretentious, and he agonized, Hamlet-like, before responding to many of my questions. But as we talked, drank tea, and ate *sajji*, the traditional, Baluch-style roast leg of lamb, he grew more expansive. Once he started to unbend, he spoke intensely for seven uninterrupted hours in breathless, staccato outbursts only loosely held together by a logical train of thought. This proved to be the first of three extensive interviews over a period of two years.

"In earlier years our struggles had been tribal," he said, "but since 1947 they have become more and more political. It has been a natural process, like a child growing from an embryo. Our people have slowly sensed that they would destroy our identity as a nation if we did not fight back." Prince Abdul Karim's revolt was "the first expression. What did he want? He was not too clear about it, but he knew he wanted a state, something separate, and what he did, when he went to jail, had its educative effect and began the growth of a Baluch consciousness that has been advancing and maturing ever since." Later, when Abdul Karim came out of jail and formed his Ustoman Gal party, "we wanted very simple things, just for our people to be educated for jobs. We were groping for some sort of nationalism, but all we asked for were our simple human rights. Yet, every time there was a price to pay—jail, confiscation of property, being blacklisted, telephones tapped, being thrown in jail, questioned—a high price for doing what was so natural."

"When Nauroz Khan went to the hills in 1958, what did he want?"

Like Abdul Karim, "it was vague, but it was also a desire for a Baluch state. He suffered, and he believed their promise of safe conduct, and then what was the outcome? What happened to him made a great impression on educated young people, on the petty bourgeoisie, on the generation coming up. Call it an eruption, an outflow, what happened is part of history. They went to the hills and other tribes followed. I wonder what was in the mind of Nauroz Khan? He could not have explained it in terms of 'nationalism' but it was to protect his traditions, his sense of identity. There was something in his mind, some vision of freedom for the Baluch."

Repeatedly, Marri's comments revealed his preoccupation with "whether the price that was paid was worthwhile." Were the Baluch patriots who suffered and died asking for enough when they limited their demands to provincial autonomy within a new Pakistani constitutional structure? Speaking figuratively, he asked, if Nauroz Khan "lost his life for an egg, as it were, wouldn't it be worthwhile asking for a poultry farm? We Baluch live in fear that we are going to be exterminated. But for what? For seeking provincial rights? If you are going to suffer in any case, why be simple enough to ask for something small? People are asking these questions increasingly."

Reticent at first to acknowledge his attraction to the idea of an independent Greater Baluchistan, he became more and more explicit as the evening wore on, constantly returning to the theme that "whatever happens, we will suffer, we will pay the same price, we will pay through the nose, so which will we choose? Why do we continue to talk of provincial rights after all that has happened? Will we have a plastic overcoat or one made of the best material? The rain will be heavy in either case."

"It's taken for granted that the Baluch must be *with* somebody else," Marri exploded. "We are expected to accept the idea of Baluch here, Baluch there, scattered in a sort of international triangle. But what is the harm of the Baluch wanting to put themselves together? It will develop, it ought to develop. Are the Baluch really not human? Are they a lower form of human being? Look at the United Nations, look at the little member states of the U.N. like Oman or the Arab Emirates. Can you wonder why we are not satisfied to talk about provincial rights? We are told we are not viable—stretching from the Indus to Iran! Are the Maldives viable? To me there is no such thing as a small people. We are human beings, and we are small only in terms of resources. Internationalism means the equal unity of nations."

Impatiently dismissing the possibility of a satisfactory future for Baluchistan within the Pakistan framework, he declared that "unless there is a plague, we'll always remain a minority, which means we will always be exploited by the Punjabis. Even when they were outnumbered by the Bengalis, before the secession of Bangladesh, the Punjabis were not willing to give the Bengalis just representation. Now, with Bangladesh gone, the Punjabis finally have become a majority and can repress the minorities in the name of majority rule." Until recently, he reflected, "there were many who didn't think of Greater Baluchistan," but as a result of their armed encounters with Pakistan, the Baluch "have learned a little more every time. There has been a certain escalation in each stage of our struggle, and this has produced a clearer recognition that what we confront is nothing less than slow death as a people. There are scars that remain from the things that have happened in the past, the guns, the killing, the rape, and they can't erase them with a smile."

Although he is known as a leftist and has often worn a Mao badge, or in later years a Lenin badge, Marri's ideas are a bizarre mixture of assorted leftist ideology and Baluch tradition. "Sometimes he's an internationalist, sometimes he's a nationalist, and sometimes he's a Marri tribesman," said Mahmud Aziz Kurd. Marri was not wearing his customary Lenin badge on the night of our Quetta meeting, but he spoke earnestly of his interest in Lenin's writings, stressing that he did not necessarily "go all the way. I could wear badges honoring others whom I also respect, for example, the Buddha. What I see in Lenin I miss elsewhere, but it doesn't mean I feel a blind attachment to the man and his teachings. Marxism-Leninism has helped me to understand politics, though being Marxist-Leninist is not easy and I am not sure that I qualify."

Marri talks of adapting Marxist-Leninist ideas to Baluch conditions in a species of national-communism. "Anyone who believes that the problems of Baluchistan can be solved with a Western-style welfare state approach is misled. If anyone thinks the Baluch is going to get his cake —Baluchistan—through parliamentary democracy—well, I doubt it. Through law, I doubt it. If we want our rights, it can't be done in the usual Western way. Capitalist nationalism is obsolete, I am afraid. Today's poor man will not follow his landlord to fight for his freedom. You have to convince him that in a new state he will get his economic rights, and that means some adaptation of what Marx and Lenin have taught."

One of the few subjects on which I could not draw Marri out was his relationship with the Baluch People's Liberation Front guerrillas, who espouse a brand of Marxism-Leninism strikingly similar to his own. He ignored questions about the Front, saying only that he was "not a regular reader" of *Jabal* and gets a copy only "now and then." Murad Khan, a Front spokesman, explained that Marri had "not yet reached the stage of becoming part of the Front, as such, but he respects the will to resist and he respects those who have the courage to resist. He likes what we are doing because he wants his people to understand what they are fighting for. He doesn't want them to fight, as in the past, simply for honor and dignity in the old Baluch tradition." My own conclusion is that Marri has close ties with the Front, like those he had with its precursor, the Pararis, but in 1978 he had not yet left Pakistan and did not want to risk government reprisals needlessly by identifying himself with a group espousing violent action. By clear implication, he accepts the Front's view that an armed struggle will prove necessary to achieve Baluch rights.

Marri hopes that Baluchistan can be independent of great power politics and that "we will not have to hitch ourselves to some bandwagon. Ideologies are shared, they are the common property of mankind, and you don't have to owe allegiance to any one power in order to pursue a certain ideology. When you become pro-this or pro-that you lose something of yourself."

Appealing for a sympathetic American attitude toward Baluch aspirations, Marri said that U.S. support for the Zia regime and its predecessors has been "part of our problem. People think that America aids the Punjabis and that therefore our only alternative is the other camp."

As he talked, Marri returned again and again to the vulnerability of small nations caught in the struggle of big powers, observing wistfully, at one point, that "if you join a bloc, you are dominated, but I suppose that is the way of the world." Then he exploded that "people should not be puppets. We would like to be a partner, not a ward. We shouldn't deceive ourselves and go from one slavery to another. Or can we say we'll *accept* this or that slavery for our own reasons? People often say they'll try the 'new evil' rather than the 'old evil.'"

At the time of our Quetta meeting, the April 1978 Communist revolution in Kabul was four months old. Alluding to the new regime's expressions of interest in the Baluch cause, Marri mused that "before we Baluch can walk, we may be carried on the feet of others. It's a pity. Before we even begin fighting, we may lose our independence. This will be the test for us." As a result of the sanctuary given by Afghanistan to Mir Hazar's guerrillas, he said, the Baluch feel a strong sense of obligation to Kabul, and "there is a danger that the Afghans will decide for us, will think for us." If Afghanistan could remain independent of the Soviet Union, he observed, close ties with Kabul might not be too risky for the Baluch, and "we might be able to have communism without being mortgaged to another power, or at least without getting a mortgage so big that we can't pay it off."

By the time I had my second meeting with Marri on March 11, 1980, he had gone into exile in London. Soviet forces had occupied Afghanistan, and his hopes for a national-communist regime in Kabul had been swept aside. I found him in a grim mood as he surveyed the stark options confronting the Baluch. "What can we, what can the Afghans, what can any small nation do?" he asked. "You need help, but when you accept it, they feel they have their investment and they take you over. You are porous, you become saturated, you become part of something larger that you can't control." Whether it is "the Russians or the Americans, can you take help from any stronger side and retain your own image of yourself? It must be possible! If we take weapons for our struggle, it is still our own blood we are shedding, isn't it? Isn't the blood we shed for our cause worth more than their weapons? Why can't superpowers help us for what we are? Why is it smaller nations must fit in a certain mold?"

Even after the Soviet occupation, he said, "the Baluch people think, 'I don't like the Punjabis, so let the Russians come.' But those with a higher responsibility have to think, 'If the Russians come, what share do I have?'" Then he turned to me angrily, adding, "Why is it the United States always works through the established structure? If the Americans pump weapons into the Punjabis, obviously we have to stretch our hand to another superpower." In January 1981, Marri paid a flying visit to Kabul, where he conferred with Mir Hazar Ramkhani and other leaders of the Liberation Front guerrillas encamped in southern Afghanistan (see chapter five) as well as with Afghan officials. On his return to London he no longer made any secret of his links with the Front. His visit was prompted, he explained, by "some minor problems" that had arisen in relations between the guerrillas and the Karmal government. Expressing gratitude for the sanctuary given to the guerrillas by Afghanistan, he noted that the Liberation Front had never formally declared its support either for the Khalq Communist faction that took power in 1978 or for Karmal's Parchamite regime, adding that "perhaps they misunderstand our reticence." He said in response to a question that he did not meet with Soviet officials during his two-week stay in Kabul.

At times, Baluch leaders have talked of a neutral, independent Baluchistan that would refuse to grant military bases to either Moscow or Washington. Asked whether the Baluch could pursue such a middle course, seeking help for a guerrilla struggle simultaneously from both superpowers as well as from other countries, Marri declared without hesitation that "if this was ever realistic, it is not now. Either you are in one camp or the other. The question is, whose aid can we get, whose aid can we accept, without selling out completely?"

When I suggested that a settlement with Pakistan would be preferable to achieving independence under superpower tutelage, he responded after a brief pause that "if the Punjabis or the Pakistani state are prepared to talk with us in a mature way, with some kind of realism and some understanding of how our people feel, we are prepared for a settlement, as we have always been. But there is no use wasting time talking of minor matters. They must be prepared to talk in terms of a national status for us, of a relationship with us based on that status. I must confess that I cannot ever remember a Punjabi talking in such terms."

Ghaus Bux Bizenjo: Elder Statesman or Secret Communist?

"That man can't live without politics. I can do without it, but he has to have it all the time or he will perish." This is how his close colleague, Ataullah Mengal, characterizes Ghaus Bux Bizenjo, the elder statesman of Baluchistan. Unlike Khair Bux Marri, who regards parliamentary politics as a charade, Bizenjo thrives on the conventional political game. Marri often has to be coaxed into conversation, but Bizenjo holds forth readily in the stentorian tones of an orator, gravely delivering well-rounded declarations that would stand up in print without a word changed. In my view, he is one of the ablest politicians in Pakistan and could have played a major role in Islamabad but for his Baluch identity and his commitment to the Baluch cause.

A portly, fatherly-looking man with a genial personality, Bizenjo, who was sixty-three in 1981, belongs to the ruling Hamalani wing of the Bizenjo tribe but lacks the solid base of tribal power that Marri and Mengal have as *sardars*. Although his father was *sardar* of the tribe, "Ghausi," as he is widely known among the Baluch, was too young when his father died to become *sardar*, so his first cousin was chosen instead. Nevertheless, because of his princely lineage, he inherited an estimated 25,000 acres of land and received special attention from the British political agent in the Bizenjo area, who arranged for him to attend a missionary school in Quetta and Aligarh Muslim University in what is now India.

As a result of his education at Aligarh, Bizenjo received much greater exposure to the broad currents of preindependence political life in the subcontinent than his more parochially educated Baluch colleagues, with the notable exception of Oxford-educated Akbar Bukti, the urbane *sardar* of the Bukti tribe. Aligarh was the breeding ground of "nationalist Muslim" politicians who supported the Congress party of Gandhi and Nehru in its advocacy of a united, secular India and who were opposed to Mohammed Ali Jinnah's call for a separate Islamic Pakistan. It was natural for a young Baluch to feel drawn to the Congress party at Aligarh, since Baluchistan, with its homogeneous Muslim population, did

Ghaus Bux Bizenjo

not share the fear of Hindu domination that motivated Jinnah's followers in other parts of the subcontinent where Muslims were a minority. Bizenjo was more attracted by the anticolonialism of the Congress party than by the anti-Hindu doctrine of the Muslim League and joined a Congress-sponsored group active at Aligarh. At the same time, he drifted into campus Communist activities. He went back to Baluchistan armed with a battery of anti-British and leftist ideas mingled with the budding spirit of a Baluch nationalist.

According to K. B. Nizamani, who was secretary of the Sind and Baluchistan branch of the Communist party in the late 1930s, Bizenjo was a Communist in 1938 and 1939, but then broke with the party over its support of the pro-Pakistan movement. As the end of British colonial rule approached, Bizenjo and other Baluch nationalists formed the Kalat National party, discussed earlier, which was dedicated to the establishment of an independent Baluchistan. At the age of twenty-nine, Bizenjo made his memorable 1947 speech (see chapter three) opposing the accession of Kalat to Pakistan. Significantly, Bizenjo has never disowned this speech, insisting that it was not treasonous, as the Bhutto regime charged, since Kalat was not yet a part of the new state of Pakistan when he made it.

As a result of his youthful championship of independence and his respected status as the eldest top-ranking Baluch politician, Bizenjo was popularly known for many years as *Baba-i-Baluchistan* (Father of Baluchistan). More recently, his militant critics, angered by his efforts to compromise with successive Pakistani regimes, have increasingly suggested that he is selling out, dubbing him *Baba-i-Negotiations*. Talking with Bizenjo, however, I was left with little doubt that he is as dedicated as Marri and other militants to the cause of Baluch autonomy or independence. His differences with the militants are not over ultimate objectives but rather over how fast and how far to go in pursuing Baluch goals in a rapidly changing regional and global environment.

In my two conversations with Bizenjo in Quetta on July 31 and August 1, 1978, he repeatedly emphasized that the Baluch problem was part of a larger, "interlocking" set of problems confronting the artificially created, multinational states of Pakistan, Afghanistan, Iran, and India. "There will have to be changes in the way that all of these countries are constituted, or there will be no peace in our region," he declared. "They will have to change because the present situation, as a result of the colonial boundaries, is one of great confusion. No one can escape this. We have to decide what to do with these inherited artificial states lumping together diverse nationalities with no rhyme or reason. What we have in so many cases is a new type of colonialism. It is not just the Baluch.

Look at the Kurds. What will become of Iran, which is, after all, a multinational state? Look at the manner in which incompatible ethnic groups have been put together in something called Afghanistan! It was only the strategic needs of the British and the Russian czars that made it possible for Afghanistan to become an independent state in the form that it took. I don't believe in a narrow nationalism. The answer for all of us lies in regional confederations."

As the first step toward a rearrangement of regional boundaries, Bizenjo calls for the recognition of Baluchistan, Pushtunistan, Sind, and the Punjab as separate nationalities and the adoption of a new Pakistani constitution giving each national unit much wider powers than those accorded in any of the constitutions that existed before Zia's martial law regime. This stand has brought him into perennial conflict with the proponents of a unitary Pakistani constitutional structure. Provoked by an attack on his autonomy demands in a Punjabi newspaper, Bizenjo issued a much quoted statement in Lahore on August 28, 1978, ridiculing the official position that Pakistanis of all ethnic backgrounds constitute a single nationality because they share the Muslim faith. Citing the Koran, Bizenjo declared that "there is no such thing as a Muslim nation on the face of this globe. The Almighty recognized tribes, clans and nationalities, as he did a universal brotherhood of all believers."[2]

Bizenjo infuriates the Punjabis by warning that it is the advocates of a monolithic Pakistan who will be responsible if the country disintegrates. "Yesterday those who spoke of the 'ideology of Pakistan' were the ones responsible for the separation of East Pakistan," he charged in his 1978 Lahore broadside. "Today they can become guilty of breaking up what is left of Pakistan as well. We have reached a crossroad in our history where we must refrain from the practice of making unfair attacks and allegations of 'secessionist' against each other. Because to me the end result of these unfair attacks could be very fatal." To Punjabis, such statements have an implicitly threatening tone. Thus, in a *Pakistan Times* article, Bizenjo warned that "if people persist in remaining unconcerned about situations like those which developed in East Pakistan and later in Baluchistan, then every four or five years the nation will go through a period of utter confusion and chaos, frustration and despair, and as a natural consequence, martial law will come in."[3]

In this article, Bizenjo envisaged "a type of federation, not a confederation," in which the central government of Pakistan would continue to control defense, foreign affairs (including foreign trade), currency, and communications and would have the power to tax the constituent units "to the extent necessary" to fulfill these responsibilities. At the same time, he explained, the federation would be "a loose one" because "only those rights which are necessary for the common interest and for mutual survival would be *surrendered voluntarily* to the center, and in all remaining matters the federating units would retain full power in their own hands." Thus, in addition to the powers stipulated under the defunct 1973 constitution, adopted during the Bhutto regime but bypassed by Zia, each unit would also have the powers on the so-called Concurrent List that were to have been shared under the terms of that carefully negotiated charter between the central and provincial governments. The four national units would have "full control and sovereignty over their own natural resources," he said, and preference would be given to local residents in jobs, contracts, and other aspects of economic development. Asked how economic planning on a federal level would be possible under such a constitutional arrangement, Bizenjo said that "all four provinces of Pakistan depend on each other and will continue to do so. The representatives of these provinces will be able to establish joint institutions to the extent that they find it necessary to do so."

Discussing the prospects for a constitutional settlement, Bizenjo often gave me the impression that he did not really expect the Punjabis to make the necessary concessions but felt that the onus for the possible breakup of the country should be kept squarely on Islamabad. "We must do our duty before history to prevent further bloodshed if we can." Even if a settlement were reached, he cautioned, "we would have to see how such a system would work, and whether the people in the minority national units would feel secure. We would have to make some arrangements in such a constitution to prevent interference in the power and authority of the autonomous federal units. We didn't have such safeguards under the 1973 constitution, and this is why it proved to be no more than a scrap of paper when Mr. Bhutto wanted to circumvent it, using the civil service, the army, and paramilitary forces to get control over us."

When I commented that many Baluch saw no hope at all of a constitutional settlement under the Zia military regime and were thinking of another armed struggle, Bizenjo responded that "if you can't solve the problem by mutual understanding and peaceful means, naturally the militant feeling will crop up. But this is not our fault, it is because of the failure of the authorities in Pakistan to deal with the problems in a reasonable manner. I'm afraid that sentiment will grow." At the mention of the Baluch People's Liberation Front, he said, "Why have these people gone to the hills? Because of the Pakistani attitude. This movement was not created by foreigners, by the Soviet Union or China; they are just Baluch fighting for their rights."

Recalling the tense months leading up to the 1973 rupture with Bhutto, Bizenjo said, "I had been struggling to avoid a confrontation and had even gone to the extent of damaging my political image because I knew that a confrontation with Bhutto would ultimately mean the rule of the army. I was able to prevent such a confrontation for nearly one year, but Mr. Bhutto was bent on a reckless course. It was obvious to me that the ultimate result of his military adventure in Baluchistan would be his removal and the sort of military rule that we now have." Since his release from prison in 1977, Bizenjo added, "I have been trying with my colleagues to find some basis for normalization with the military leaders, but we have not been successful, and it will be damaging to me as well as to my people if we fail. I do not see any other moderating force in the picture."

In contrast to Marri, who is uneasy and ambivalent about seeking Soviet or other foreign help for an independence struggle, Bizenjo stated that "in a crisis, naturally we will seek help from somewhere, and if we get it, we will accept it. When a nationality is fighting for survival, what do you expect? If any nationality in any country faces permanent exploitation by majority nationalities, and those majority nationalities are protected and helped by the Western bloc, then in order to fight for their survival the minorities will naturally not hesitate to have help from anywhere."

Even if the Baluch did accept Soviet help to achieve their independence, Bizenjo hastened to add, "taking help and support is one thing, and the way you do things in your own country is something quite different. In most respects, we would not emulate the Russian model in our country. Of course, when other countries help, it's not a charity. They are trying to influence you politically and you incur certain obligations. But we would not forget the interests of our own people. We feel we have the capacity to stand up for our interests."

One area in which the Baluch do admire the Soviet model, Bizenjo indicated, is "their approach to the national question. We have been inspired by their idea that the existence of separate nationalities should be recognized and that each nationality should have the ultimate right of secession. However, we also recognize that the way the system works in practice is different from theory. Russia is centralized, and to them the national question is subordinate to the communist ideology. But if socialism is working there correctly, then the people of the non-Russian nationalities will be satisfied. Socialism and communism, if practiced properly, have the capacity to solve the national question."

Until recently, Bizenjo has carefully omitted references to the ultimate right of secession from his demand for a Pakistani constitution based on the recognition of four nationalities. This position was consistent with the Soviet line, which emphasizes the goal of a "united, socialist, federal" Pakistan and opposes separatism as a weapon of "bourgeois nationalists." In April 1980, however, Bizenjo explicitly included the right to secede in his response to a proposal for an antigovernment alliance between his Pakistan National party and former air marshal Asghar Khan's Tehriq Istiqlal (Movement for Integrity). A proposed joint manifesto submitted by Bizenjo for Asghar Khan's approval would have called for strictly limiting the powers of the central government to defense, foreign affairs, communications, and currency, while providing for the right of provincial units to secede if Islamabad violated their constitutional prerogatives. Before Asghar Khan could respond, he was arrested by Zia for his attacks on the martial law regime. In the meantime, Bizenjo had circulated copies of his draft, which was never published, to a small circle of Baluch leaders.

Various Baluch sources who described this highly significant change differed about its meaning. Some felt that since Bizenjo keeps in close touch with the pro-Soviet lobby in Pakistan, his shift indicates that Moscow is moving toward a newly flexible position on the issue of an independent Baluchistan. Others thought that Bizenjo simply wanted to remain in step with the militant temper of Baluch opinion and acted entirely on his own.

Bizenjo's links with pro-Soviet Communist activists have led some of his political opponents to charge that he is more of a Communist than a nationalist and that, someday, he will be Moscow's most valuable ally in Pakistan. In particular, his detractors emphasize his ties with Nawaz Butt of Karachi and Shameem Malik of Lahore, leaders of the Communist-sponsored National Progressive party. They point out that he consistently advocated a Soviet-tilted brand of neutralism as a leader of the Pakistan National party and its predecessor, the outlawed National Awami party, and opposed attempts by the Pushtun NAP leader, Abdul Wali Khan, to promote a centrist policy. These critics also point to his strong support of the "progressive" 1978 Afghan revolution and to his vocal opposition to Pakistani support of the anti-Communist Afghan rebels. Warning in early 1979 that pro-Kabul Baluch and Pushtun insurgent activity would be unleashed in the border areas if Islamabad and its Chinese and Western allies continued to support the Afghan rebels, Bizenjo urged "all concerned to take note of the delicate nature of the geopolitical situation in our region. You are playing with fire. I must make it explicitly clear that we Pakistanis, especially the Baluch and Pushtuns who live on both sides of the borders of these three neighboring countries, will resolutely oppose all attempts to push us over the precipice to disaster."

Comparatively, Bizenjo is undoubtedly more pro-Soviet in his outlook than Marri or Mengal, but it would be a mistake, in my view, to write him off as a captive of Moscow. Many student leftists and nationalist militants in Baluchistan thoroughly distrust him, branding him as a chameleonlike opportunist who would have betrayed the Baluch cause in his 1977 negotiations with Zia in return for tokens of political power and economic largesse if Marri and Mengal had not stopped him. To these leftist critics, his sympathies with Marxism-Leninism are only superficial. They charge that he has become increasingly beholden to big business interests which have backed his political activities, notably the Haroun conglomerate and Mustikhan Transcontinental, controlled by Akber Y. Mustikhan, the millionaire Baluch contractor.

Despite his long-standing criticism of the Iranian Shah as a Western puppet, Bizenjo jumped at an invitation to visit Teheran in June 1972, during his tenure as governor of Baluchistan. He had several private talks with the Shah and proudly unveiled an economic aid package for Baluchistan on his return. This visit brought sharp attacks from leftist leaders throughout Pakistan, who charged that he was plotting with Teheran and Washington to bring the Pakistani Baluch areas under Iranian hegemony. At the time of our conversations, the Shah was still in power. When I asked Bizenjo whether he could imagine circumstances in which Iran could provide help for the achievement of Baluch aspirations, his response was an enigmatic "beggars can't be choosers, after all," a smile, and a quick change of the subject.

As for his Soviet-tilted foreign policy declarations, closer examination shows that many of these were inspired directly or indirectly by American military aid policies that have bolstered Pakistani military regimes over the years and have facilitated Islamabad's repression of the Baluch. Commented Ataullah Mengal, "If strong criticism of misguided American policies that have affected us as Baluch is 'pro-Soviet,' then many of us are guilty of that." While Bizenjo might have been "more favorably disposed" toward the Russians in earlier years than some of his Baluch colleagues, Mengal said, he "cooled off considerably, like the rest of us," when Soviet representatives in Pakistan gave their blessing to the Bhutto regime at the expense of the Baluch, tacitly approving Bhutto's military offensive in Baluchistan and even belaboring Bizenjo, at one point, for opposing him. Bizenjo's disenchantment has grown, Mengal added, since the Soviet occupation of Afghanistan, though he has stopped short of open criticism of Moscow "because the Americans are also involved in the region and it is certainly not a black and white situation." If he were serious about his socialism, Mengal reflected, Bizenjo would not have objected so self-righteously when Bhutto confiscated his lands during the insurgency. "I often tease him, 'You are a socialist as long as it doesn't affect you personally.' What kind of socialist is it who prays five times a day and recites from the Koran? Ghausi is a nationalist. We are all nationalists."

Akber Y. Mustikhan, who has backed both the National Awami party and the Pakistan National party, said that Bizenjo has regained most of the lands taken by Bhutto but still owns at most a few hundred acres of cultivable farmland. Only recently has he begun to show some interest in developing his extensive mountain tracts, which have a "great potential" for orchards and dairies. "He is not interested in money," lamented Mustikhan. "He is a completely political animal, and a very pragmatic man in his sphere. He has absolutely no illusions about the Russians. He will not play their game unless you Americans, and the Pakistani authorities, force him to do so, unless there is no other alternative. You can say that Ghausi is an opportunist, in the positive sense of the word, in the sense of what is best for the Baluch. But don't forget that he has been brought up in Western-style parliamentary politics. This is what he knows best and loves best. It is too bad that it has never been possible to play this kind of politics for very long in Pakistan."

Bizenjo himself guffaws at suggestions that he is a Communist, roaring, "Which of the ninety Communist factions in Pakistan would I join? They all want to be the leader, they all want Moscow to support them, and Moscow laughs at all of them. It is one thing to understand the experience of socialist countries and what this means for us. It is quite another to talk of the type of Communists we have in Pakistan."

My own conclusion is that Moscow has been seriously cultivating Bizenjo as its principal potential ally in Pakistan. Communist leaders consciously flatter his ego by treating him not as a mere Baluch leader, but as the future prime minister of a "socialist, federal" regime in Islamabad. Bizenjo, for his part, is still ready to strike a bargain with Zia for an autonomous Baluchistan, but he no longer believes such a bargain is possible. Moscow, he calculates, is likely to become increasingly influential in South Asia once it has secured its hold in Kabul. He hopes that Soviet objectives will prove to be "much more limited" in Pakistan than they were in Afghanistan and that the Baluch will be able to turn events to their advantage if they are sufficiently adroit. Thus, he suggests, the most promising way to break the grip of the Punjabi-dominated military on the country may well be to promote a "national democratic" government with Communist participation that will grant autonomy to the provinces, including the ultimate right of secession. If such a government pursued a neutralist foreign policy, he argues, the West should not object, since the only acceptable alternative in Soviet eyes may well be the dismemberment of Pakistan.

Solemnly recalling the "terrible horrors" of the 1973–1977 period, "the terrible suffering of so many innocent people," Bizenjo continually stressed the theme that it is "our duty to do what we can in the political and diplomatic arena" before countenancing another bruising military struggle for independence. In the wake of the Soviet occupation of Afghanistan, he fears that Baluchistan could become the focus of a superpower collision that could greatly damage the Baluch cause. "Now that Afghanistan can no longer play the role of a neutral buffer," he observed, "perhaps Pakistan, which is very much affiliated with the Western powers, should change its course and should play that role. If it fails to do so, there may well be a series of upheavals and conflicts leading to the breakup of Pakistan, and the superpowers will have to create a new buffer zone to preserve peace in the Persian Gulf area. We would rather become this new buffer state, with the concurrence of the superpowers, than achieve our independence through alignment with one or the other of them. The cost in blood and tears would certainly be much less for us."

Ataullah Mengal: "Let Them Come to Us"

Lean and wiry, with blazing black eyes and a carefully preened black beard, Ataullah Mengal, who was fifty-one in 1981, is a more "typical" Baluch than his two colleagues. He speaks in the straightforward and often fiery manner traditionally esteemed in Baluch culture, looking you directly in the eye. Less sophisticated in his educational background than Marri or Bizenjo, he shuns their intellectual and ideological pretensions. Like Marri, Mengal is bitter and unrelenting in his suspicion of the Punjabi-dominated Pakistani establishment. Like Bizenjo, however, he is calculating, cunning, and coldly pragmatic. He is the symbol of uncomplicated Baluch patriotism and commands broad respect in all political factions.

Next to the Marris, the Mengals are probably the most numerous Baluch tribe, with some 85,000 people spread over the Khuzdar, Kalat, and Las Bela districts (see Figure 2). Ataullah's father, Rasul Bux, was a popular *sardar* who concentrated on building the power of the ruling Shahizai clan and tending to his farmlands and orchards. Rasul Bux remained aloof from politics, but his son soon began to show an interest in liberal and nationalist ideas as a student at a small Islamic college in Karachi. Even though he was repelled by the rigidity of the Marxist thought then fashionable on the campus, he was moved by the arguments of moderate reformers who attacked the inequities of the feudal economic structure in Pakistan.

Mengal dramatically divested himself of nearly half of his inherited lands, parceling them out among his tenants. Like Marri, he earned a reputation as an incorruptible, progressive *sardar*. During the 1950s, horrified by army excesses in Baluchistan, he gradually drifted into political life. Baluchistan did not yet exist as a provincial entity under the Ayub regime, but the Baluch areas were represented in the National Assembly. Mengal ran successfully as an independent for the assembly and promptly collided with the Ayub regime by denouncing military rule and demanding autonomous provincial status for Baluchistan. Ayub then attempted to depose him as *sardar* in 1962, appointing in his stead a distant cousin, who was murdered by irate tribesmen on the day of his inauguration ceremony. Although Mengal pleads innocence, pointing out that he was far from the scene, the Ayub regime jailed him for complicity in the murder. He was released after two months, and Islamabad once again acknowledged him as *sardar* in the hope that he would prove more cooperative. But by April 1963, he was imprisoned again, this time for allegedly seditious statements, and was not released until January 1967.

Mengal emerged more politically conscious than ever from his four-year imprisonment and joined Marri and Bizenjo in organizing the Baluchistan branch of the National Awami party and in campaigning for the unification of the Baluch areas in Baluchistan province, a demand formally granted by Yahya Khan, who deposed Ayub in 1969. When the National Awami party won the 1970 elections in Baluchistan, Mengal became chief minister. When Bhutto ousted him, triggering the 1973–1977 insurgency, the Mengal tribe played a major role in the fighting. However, the Mengals proved to be less united than the Marris. Several of Mengal's five brothers sabotaged his efforts to mobilize the tribe against the government.

Mengal suffered a shattering personal tragedy during the course of the fighting when his second son, Asadullah, was shot down in broad daylight on a Karachi street by Bhutto's agents. Although Zia promised Mengal that he would find and punish the killers, Zia has never done so, claiming that the evidence has all been destroyed. Citing information supplied by former Bhutto aides, Mengal alleges that the real reason for Zia's unwillingness to deliver on his promise is that army personnel were involved, including a brigadier general.

During the three years I have known Mengal, his nationalist attitudes have progressively hardened, and he has gradually abandoned his hopes for accommodation between the Baluch and Islamabad. When I first met him, on October 14, 1977, in New York, he had just been released from prison for medical reasons by the newly installed Zia regime and had come to the United States for open-heart surgery. Marri and Bizenjo were still being held on treason charges, despite the fact that Zia had halted many of the other politically motivated judicial proceedings initiated by the Bhutto regime. Shortly before releasing Men-

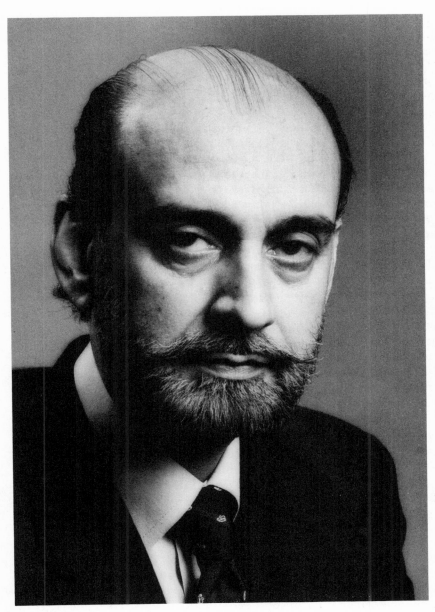

Ataullah Mengal,
former Chief Minister
of Baluchistan
(Pakistan)

gal, Zia went to the prison, summoned the three leaders for a "friendly chat," and offered to improve the conditions of their confinement. "It was clear even then," Mengal said, "that the General didn't think what Bhutto had done to us was so terribly bad, after all, even though he made some comments critical of Bhutto." The meeting ended in an atmosphere of considerable tension, recalled Mengal, after Zia told his captives that "we are all Muslims, and we should not say that we are Baluch or Pushtuns." Bizenjo angrily rejoined that "we are Baluch and Pushtuns and we will never make a viable Pakistan except on that foundation."

Marri and Bizenjo were released eventually, but by freeing other political prisoners so much earlier than the Baluch, Mengal declared, Zia had "reinforced the feeling of our people that they are second-class citizens of this country. Before, we could say that it was just Bhutto, but now they can see that the Pakistani government and the Punjabis are all the same, regardless of who is in power." A delegation of student leaders came to meet him in Karachi after his release, Mengal said, and "were all talking to me about independence. They said they could see no future in Pakistan. They belittled the meaning of elections for the Baluch, even if they were ever held, since we are so few in number compared to the rest of Pakistan. They said that our vote does not count." When Mengal argued that justice could still be obtained in Pakistan through political means, Moem Khan, then president of the Baluch Students Organization, posed question after question about the circumstances of his 1973 ouster to demonstrate the futility of attempting to work with a Punjabi-dominated central government. "Then they abused the Zia regime and said that it was not just Bhutto or Zia who was to blame for what had happened, it was the Punjabi mentality. I advised them to work for a new constitution and a new type of federalism. They said nothing doing, they can't adjust to this country. They said, we will have oil, we will have uranium, so why can't we be independent?"

In 1978, when I next met Mengal in Karachi on July 19 and in Quetta on July 30, I found him increasingly disturbed by the polarization that was developing between Bizenjo's supporters, on the one hand, and hard-liners who looked to Marri as the probable leader of a new armed struggle. Mengal found himself in the middle, trying to hold the triumvirate together.

Mengal was also more doubtful of Zia than ever. The three leaders had held repeated meetings with Zia and his advisers, he said, and had been unable to get clear responses to their demands. These included "at least $10 million" in compensation for damages suffered by the Baluch during the insurgency, a comprehensive amnesty for political prisoners, and the complete withdrawal of Pakistani army and paramilitary units. Mengal was bothered most of all by the lack of any clear movement from military government back to civilian rule under a stable constitution that would protect the interests of the Baluch and other minorities. "Assuming that we could get understandings with them on immediate issues, how could they assure us that what they accepted would be honored by their successors?" he asked. "Even Zia is not a free man. He is surrounded by a tight circle of advisers and it takes a long time to implement even the smallest concession that he makes to us. That gives a handle to our hawks, who can charge with considerable credibility that he is not living up to his undertakings."

What the Baluch face, Mengal said, is a "whole gang of Punjabis" in the bureaucracy and the army, "a network that has complete control of the civil service machinery in Baluchistan and has no sympathy for the agreements we have been discussing with General Zia." This "gang" actively sabotaged the negotiations with Zia when the Baluch demanded a Baluch-controlled administrative structure for handling compensation payments. They also "put a lot of pressure on Zia" when the Baluch insisted that the Punjabi chief secretary of Baluchistan province be dismissed and replaced by a Baluch.

"They take the attitude that we have to prove our patriotism," said Mengal, "but we have had enough of this cringing. We're not going to continue going to them, paying homage to them to get their certificate of patriotism and approval. Let them come to us. If they call me a traitor a thousand times, it means I'm loyal to my people, the people of Baluchistan. I'm going to tell them that in the eyes of the Baluch, the Punjabi is enemy number one. I'll tell them, 'You satisfy the younger generation. They are deadly against you and they say to hell with Pakistan.' "

Mengal spoke grimly of the "impossible choices" confronting the older generation of Baluch leaders, who are caught between "Punjabi bullheadedness" and the demands of militant student groups pushing for an independence struggle. As a result of the intransigence shown by Pakistani leaders, he said, "I have no grounds left to plead the case for further efforts to come to an understanding with Pakistan. I tell the students that independence is not possible without a terrible price and might not be possible at all. I tell them that our location makes others feel it is necessary to control us. I ask them: 'Would you like to change masters? Will that suit you?' But still, they go on talking about independence and working secretly for independence. I tell the students, 'I won't oppose you, but I won't lead you. I'll be an ordinary follower. Let history judge who is right. You take the responsibility for the blood bath that a struggle for independence would involve. I can't take the responsibility for leading you in that direction.' "

In our 1978 conversations, Mengal talked gloomily of retiring from politics, declaring that "we will slip out of the scene, relax in our homes, and leave the whole thing to the young men. There is nothing for us to do if we are forced to choose between the betrayal of our honor and a course of reckless adventurism." By mid-1979, however, he and Marri had decided to carry on their struggle as political exiles and had left the country, ostensibly for medical treatment. Mengal's heart problems were well known, and Marri had been seeing internal medicine specialists in Pakistan, complaining of a digestive ailment. When they asked for permission to go to London, Pakistani officials could find no plausible reason for refusing. By all accounts, Islamabad concluded that the two leaders would be less of a nuisance outside the country than inside. However, the government began to have second thoughts after more than a year had passed and the leaders showed no signs of wanting to return.

In subsequent conversations with Mengal, by telephone and in London during the course of 1980, it became clear that he was reappraising his attitude toward an independence struggle. He no longer felt it would be "reckless" to pursue guerrilla activity if adequate foreign support could be arranged on acceptable terms. By remaining abroad, he felt that he could make contacts more easily than in Pakistan and could speak out more freely if, at some stage, he and Marri gave up all hope of a settlement with Islamabad and decided to establish a Baluch government-in-exile.

I also found that Mengal had radically upgraded his conditions for a political settlement with Pakistan. In 1978, he was still ready to accept a loose federation of the type advocated by Bizenjo, although he demanded built-in constitutional guarantees to safeguard provincial rights. In 1980, he insisted that the Baluch could only feel secure in a confederation based on complete parity for the four constituent units, irrespective of the size of their populations. "We can't live in a federation," Mengal said, "because the Punjabis would always dominate us. Suppose we get our rights—we would only be 9 people in an assembly of 300. They *insisted* on the principle of parity between East and West Pakistan when it was in their interests, when the western wing was outnumbered by the Bengalis. They said the Bengalis should sacrifice in order to hold the country together. Well, let them sacrifice now."

In his proposed confederation, each of the provinces would have equal representation in the armed forces and the civil service. Most of the taxing powers now wielded by the central government would be trans-ferred to the provinces, thus assuring "equitable and adequate" revenues to the more populous provinces, while giving the minority provinces the benefits of their natural-resource endowments.

Bridling at my observation that Islamabad would be likely to reject such proposals out of hand, he exploded that "they are so arrogant, so self-centered, that they don't seem to care whether we go or stay. If they can't control us, they don't want us in Pakistan. It is true that we don't hope for much from them. But it is not our fault. It would have been acceptable to remain with them if at any stage in the last thirty years they had given us any respect."

Punjabi domination, he went on, means "tens of thousands of them coming in, civil servants and army fellows telling you what to do, people from Lahore buying up our farms, buying the best land in Quetta, more and more of them crawling all over us, annihilating us." We Baluch must choose, he concluded with a shrug, between "losing our identity at the mercy of the Punjabis or stretching our hand to others."

"If the Russians come," he said, "if it comes to that conclusion, we might at least have some kind of conditional freedom. They may send their technocrats and their soldiers, but they would not send a whole population to occupy Baluchistan as the Punjabis are doing, step by step. Russia is too far away. They might do some good things, they might educate our children. What 'freedom' do we have to lose?" Then, lament-ing the fate of Afghan president Babrak Karmal, he hastily added that "we know the power would lie with someone else if the Russians came. We know there is a difference between getting freedom and changing mas-ters. But would the Americans be better?" While Moscow would be un-likely to tolerate a neutral Baluchistan, he speculated, and would no doubt insist on having military bases, "perhaps the Americans would be satisfied if they could just keep the Russians out. They might not be as bad."

Denouncing the American role in Pakistan, Mengal urged the United States to withhold further economic and military aid to the Zia regime "until democratic values are restored, not only in the form of elections, but in fair treatment for the minority provinces. You have no reason to give assistance to such a regime, and to continue to do so would conflict with your professed dedication to human rights." He pointed to the economy as Pakistan's area of greatest vulnerability, insisting that "if the Iranians, the Arabs, and the United States would stop pumping in money, this government wouldn't last for two years. It's living on blood transfusions and glucose drips." Even with continued help, he predicted, Pakistan is in for a series of military coups which will lead to a divided, politicized army and more frequent clashes between the military and antigovernment demonstrators. Coupled with further economic deterioration, such a breakdown of authority could lead to endemic violence and strife, "a continual state of near civil war in which the Baluch, the Pushtuns, and the Sindhis will sooner or later see their opportunity to overturn the present power structure."

Much will depend, Mengal reflected, on developments in Afghanistan, since continuing border tension would enable Zia to "frighten some of the people into supporting the status quo" and would help to keep the flow of Western aid coming. Conversely, if there is some sort of diplomatic settlement, the West will "lose interest in Pakistan" and the situation will be more fluid. As Pakistan begins to collapse of its own weight, Mengal concluded, the West "might begin to see things from a different angle. After all, why should you assume that your interests can only be protected by the continuance of Pakistan in its present form? Why should the United States let the Soviet Union be the only champion of national liberation?"

The election of Ronald Reagan brought a further hardening of Mengal's position. In a London conversation in December 1980, he said angrily that "whatsoever chance of American support for our cause had existed previously has all but vanished, since the United States is more likely than ever to support reactionary regimes everywhere." By February 1981, he had decided to come out openly for Baluch independence, and to the extent that he held out hope for foreign support, it was for Soviet support.

"There was a time when we deluded ourselves with the belief that the Baluch could live in Pakistan as a respected nation," he told an interviewer for the London Baluch monthly *Nedae Baluchistan* (Voice of Baluchistan). "But now every Baluch, whether he says it or is forced to keep quiet, has reached the conclusion that there is no place in Pakistan for a self-respecting Baluch. We want to see Baluchistan as a sovereign state and the Baluch as an independent nation."

History has made clear, Mengal declared, that "the only way to gain freedom is through the muzzle of a gun." However, he saw little imminent prospect of obtaining foreign military help, especially from China, which "no longer supports socialism or people's movements and thinks only of opposing the Soviet Union," or from the United States, which "we regard as our enemy number one on the basis of past performance and which we will continue to regard as our enemy unless it proves to us, in practice, that it has changed its attitude." India, he said, "is forever trying to promote friendship with the Islamabad rulers, so why would it support the Baluch?" As for the Soviet Union, Mengal was notably milder, observing only that Moscow "has to date expressed no interest in the Baluch struggle. Perhaps they do not consider the Baluch mature enough to fight for their freedom." Referring to Afghanistan, Mengal said that "no matter how much one may disapprove of one country's interference in the affairs of another country, it would not be fair or objective to hold Soviet Russia alone responsible in the case of Afghanistan."[4]

Pakistani newspapers were not permitted to publish dispatches on Mengal's pronouncements, but news of his open advocacy of independence quickly reached Baluchistan through the underground. "Think of the irony," Mengal reflected. "When we were not in favor of independence, they claimed we were, and now that it is true, they want to keep it quiet."

Baluch People's Liberation Front guerrillas

The Baluch Nationalist Movement in Pakistan   5

The Baluch rose up swiftly and unquestioningly in 1973 to avenge what they perceived as an assault on their tribal and racial honor. Given their lack of preparation and centralized direction, however, they dissipated much of their energy fighting on a localized, ad hoc basis under free-wheeling tribal commanders. Student leaders and other urban nationalists attempted to channel this sporadic tribal resistance into organized guerrilla activity, but their efforts, too, were largely uncoordinated. Seven separate guerrilla groups operated independently in the hills under seven separate sets of leaders. Except for the Pararis, all of these groups were hastily assembled at the outbreak of the conflict and all of them were gradually disbanded following the 1977 cease-fire.

Nationalist leaders are proud that the Baluch were able to pin down Pakistani forces vastly superior in number for so long, arguing that they would have triumphed, despite their organizational deficiencies, if they had been armed with modern weaponry. Nevertheless, there is now a widespread recognition among the Baluch that their cause suffered greatly from its disorganized character. This realization has led to greatly accelerated nationalist activity designed to build upon the organizational networks established during the insurgency.

War-born political consciousness has excited unprecedented ferment in Baluch society. Newly politicized elements in the countryside are swelling the nationalist ranks. In many cases, these new elements are challenging the authority of urban-centered activists, and significant differences are developing within and between nationalist groups over issues of ideology, strategy, and tactics. Tribal animosities and personal rivalries also continue to plague the nationalist movement. Conceivably, internecine conflict will make it impossible for contending nationalist factions to cooperate effectively, but tensions have been alleviated to a great extent by the emergence, for the first time, of a broadly accepted high-level Baluch leadership, discussed in the preceding chapter.

In 1980, there were three principal vehicles of organized Baluch nationalist activity in Pakistan: the Baluch People's Liberation Front, which believes in the inevitability of a military confrontation with Pakistan and Iran; the Baluch Students Organization (BSO), which subdivides, in turn, into two rival factions; and the Pakistan National party, a moderate, nonviolent group favoring a restructured Pakistani constitutional system in which Baluchistan would have an autonomous, loosely confederated relationship with Islamabad.

The Baluch People's Liberation Front

The Baluch People's Liberation Front is an exotic amalgam of Baluch nationalism and independent Marxist-Leninist thought which explicitly rejects the primacy of either Moscow or Peking. The Liberation Front is a direct outgrowth of the Parari guerrilla movement founded by Sher Mohammed Marri in 1963 and did not adopt its present name and organizational structure until 1976. It still has close ties both to Sher Mohammed and to his tribal ally, the Marri *sardar* Khair Bux Marri, although Mir Hazar Ramkhani, who headed the Pararis during the 1973–1977 insurgency, has now been formally crowned as leader of its People's Revolutionary Command.

The Pararis were organized primarily to wage a guerrilla struggle and had only an inchoate political program. Their evolution into the more ambitious Liberation Front, which espouses political as well as military objectives and policies, began during the period of ideological reappraisal in Pakistani leftist circles that followed the 1969 cease-fire. Pointing to Parari successes on the battlefield, Sher Mohammed argued that the power structure in Pakistan could be overturned only if other minorities joined the Baluch in waging simultaneous and coordinated armed struggles to win their demands for regional autonomy. Although he was joined by like-minded allies in Bengal, Sind, the Pushtun areas, and even the Punjab, most of the entrenched leftist leadership believed that the Pakistani Left was not strong enough for a confrontation with the establishment. This group included the Communist party, which is dominated by *mahajirs* (refugees) from areas now in India and which does not have strong local roots in any of the minority provinces, including Baluchistan.

Sher Mohammed and his allies contended that nationality demands should be the cutting edge of leftist strategy in Pakistan because the economic deprivation of the masses in the three minority provinces is the result of Punjabi domination. Only by achieving autonomy within a loosely federated, socialist Pakistan, he said, or by seceding from Pakistan altogether, could these provinces escape from the economic oppression inflicted by the Punjabi-dominated political and economic hierarchy. Traditional Marxist-Leninists were deeply suspicious of this emphasis on the nationality issue, charging that leftist elements would become the tools of "bourgeois nationalist" politicians who were merely using ethnic grievances as a means of exacting economic concessions from the Punjabi elite for their own narrow class benefit.

This debate over the related issues of an armed struggle and what is known in Marxist-Leninist parlance as the "national question" echoed among Pakistani students abroad. In 1969, a group of influential non-Baluch leftist intellectuals attending various British universities rallied to Marri's standard. Baluchistan, they concluded, should be the testing ground for an armed national liberation struggle. Such an insurgency would provide a model for the rest of Pakistan and therefore should be initiated whether or not Marxist-Leninists in other parts of the country were ready to launch their own struggles. All seventeen members of the clandestine London Group are well-connected sons of prosperous businessmen and civil servants. The ringleader, Mohammed Bhabha, is the son of a Karachi import-export magnate who belongs to the Aga Khan's wealthy Ismaili sect. Two of the members of the group, Asad and Rashid Rahman, are sons of the late Justice S. A. Rahman of the Punjab High Court. Another, Najam Sethi, is a scion of the multimillionaire Sahgal family, one of the "Twenty-two Families" who were the principal targets of the Left during its successful campaign to overthrow the Ayub regime.

"We were not completely homogeneous ideologically," commented one of the members, Ghulam Mohammed, in a Kabul interview in August 1978. "But what linked us was an independent point of view in relation to the other Left tendencies then in existence. We were the kind of people who were not prepared to be linked with foreign axes. We were seeking something new, and we were all sympathetic with Baluch nationalism even though we were not Baluch." Some were admirers of the Chinese and Vietnamese models, he recalled, and wanted to create a new Marxist-Leninist party that would oversee guerrilla activity. Others were influenced by Che Guevara and by the French leftist theoretician Regis Debray, who argued that the guerrillas themselves should be the focus of political power in revolutionary movements and should not be subject to the discipline of a noncombatant political party. Ultimately, it was the Debray approach that proved most influential.

The London Group went to the hills in 1971. When word got around in the coffee shops of Karachi and Lahore, another twenty to twenty-five young leftists soon followed, including two sons of a prominent Sind politician, Mir Ali Ahmed Talpur, who was to become defense minister under Zia. For Mir Hazar Ramkhani, it was not an easy task to integrate these soft, city-bred intellectuals into his Parari ranks. Several left within a matter of months after tasting the hardships of fugitive life in the mountains. However, most of them adjusted to tribal ways, learned

Baluchi, adopted Baluch names, and eventually won the trust of their skeptical Baluch comrades by demonstrating their willingness to share the risks of combat during the war years. Mohammed Bhabha took the name Murad Khan. Asad Rahman, who called himself Chakkar Khan (a legendary leader of the Dombki tribe), played a key wartime role as one of Mir Hazar's zonal commanders. Another Punjabi, Ahmed Rashid, who adopted the name of Balach (a sixteenth-century warrior hero), led several successful Parari operations against an Amoco oil-drilling venture near Bambore, forcing a suspension of oil exploration in the Marri area for two years. The new recruits proved invaluable to Mir Hazar in organizational and propaganda activities. Their affluent sympathizers in Karachi and Lahore sent food, medical supplies, and funds to the hills. Murad Khan had contacts with George Habash's Popular Front for the Liberation of Palestine and arranged for the training of forty-odd Baluch guerrillas in Beirut in 1973.

As the insurgency began to lose steam in 1975 and 1976, it became apparent that the Pararis and the leaders of the six other organized guerrilla groups engaged in the struggle did not share the same long-term objectives. Most of the others hoped for some sort of truce with the central government and had no clear vision of the future beyond that. However, Mir Hazar and his increasingly influential brain trust from the London Group felt that the insurgency had shown what a relatively small, disciplined force could do in the face of overwhelming odds and were more committed than ever to a continuing armed struggle. This approach was also shared by many of the more militant activists in the other groups. In late 1976, Mir Hazar formally reconstituted the Pararis as the Liberation Front in order to facilitate the absorption of these militants within a broadened and restructured organizational framework. Khair Bux Marri gave his blessing to this move, and Sher Mohammed Marri was actively involved in the reorganization process. The Front subsequently attracted several hundred of the discontented followers of those guerrilla leaders, such as Khair Jan Baluch and Aslam Gichki, who accepted Zia's 1977 amnesty offer and returned to Pakistan. More recently, it has also provided a rallying point for a steady trickle of militant nationalists, especially in student groups, who want to prepare for a renewed guerrilla struggle.

On visits to the Liberation Front's base camps in southern Afghanistan between 1977 and 1980, I detected signs of tension between the strikingly divergent elements that make up the movement. Some 40 percent of its fighting forces are Ramkhanis, the Marri clan of which Mir Hazar Ramkhani is the hereditary chieftain. Marris belonging to other clans make up another 20 percent or more of the combat forces and hold most of the Liberation Front's key military command posts. A vast cultural gap exists between these largely uneducated tribesmen and the younger, detribalized nationalists from a variety of different tribes, many of them recent college graduates, who constitute the remaining 40 percent of the guerrillas. Khair Jan Baluch, one of the guerrilla leaders who broke with the Liberation Front after the 1977 truce, observed that an even more important source of tension is Marri chauvinism. "At heart, they think they are a superior race and are not really willing to share power with people from other tribes, or with the progressive Punjabis and Sindhis, like the London Group, who have joined up with them."

Since Mir Hazar will not reveal the identity of the members of his People's Revolutionary Command, it is difficult to determine the degree of non-Marri representation in the Liberation Front's top leadership. The leaders vigorously deny charges of Marri domination, citing as evidence their non-Marri zonal commanders and their explicit repudiation of tribalism as the basis for the organization of combat units. During the 1958–1960 fighting, they note, Nauroz Khan's guerrillas, primarily from the Zehri and Mengal tribes, were organized by clans. Similarly, most of the guerrilla activity from 1973 to 1977 was conducted by separate tribal groups fighting under their own tribal leadership. By contrast, as the London Group leader Balach stated, the Liberation Front combat units integrate not only different sections of the Marri tribe but also an "even balance" of members from other tribes. With the continuing influx of younger nationalists from the student movement, the Liberation Front "will become more and more a truly national movement."

While the movement's leaders make more sweeping claims, I have concluded that its presently organized combat units number at most 7,500 men. More than 2,700 (not including family members) are based in the Afghan camps, while some 1,700 are scattered in different parts of Pakistani Baluchistan and another 3,000, mostly Marris, are "active reservists" who work in Karachi and other parts of Sind. The largest single concentration that I personally have inspected—some 1,700—was encamped near Kalat-i-Gilzai, a lonely, rocky cul-de-sac deep in the Afghan hills. The camp is sixty-five miles from the nearest village and is reached only after a four-hour jeep ride from the nearest highway over a maze of bumpy mountain trails. According to Mir Hazar, the Liberation Front's organized units constitute a skeleton command structure capable of mobilizing thousands of additional troops in a future insurgency. "We could field 15,000 or 20,000 in a matter of weeks," he said, "if we had the weapons."

Despite its Marxist-Leninist rhetoric on many issues, the Liberation Front's organizational structure is not modeled after Communist parties.

When the Front was launched in 1976, Balach said, "we decided after a rather difficult debate that we would not attempt to have an elaborate organization based on democratic centralism. We made a conscious departure from the traditional way that Communist parties operate. Experience has shown the dangers of bureaucracy and egoism in Communist parties, and in a tribal society, with its hierarchical structure, we felt that the dangers of a bureaucratic approach would be peculiarly great." The organization described by Balach and other Liberation Front leaders is loosely structured and does not incorporate formal party units at the local level. Following the Debray model, the guerrilla combat units also serve as the party organization, functioning cooperatively without an internal chain of command. "If you give a man a title and a place in a structure," said Balach, "he begins to take himself too seriously, to lord it over others in a way that he would not otherwise do." Each guerrilla has a specific locale or task for which he is responsible. He reports only to a zonal commander, who reports, in turn, only to the People's Revolutionary Command.

The Liberation Front's irreverent attitude toward doctrinaire Marxism-Leninism is apparent in its acceptance of nomadism as part of its revolutionary doctrine. "We want to modernize tribal society, not to destroy it," declared Murad Khan, external affairs secretary. "We want to keep what is healthy in the tribal ethos, introducing industrialization gradually." One of the distinctly unhealthy elements in Baluch society, he added, is its denigration of women. The Liberation Front program defies traditional Baluch attitudes concerning the role of women and states that women members play a role in noncombatant educational and health programs. The Front even tried to use male paramedics to give treatment to women but has backed away from this after angry protests. On my visits to the camps, the women and children stayed in their tents, and my impression is that there are only a few women activists in the movement.

Reviewing the Liberation Front's policy pronouncements, I found a consistent emphasis on the need for an armed struggle to "liberate" Baluchistan, but a deliberate ambivalence, until recently, on the issue of whether or not liberation must come in the form of sovereign independence. In its first manifesto, the Liberation Front stressed that it was "not fighting a secessionist war for the Baluch alone, but a war of national liberation for all the nationalities of Pakistan." The manifesto pointed to Iran's growing military power and concluded that "a struggle for 'Greater Baluchistan' is not feasible in the face of the realities of the situation in this region."[1] Similarly, in the initial issue of *Jabal* in December 1976, the Front emphasized its identity with other leftist forces in Pakistan, describing Baluchistan as "a reliable base area for the liberation

Mir Hazar Ramkhani (center, seated), chairman of the Revolutionary Command of the Baluch People's Liberation Front, with followers at the Front's Kalat-i-Gilzai base camp in southern Afghanistan. The author found that the guns pictured here include British NATO-model Parker-Hale rifles captured from the Pakistan Army.

Aslam Gichki, leader of Baluch guerrilla activities 1973–1977 in the Makran Hills of Pakistan

The author joins Mir Hazar Ramkhani in a feast of sajji, *or Baluch-style roast leg of lamb, at the Baluch People's Liberation Front base camp in Kalat-i-Gilzai, southern Afghanistan*

struggles of the other oppressed nationalities, classes and democratic forces in Pakistan."[2] "We do not deny, but rather uphold, the right of nations to self-determination, including secession," *Jabal* declared in February 1977. "However, in the concrete circumstances of our country there is as yet no secessionist movement in Baluchistan. To the extent that we are able to explain the nature of the struggle and its perspective to the people of Pakistan as a whole and win their moral, political, and practical support, to that extent we shall have laid the basis for a *voluntary* union of the nationalities in Pakistan."[3]

By April 1978, Liberation Front leaders were beginning to display growing impatience with Baluch moderates and leftists in other parts of Pakistan, bemoaning their apparent readiness to accept a strengthened version of the prewar, 1973 constitution if the Zia regime could be induced to grant increased autonomy to the minority provinces. Calling once again for an armed struggle, *Jabal* declared that:

> In Baluchistan today, the armed revolution is fighting the armed counterrevolution. Here, it is no longer a question of "one unit or its breakup," or of "constitutional safeguards for the minority nationalities" or "greater power to the provinces." These are mere platitudes and totally pointless starters for resolving the problem, because the Liberation Front has raised the question to its highest point—that is, armed struggle for the national and democratic rights and the total liberation of the people of Baluchistan.[4]

This proved to be the last issue of *Jabal.* Publication was "suspended" following the 1978 Communist coup in Afghanistan and it has yet to be resumed. "We want maximum flexibility," explained Murad Khan. "The situation has been so fluid that we have felt it best to say little, while watching and waiting." In interviews with Liberation Front leaders since the suspension of *Jabal,* however, I found an increasingly explicit acknowledgment that the movement is working for independence. "We would like to see a liberation struggle in other parts of Pakistan," said Chakkar Khan, one of the founders of the London Group, interviewed in Kabul in August 1978. "But quite frankly, we do not expect this to happen very soon in Sind or the Punjab, at least not in the near future. Maybe in ten or fifteen years it may happen, but by then we'll be independent." External Affairs Secretary Murad Khan, in an interview in Paris in March 1980, said that "we are giving up our old idea of a federation of socialist republics in an all-Pakistan revolutionary structure, with Baluchistan in the vanguard." Increasingly, he explained, "new developments in the region" have pointed toward the desirability of an independent Greater Baluchistan that would unify the Baluch in Pakistan,

Afghanistan, and Iran. Militarily, the erosion of centralized authority in Iran following the Khomeini revolution has made this goal a "much more realistic one" than it was during the Shah's regime. Moreover, confronted by the Soviet military presence in Afghanistan, the Baluch in all three countries now recognize that they could well become pawns in superpower politics if they fail to unite. The Liberation Front "does not wish to take a position either for or against the Soviet presence," he said, "but we know that if the Baluch stand together, their interests will be best protected under the new circumstances."

What if Moscow should seek to promote an independent Greater Baluchistan and offer to provide military equipment? Since the Soviet occupation of Afghanistan, Front leaders have become extremely circumspect on this issue, but they had left the door wide open for Soviet assistance in earlier interviews. "We would welcome help from any side, from any government," declared Mir Hazar in August 1978, "and if any government helps those who oppress us, we will be against them." Chakkar Khan stressed that "we don't want to get involved in global blocs if we can avoid it, and we don't want to become dependent on anyone." If Iran could be neutralized, he claimed, the Baluch could defeat the Pakistan Army without much outside help, since "we would get many of the weapons we need by capturing arms in battle and through the black-market, as in the past." At the same time, he acknowledged that some source of sophisticated hardware would have to be found. It would not be possible to establish a liberated base area similar to Mao's Yenan, he reflected, "unless and until we can get more modern forms of hardware than we had the last time. We need especially something like the SAM-7, a portable anti-aircraft gun that we could use against the Pakistan Air Force."

Initially, when the Khalq wing of the Afghan Communist movement took power in 1978, the Liberation Front liked the national-communist tenor of the new Kabul regime. Murad Khan frankly expressed the hope that Afghanistan would become "a stronger and stronger ally of ours," serving as a conduit through which Soviet arms could be obtained without direct dependence on Moscow. As for the Soviet Union itself, he was more ambivalent, observing that "the shadow of the Russian bear is over us all the time, and they will either be our closest ally or our greatest foe." Two years later, when the Soviets marched into Afghanistan, Liberation Front leaders were clearly distressed. But they avoided open criticism of the Soviet presence and still appeared ready to accept Soviet aid if it were offered, albeit with greater misgivings.

Some of the Liberation Front's Soviet-leaning critics, notably former student leader Khair Jan Baluch, suggest that the Front is "basically Maoist in its ideology" and has received Chinese help. It has distributed Chinese literature in the Marri areas, Khair Jan claimed, and he had himself seen a photograph of Chairman Mao, together with boxes of Chinese Communist books, in the apartment of a Liberation Front leader in Kabul. Whatever may have been true in the past, however, I have found no evidence that the Liberation Front has a special ideological affinity with the present Chinese regime or is receiving material help from Peking.

Since setting up his camps in Afghanistan in 1975 during the Mohammed Daud regime, Mir Hazar has received a subvention of $32 monthly per person from successive Afghan governments, totaling some $875,000 per year in mid-1980. This support stems from the tradition of Baluch-Pushtun kinship dating back to Nasir Khan's tributary ties with the first Afghan kingdom in Kandahar.

Daud, who was under pressure from the late Mohammed Reza Shah Pahlavi of Iran to make peace with Pakistan, only grudgingly admitted the Baluch. He then refused to grant the guerrillas political asylum, giving them a more uncertain status as refugees. His government also declined to recognize the Liberation Front as the legitimate representative of the Baluch in the camps. Throughout his regime, he continued to give monthly subventions to the Baluch who had come in 1975. However, as a gesture to Pakistan, Daud withheld food and other assistance from 625 new recruits and their families who came to join Mir Hazar in mid-1976, forcing them to live in a makeshift camp at Shorawar, just inside the border. He hoped they would go back voluntarily. Shortly before his assassination in 1978, he was on the verge of concluding a deal with Islamabad providing for the forcible return of all Baluch "refugees" to Pakistan. By contrast, the Khalq government promptly granted the guerrillas political asylum, started giving food and other welfare aid to the Shorawar camp, and formally recognized the Liberation Front. At the annual Pushtunistan and Baluchistan National Day celebration in Kabul on August 31, 1979, Mir Hazar was invited to speak on behalf of the "Baluch liberation movement."

Even during the Daud period, Mir Hazar's followers were not treated as bona fide refugees by international relief agencies. While he has been able to feed and clothe his followers with his Afghan government subventions and from funds supplied by Liberation Front supporters in Pakistan, Mir Hazar has not been able to obtain International Red Cross medical help to combat widespread typhoid fever and tuberculosis. The Red Cross has justified its rejection of his pleas by pointing to the political and military character of the camps. Since 1975, more than 465 men, women, and children have died, including some 40 guerrillas and another 70 older men.

The guerrillas have not been treated any better or worse by Kabul since the advent of the Soviet-installed Parcham regime. However, the bitter conflict between the Khalq and Parcham factions, together with the continuing rebellion against Kabul since the 1978 Communist coup, has placed the Liberation Front in an increasingly awkward position. The feuding Afghan Communist leaders are preoccupied with their own survival and have shown little interest in the Baluch cause. The Liberation Front has attempted to keep on good terms with both factions, never knowing for sure who would come out on top. Yet at the same time, it has had to avoid overly close identification with all Kabul leaders because many of the Afghan Baluch tribes have been angered by heavy-handed Communist reform efforts, especially during the Khalq period.*

Further complicating the picture, the Liberation Front's Kalat-i-Gilzai camp is located in an area where anti-Communist rebels have been extremely active. At least one clash has occurred between the Baluch guerrillas and the Afghan resistance groups who accuse the Front of pro-Communist sympathies. By early 1981, Mir Hazar had made his peace with the resistance, but it was unclear whether the Soviet-installed Parcham regime would survive and what policy Moscow would pursue toward the Liberation Front if and when it succeeded in consolidating its control in Kabul.

The political paralysis of the Front produced by the Soviet occupation of Afghanistan, together with a simmering controversy over whether to work for independence or to cooperate with other anti-government groups in Pakistan-wide political struggles, led to the defection of several leading non-Baluch members of the London Group in March 1981, among them Asad Rahman (Chakkar Khan), a Punjabi. Mir Hazar and the Marri hard core of the Front were staunchly committed to an independent Baluchistan and were working closely with Khair Bux

---

* In the Baluch areas of isolated southwest Afghanistan, as in the Pushtun areas of the southeast, Khalq officials attempted to circumvent the established tribal leadership structure, evoking a powerful backlash. Some 10,000 of the 90,000 Afghan Baluch, notably the Nahrni, Reki, Sanjrani, and Ghur Ghesh tribes, have ancestral ties to the Baluch tribes living across the border in Iran and migrated there during the Khalq period. Some 500 Baluch from these tribes have carried on anti-Kabul resistance activity, receiving food and medical help from Afghan Baluch kinsmen now living in Zahedan and Sistan. However, this group operates independently from the Islamic fundamentalist resistance organizations based in Pakistan, which are regarded as tools of the "anti-Baluch" Zia Ul-Haq regime in Islamabad. Most Afghan Baluch have sought to keep their options open, avoiding either open identification with, or direct opposition to, the Kabul Communist regime.

Marri, who favored independence, following his exile from Pakistan (see chapter four). By contrast, some of the London Group members, echoing the current Soviet line, felt that the Baluch should join with other leftist groups in seeking to overthrow the Zia regime and build a new "anti-imperialist" Pakistan.

The Baluch Students Organization

Discussing the future of Baluchistan with President Zia in an interview (see chapter eight), I pointed to the intense nationalist feeling that I had encountered among students of all factions and the strength of student support for an armed independence struggle. Disgustedly throwing up his hands, Zia responded that "there are only a few thousand students in the whole of Baluchistan. What can *they* do?"

To be sure, the Baluch student movement, as such, does not pose a direct threat to the central government, because there is a continual turnover in its membership and government-controlled educational institutions exercise considerable leverage over individual students. In a tribally-based society like that of the Baluch, however, students play a peculiarly important political role, helping to fill the vacuum left by the absence of a significant middle class. The Liberation Front and other nationalist groups draw a steady stream of young recruits from the student movement. Moreover, the student movement is, in effect, a way station for many politically conscious young Baluch who have passed through the educational system but do not yet feel drawn to any of the existing nationalist groups. In addition to their formal membership, the two leading student organizations have almost as many active sympathizers, especially among the growing thousands of educated unemployed.

Next to the Liberation Front, the Baluch Students Organization, or BSO, and its militant dissident wing, the Baluch Students Organization–Awami (People's), or BSO-Awami, are the best organized and liveliest political forces in Baluchistan. Originally established in 1967 to combat the One Unit system, the student movement has grown steadily in strength, stimulated by the heightened political consciousness resulting from the 1973–1977 insurgency. Allowing for the turnover from year to year as students have graduated, more than 25,000 young Baluch have received their political conditioning as BSO members between 1967 and 1981.

Ironically, the expansion of student political activity has been accelerated by Pakistani government development efforts in Baluchistan. Seeking to rebut Baluch charges of neglect in the educational field,

Bhutto ordered a rapid expansion of educational facilities in the province. Twenty-seven new colleges and junior colleges were opened over a six-year period in a crash program to neutralize the insurgency by winning the "hearts and minds" of the Baluch. To keep politics off the campus, Bhutto decreed that there would be no student governments in these colleges until the end of the insurgency. Since many of these hastily launched institutions lacked adequate housing and other basic facilities, however, the net result was a restive collegiate population that flocked into the student movement not only to protest campus conditions but also to demonstrate sympathy with the insurgents.

In mid-1980, the BSO claimed a membership of 4,300 students, organized in forty-six chapters, including thirteen in Sind. It has a national council of 200 members that meets twice a year and publishes a monthly newsletter, *Girukh* (Lightning), a doctrinal monthly, *Sangat* (Truth), and a monthly literary journal, *Bam* (Morning Star). The BSO-Awami has a smaller membership, slightly less than 2,000, and a loosely knit organizational network that embraces all major campuses in Baluchistan. It has a national council of 110 members and publishes a monthly newsletter, *Pajjar* (Awakening), and a monthly literary journal, *Labzank* (Treasure of Language).

Based on the results of four meetings with thirty-two assorted student leaders in Quetta and Karachi from 1977 to 1980, I have concluded that the BSO and the BSO-Awami are strong, independent organizations and are not controlled by other groups. Nevertheless, both of them are continually subject to outside pressures, as well as a conspicuous internal tug-of-war between ideologically disparate student leaders. Some leaders are sympathetic to student and labor groups outside Baluchistan linked with the Pakistan Communist party; others lean toward the Liberation Front, and a minority prefer Bizenjo's moderate Pakistan National party.

Initially, it was the now outlawed National Awami party (NAP) that stimulated the creation of the BSO in 1967. Some of the first student leaders were NAP sympathizers. Then, in March 1978, student militants were outraged by Ghaus Bux Bizenjo's attempts to negotiate a political settlement with Zia and staged a successful revolt at the biennial BSO convention. The first leaders elected by the triumphant rebels were Razik Bukti and Habib Jalib. Bukti, then twenty-seven, generally regarded as Communist-oriented, was chosen as president. Jalib, who was five years younger and somewhat more sympathetic to the Liberation Front, was named secretary-treasurer and succeeded Bukti as president two years later. Both leaders promptly accepted invitations to the Soviet-sponsored World Conference of Students in Havana in July 1978, but the Pakistani government refused to grant them visas.

Figure 1

ETHNIC MAJORITY REGIONS: IRAN, PAKISTAN AND AFGHANISTAN

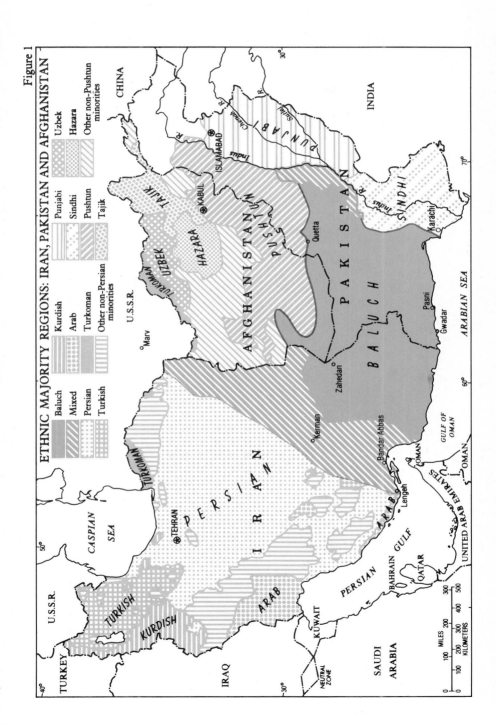

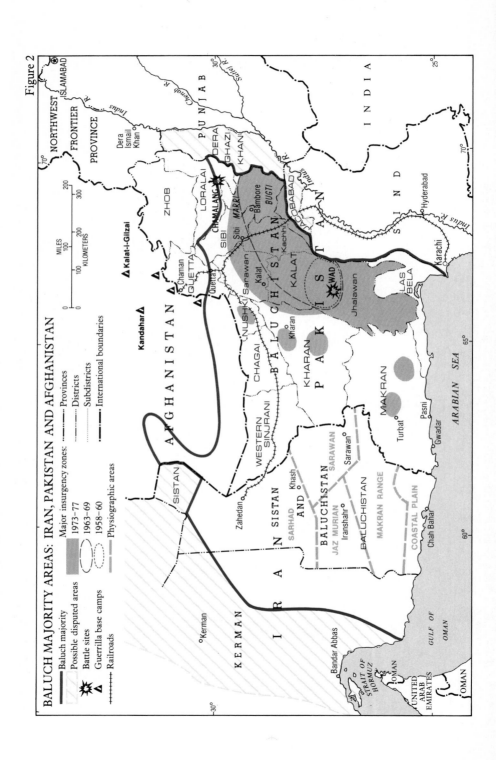

Figure 2

BALUCH MAJORITY AREAS: IRAN, PAKISTAN AND AFGHANISTAN

Figure 3

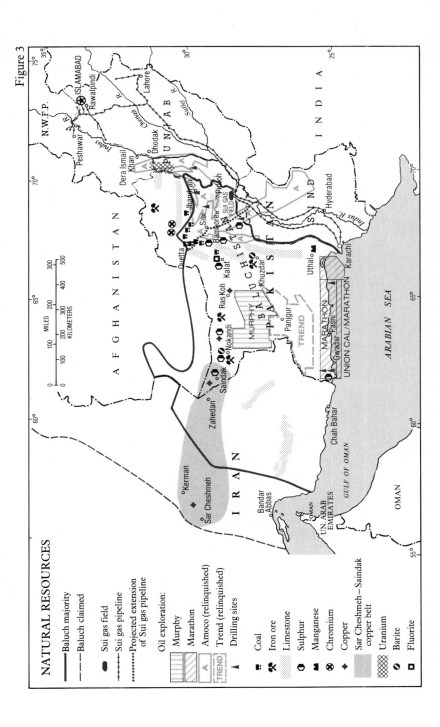

NATURAL RESOURCES

Baluch majority
Baluch claimed

Sui gas field
Sui gas pipeline
Projected extension of Sui gas pipeline

Oil exploration:
Murphy
Marathon
Amoco (relinquished)
Trend (relinquished)
Drilling sites

Coal
Iron ore
Limestone
Sulphur
Manganese
Chromium
Copper
Sar Cheshmeh – Saindak copper belt
Uranium
Barite
Fluorite

Figure 4

The Iraqi-supported Baluchistan Liberation Front, which conducted an insurgency against Mohammed Reza Shah Pahlavi's regime in Iran from 1968 to 1973, made far-reaching territorial claims in the above map depicting an independent "Greater Baluchistan." Many Baluch nationalist leaders today make less extensive claims (see chapter nine). In the redrawn and translated version below, solid red lines show existing national boundaries, and dotted lines indicate the extent of Baluch-majority areas as defined in Figures 1-3.

Figure 5

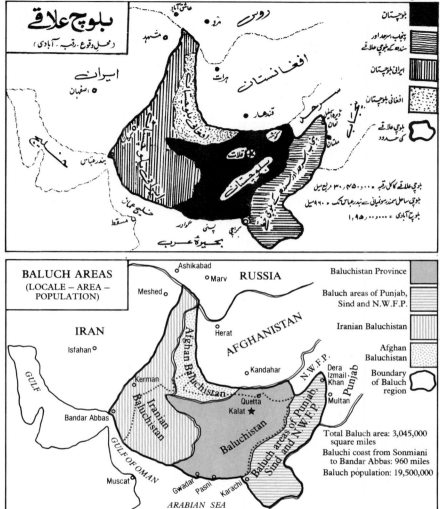

While not openly advocating an independent "Greater Baluchistan," the late Khan of Kalat, Mir Ahmed Yar Khan Baluch, ruler of a Baluch principality that existed for four centuries before the creation of Pakistan, depicted "Baluch Areas" on the cover of a book published in 1970 (see footnote 10, chapter 3). These areas, the Khan wrote, were encompassed by the eighteenth-century domain of Kalat and its tributaries. Two years later, when he was appointed governor of Pakistani Baluchistan, his book was banned. The redrawn and translated version (below) shows existing national boundaries in solid red lines. Dotted lines indicate the extent of Baluch-majority areas as defined in Figures 1-3.

Bukti, a "professional student" working intermittently for a law degree, has extensive connections in Karachi and Lahore leftist circles, especially with leaders of the Communist-sponsored National Progressive party. Under his leadership, the BSO spearheaded the formation of a new, countrywide student group, the Pakistan Federal Union of Students, which echoes the Progressive party line on many issues. Bukti insisted in an interview that there is "no need to be pro-Moscow or pro-Peking, and we do our work after analyzing the conditions of this country and devising programs to change the system of this country." However, he said that the Soviet Union is "very progressive, and we support progressive movements. There are two superpowers in the world, and the role of these superpowers is very different. One supports the majority while the other supports the minority and reactionary movements. People here feel that America is not the friend of the masses of the world."

Jalib, the son of a day laborer, is a political neophyte who talks more about Baluch nationalism than about ideology. When I pressed Bukti and Jalib about the BSO attitude toward the Liberation Front, Bukti was quick to say that the BSO had "no connection" with the Liberation Front, while Jalib shook his head vigorously, observing that "everyone is trying to struggle in a manner reflecting his own type of political consciousness. They are our friends, they are against the opportunist class of Baluch leaders." Similarly, while Bukti reacted negatively to mention of the Front's "armed struggle" line, Jalib was more equivocal. "We hope that we will be able to defeat the military and the bureaucracy by the strength of our united political action," he said. "But remember, it is the government that is using force. They have created the present situation, and if the Baluch people are confronted with violence indefinitely, naturally they will react in kind. The time will come when the defense will come into the offense." Jalib expressed his admiration for the Liberation Front's mentors, Khair Bux Marri and Sher Mohammed Marri, dismissing charges that they have a narrow Marri tribal outlook. "When a person has a progressive ideology," he asked, "how can anyone say he is a tribal man?" Khair Bux, he added, "has a broad outlook. He is an honest man who stands for the Baluch nation."

In contrast to the diversity of views within the BSO leadership, the BSO-Awami leans unambiguously toward the Liberation Front, an orientation which goes back to the controversy among Baluch leaders over the terms of the 1969 cease-fire. Although Sher Mohammed and the Pararis agreed to lay down their arms, they were dissatisfied with the political concessions obtained in return for the truce. Their sympathizers in the student ranks formed an "anti-*sardar* group" within the BSO to protest what they regarded as an overly soft posture on the part of Bizenjo, Ataullah Mengal, and the other tribal *sardars* who had negotiated with Islamabad. At first, the dissidents did not intend to leave the BSO, but factional lines soon hardened, and they formally seceded to form the BSO-Awami in December 1972.

Although the BSO-Awami guards its independence and is not openly linked with the Liberation Front, it makes little secret of its sympathy for the Front. An official BSO-Awami review of the group's history praised the role of Sher Mohammed and the Pararis for "reshaping the armed struggle on organized, scientific lines." The historical review saluted "those patriotic and nationalistic leaders who were not taken in by compromises" in 1969 and expressed the hope that "with their foresight, they will lead the oppressed Baluch nation until the end."[5] Similarly, condemning Bizenjo and Mengal for their "sham negotiations" with Zia in early 1978, *Pajjar,* the BSO-Awami organ, lauded Khair Bux Marri for his refusal to participate in those negotiations.[6] Sher Mohammed Marri made the major address at the annual BSO-Awami national council meeting in 1978, and I found BSO-Awami activists pouring in and out of his Quetta home on two successive visits. A former BSO-Awami president, Abdul Nabi, has served as the Liberation Front's key contact man with the student movement.

Stressing that neither student group "will let outsiders tell us what to do," Rahim Bux Baluch, a member of the BSO central committee, complained that "no existing party is really progressive in a way that the younger generation of Baluch can fully accept. We feel there is a vacuum, and we are trying to fill it ourselves with our own thinking. We don't agree with the Communists, who tell us that the Liberation Front is betraying progressivism by preparing for an armed struggle to win independence. We accept the relevance of armed struggle for the Baluch, but what the Liberation Front is doing is only part of the struggle at this stage. If we find that we cannot win our rights in Pakistan, then only will we go to the hills and fight for independence."

The student movement was an important source of guerrilla recruits during the 1973–1977 insurgency. Khair Jan Baluch, then BSO president, organized a guerrilla group of his own, and was later followed by five other erstwhile BSO veterans who drew their recruits, as he did, largely from their former colleagues in the movement. "I got more than 300 right away," he recalled, "and I could have had hundreds more if I had been able to give them guns. You see a lot of them in the coffee houses and discos now, but they're not all soft. There are plenty of young men in the movement ready to fight if we give the call and they see that it's serious."

Mahmud Aziz Kurd, a veteran Baluch politician of the older generation with moderate views, told a BBC correspondent in early 1980 that "already, quite a few of the students have gone to the hills in recent months to begin organizing themselves for an armed struggle against the present government."[7]

When I asked directly whether they favored independence, student leaders would often exchange significant glances and speak vaguely, obviously fearful that any explicit public endorsement of the independence objective would expose them to treason charges. As the hours wore on and conversation became less guarded, however, I generally found that they were fervent nationalists. Their doubts and differences concern when and how to pursue independence. Pro-Liberation Front elements favor active efforts to prepare for an insurgency now, while pro-Communist elements envisage a gradual process of political disintegration in Pakistan leading to the emergence of autonomous but closely linked leftist regimes in Baluchistan and each of the other three ethnic regions of the country.

The 1978 Communist coup in Afghanistan strengthened hopes for a leftist uprising throughout Pakistan. Baluch student leaders spoke enthusiastically to me about the "genuinely progressive" and "national" character of the Kabul government and its leaders, Nur Mohammed Taraki and Hafizullah Amin. However, when I visited Pakistan in March 1980, after the murders of Taraki and Amin in palace shootouts and the Soviet occupation of Afghanistan, many student leaders in Baluchistan were no longer confident that Pakistanis in other regions would emulate the Afghan revolutionary model. They expressed fear that the Zia regime would be able to exploit the Afghan "threat" to remain in power and that the Baluch would have to take up arms on their own against Islamabad. Most BSO and BSO-Awami leaders had gone underground after Zia's ban on political activity in October 1979, followed by periodic roundups of student activists.

Baluch student leaders were visibly less enthusiastic about the Soviet-installed Babrak Karmal regime than they had been about the Amin regime. "We don't want to be a satellite of the Soviet Union," said one of those I was able to meet clandestinely, Hamid Baluch, president of the Karachi BSO. "But we can accept their aid. The Russians will support us with modern weapons, we are sure. When the time comes, if they won't, it would mean they are not progressive, not socialist."

The Pakistan National Party

If the Zia regime were to permit elections in Pakistan, the strongest electoral force in the Baluch areas would be Ghaus Bux Bizenjo's Pakistan National party (PNP), successor to the National Awami party

(NAP), which was outlawed during the insurgency. "National" in name only, the PNP is primarily Baluch in character, but was launched as a Pakistan-wide group in order to circumvent martial law regulations banning the formation of regional parties.

Less than six months after the formation of the PNP in March 1979, Islamabad banned political activity, forcing the group to suspend overt activities. Nevertheless, according to one of Bizenjo's lieutenants, Mahmud Aziz Kurd, the party is attempting to keep its organization intact and had more than 2,200 members on its rolls in mid-1980, including 200 "very active workers." In contrast to the BSO and the Liberation Front, which draw on the more adventurous young Baluch and politically aroused tribesmen from the hinterlands, the PNP represents the detribalized Baluch middle class, not only in Quetta and smaller urban centers in Baluchistan itself, but also among Baluch migrants in Karachi and other parts of Sind. While favoring moderate, nonviolent action through parliamentary processes, PNP partisans are strong nationalists who supported the 1973–1977 insurgency and echo Bizenjo's readiness to fight once again if necessary.

As the heir to the NAP tradition, the PNP enjoys considerable prestige in Baluch eyes, because the NAP provided the only sustained organizational vehicle for the pursuit of Baluch aspirations prior to the insurgency. For two decades, the NAP, with its separate regional units in the Baluch, Pushtun, Sindhi, and Bengali areas, attempted to wrest power from the Punjabi-dominated establishment. The Bengalis alone constituted a clear majority of the Pakistani population, but the Punjabis had been able to block their assumption of power in Islamabad by playing off one Bengali political group against another and by diluting Bengali parliamentary strength through gerrymandering. The NAP strategy was to join forces in the National Assembly with the principal Bengali political party, Sheikh Mujibur Rahman's Awami League, and thereby gain control of the national government. Working closely with the Awami League, the NAP spearheaded the popular agitation that led to President Ayub Khan's overthrow in 1969, emerging as the strongest party in the Baluch and Pushtun areas in the 1970 elections.

In retrospect, it might be said that this united-front strategy was too successful, for the prospect of a dominant NAP-Awami League alliance in the National Assembly prompted Ayub's successor, Yahya Khan, to nullify the assembly's role in early 1971, heading off the possibility of a government headed by Sheikh Mujibur. This led, in turn, to the ugly chain reaction of violence that culminated in the secession of Bangladesh, a disastrous blow to the Baluch, Pushtuns, and Sindhis, who were reduced, even collectively, to minority status in what was left of Pakistan.

The NAP continued to champion the cause of Baluch autonomy, albeit shorn of Bengali support, when Bhutto took over in Islamabad following the Bangladesh debacle. Bizenjo as governor, Mengal as chief minister, and Marri as party chairman were all united behind the NAP banner during the short-lived period of Baluch self-rule during 1972 and 1973. They all proudly identified themselves as NAP leaders when Bhutto dismissed their government and arrested them in 1973. By the time they had emerged from prison, however, four years of guerrilla war had made the NAP seem obsolete, not only because its moderate, parliamentary methods had been discredited as a means of achieving Baluch rights, but also because the very idea of Baluch participation in Pakistan-wide politics was increasingly open to question.

A split had developed during the 1973–1977 insurgency between NAP's Baluch leaders, who were more embittered than ever toward Islamabad, and their Pushtun allies, who were more accommodating to the Zia regime. Even Bizenjo, anxious as he was to negotiate a Baluch settlement with Islamabad, remained staunchly committed to the concept that the minorities were separate "nationalities" and were thus entitled to autonomy. This view pitted him against Abdul Wali Khan, the Pushtun leader, who favored using terminology less objectionable to the Punjabis and moderating autonomy demands. Wali Khan hoped his approach would open the way for power-sharing in Islamabad.

The breaking point between the Baluch and Pushtun leaders came in early 1979 when they attempted to draw up a platform for a resurrected and rechristened version of the outlawed NAP, known as the National Democratic party. Wali Khan objected to Bizenjo's proposed use of the word "nationalities" to describe the provinces of Pakistan, urging instead that they be characterized as "distinctive cultural and linguistic entities." The two delegations also differed on how hard to push their autonomy demands. Equally important, Bizenjo was openly critical of the Zia regime's support for the anti-Communist rebels in Afghanistan, while Wali Khan was more equivocal. Amid angry recriminations, the Baluch abruptly walked out, called a separate convention, and formed the PNP.

Despite his past ties with the NAP, Marri refused to join the new group, declaring that there was no longer any point in participating in Pakistan-wide politics. Mengal joined the new party briefly, but withdrew soon afterward on the eve of his decision to go abroad. At the other extreme of the Baluch nationalist spectrum, Sher Baz Mazari, a leading moderate, joined Wali Khan in the National Democratic party.

The six-point manifesto adopted by the party at its founding convention stressed "constitutional and practical guarantees of equal internal autonomy to all federating units" in Pakistan, a "positive, non-aligned foreign policy" and a "national democratic revolution" designed to achieve "economic independence" and an end to "the remnants of feudalism and monopoly capitalism."[8] Zia's ban on political activity silenced the voice of the PNP almost before the ink was dry on its platform. Nevertheless, with its organization still largely intact, it could be quickly reactivated in the event of a return to parliamentary politics in Pakistan. Given Bizenjo's following, the PNP would undoubtedly win strong Baluch support even if militant Baluch groups were to boycott the elections.

Next to Bizenjo, the most important figure in the PNP is its millionaire backer Akber Y. Mustikhan, who has also given quiet help at times to Marri, Mengal, and other nationalist figures. A member of an Iranian Baluch branch of the Mengal tribe, Mustikhan's father was a self-made man who migrated to Karachi, got his start in road-building during the British Raj, and went on to become one of the biggest rubber and rice plantation owners in Burma. Mustikhan has multiplied the family fortune, partly through partnerships with the Harouns, one of Pakistan's leading business families. He now presides over his own miniconglomerate that embraces Mustikhan Transcontinental, a construction firm operating throughout the Middle East, Frigid Fish Limited, which exports shrimp, and assorted enterprises ranging from oil-marketing ventures with Gulf sheikhs to dairying, truck farming, and shipbuilding.

Until 1979, Mustikhan had kept carefully in the background, leaving open political advocacy to his son Yusuf, president of the Karachi PNP unit. Recently, however, he has started to register his political views openly in conversations with diplomats and foreign journalists and is even writing a book, to be entitled *The Baluch and Pakistan*. He is going public, he explained, because he foresees a growing danger that Islamabad's insensitivity to Baluch sentiment will open the way for Soviet-supported secessionist activity.

In an unpublished letter to General Zia on March 8, 1980, Mustikhan warned that "both of the superpowers are showing a positive interest in Baluchistan, strategically the most important and sensitive area of Pakistan, which should not be allowed to become a subject of power politics." Mustikhan set forth a detailed "Plan for National Consensus" outlining, step by step, a way for Zia to preside over a gradual transition from naked military rule to a more broad-based regime. Even though it was an extremely conservative proposal, he recalled acidly, with elections deferred until the last of four slow stages and limited initially to the federal level, Zia did not respond. Mustikhan was also instrumental in promoting an unpublished exchange of letters between Zia and Bizenjo in late 1980 in which the two leaders made an abortive attempt to define an agenda for negotiations on a restructuring of the Pakistani constitution (see chapter nine).

"We are in for trouble, lots of trouble, unless things change," he commented after a 1980 Washington visit. He had urged U.S. officials to put pressure on Zia for a more conciliatory approach to the Baluch "before it is too late," he reported, but found a tendency to discount his warnings and even to minimize the potential of the Baluch movement. Like Stalin, who asked how many divisions the pope had, some of the Americans he had encountered were "unduly influenced" by the fact that the Baluch leaders had organized guerrilla forces of less than 8,000 men in a state of combat readiness. "In the West, you think in terms of organization," Mustikhan reflected. "If you don't see a formal organization, you think we don't have a movement. But with us, the whole of Baluch society is the movement, and when the leaders give the call, and provide weapons, the people follow."

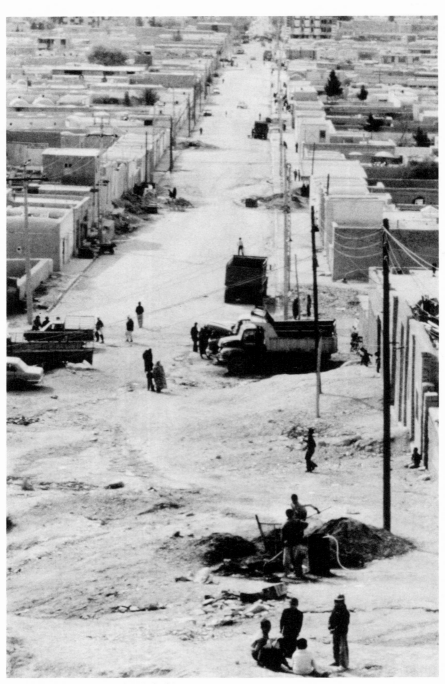
Zahedan street scene, Iranian Baluchistan

The Baluch Nationalist Movement in Iran

6

At first glance, the erosion of central authority in Iran following the overthrow of the Shah made the prospects for Baluch nationalism appear more promising in Iran than in Pakistan. The outbreak of war between Iraq and Iran strengthened that impression, leading to widespread predictions that Baghdad would seek to dismember Iran and would, therefore, support Baluch separatists in the east as well as Khuzistani Arab and Kurdish separatists in areas directly contiguous to Iraq. In reality, however, the Baluch nationalist movement in Iran was not yet sufficiently well organized in early 1981 to take advantage of Teheran's weakness or to attract large-scale Iraqi support. In marked contrast to the nationalist movement in Pakistan, it lacked a broadly accepted leadership linking the rural Baluch tribes with politicized urban activists. Indeed, the Iranian Baluch generally looked to Pakistani Baluch leaders as their "national" leaders and waited impatiently for the call to arms while gradually building up their own organizational strength.

The relatively inchoate state of Baluch nationalism in Iran at the advent of the Khomeini revolution did not indicate that the underlying political climate in Iranian Baluchistan was less favorable for nationalist activity than in the Pakistani Baluch areas. Rather, it reflected the fact that Reza Shah and Mohammed Reza Shah Pahlavi had made a more thoroughgoing effort to contain Baluch nationalism than their British and Pakistani counterparts.

Suppressing the slightest assertion of Baluch identity, the Pahlavi dynasty used the carrot as well as the stick to control the Baluch, channeling development funds into the hands of cooperative tribal chiefs and benignly tolerating a lucrative smuggling trade. Beneath the surface, however, rebellion continually smoldered, bursting into the open from 1957 to 1959 and again from 1968 to 1973. Once the Shah left the scene, the Baluch, like the Kurdish, Arab, and Turkish minorities in Iran, soon reverted to the posture of resistance that had prevailed prior to the Reza Shah period. For the first time in fifty years, the Iranian Baluch attempted to organize open political activity. While cautiously testing the intentions and capacities of the weakened central government in Teheran, they intensified their links with the growing nationalist movement across the Pakistani border.

The Pahlavis and the Baluch

Talking with Baluch and Persians in Iran, I soon detected undercurrents of racial hostility even more powerful and deeply rooted than the tensions between the Baluch and their Punjabi overlords in Pakistan. Although the Punjabis are despised, their domination over the Baluch dates back little more than three decades. By contrast, the Baluch in Iran have been battling Persian monarchs for nearly 2,000 years. To the Baluch, the Persians are a *taarof* (effete) breed who do not deserve to rule them. To the Persians, who look with cultural and racial disdain even on the surrounding Arab states, the Baluch are virtual savages, fortunate to have the blessings of Persian conquest.

Geographically, Iranian Baluchistan is divided into five distinct areas separated by natural barriers: the Jaz Murian agricultural heartland; the wild Sarhad desert country to the north; Sarawan, punctuated by oases, to the southeast; the Makran hills; and the coastal plain (see Figure 2). Trade has been confined throughout history within each of the five regions. Even as late as 1978, travel between these different natural compartments of Iranian Baluchistan was so difficult that in order to go from Khash to Bandar Abbas, it was necessary to go circuitously by way of Zahedan to the north and Kerman to the west. It is this segmented character of the Iranian Baluch areas that has made it so difficult for would-be Baluch nationalists to establish enduring political entities comparable to Nasir Khan's Kalat Confederacy. To make matters worse for the Baluch, the Jaz Murian heartland lies on the direct access route from Kerman, the nearest Persian province, and has always been extremely vulnerable militarily to Persian conquerors. Reza Shah sent his forces over this route in 1928 when Dost Mohammed made his abortive attempt to establish an independent Baluch principality.

In his controversial study of the geopolitics of Persian Gulf oil, *The Wells of Power,* Sir Olaf Caroe observed that Baluchistan is "an empty porch to the Persian mansion, but porches, though empty, must be held by the owner of the house."[1] This was the passionate conviction of Reza Shah and later Mohammed Reza Shah Pahlavi, who displayed a relentless determination to subdue the Baluch tribes and to make Baluchistan an integrated part of a centralized Iranian state.

For most of the fifty years of Pahlavi rule, Teheran had to depend primarily on the use of overt military force to keep the Baluch areas under control, even when there was little coordinated insurgent activity. Army units permanently stationed in Iranian Baluchistan waged intermittent punitive expeditions against scattered bands of rebellious tribesmen, who often raided military camps and persistently refused to turn over hidden stocks of guns as required by law. In addition to using military power, however, Teheran enforced its authority by buying off some of the Baluch tribal chieftains and using them as middlemen. These co-opted *sardars* not only received substantial annual stipends from the Shah's regime but also handled the influx of development resources from Teheran, which provided ample opportunities for lucrative rake-offs. Describing the case of an irrigation pump in a Sarhad village where he lived for two years, Philip Salzman, a Canadian anthropologist, noted that the *sardar* kept 60 hours of pump time for himself and another 30 for his brother out of a total of 168 hours per week, selling the remaining 78 hours to his tribesmen.[2] As Salzman observed, the government had to establish its control indirectly, by co-opting as many *sardars* as it could, in those areas where the nomadic character of tribal society made it virtually impossible to set up a direct centralized administration. By contrast, in the case of the sedentary agricultural settlements in relatively fertile areas of the south, the local variant of *sardars*, known as *hakoms*, were more vulnerable, and Teheran completely displaced them, ruling through the army and the gendarmerie. This assertive central policy was in marked contrast to the pattern in Pakistan, where the British permitted the tribal chieftains to retain their power.

By the time Reza Shah's reign ended in 1941, Teheran had largely subdued the Baluch tribes, but Mohammed Reza Shah faced a new challenge in the emergence of Baluch nationalism across the border. Fearful that the Baluch in Iran would be infected by the Greater Baluchistan movement developing in Pakistan, the Shah pursued a ruthless, hard-line policy toward the Baluch designed to stifle any expressions of Baluch identity. In particular, he was determined to prevent the growth of a politicized Baluch intelligentsia. Sharply limiting education in the Baluch areas, he banned the use of the Baluchi language in the few schools attended by Baluch students and made the use of Persian mandatory. He compelled Baluch students to use history textbooks in which the Baluch were described as Persian in ethnic origin and prohibited the use of Baluchi in government offices. He also made it a criminal offense to publish, distribute, or even possess Baluchi-language books, magazines, and newspapers, a prohibition which curtailed but did not entirely choke off the flow of underground publications from Pakistan.

One of the most bitterly resented aspects of the Shah's repressive approach to the Baluch was his ban on the wearing of traditional Baluch attire in schools and other public places. James Ricciardi, a former Peace Corps volunteer who taught English in a Baluch school in Zabol, was astonished to see this rule brutally enforced on one occasion by a Persian teacher. When a Baluch seventh grader came to school wearing a typical Baluch black tunic over his bright blue Baluch pantaloons, the enraged teacher kicked him in the groin, shouting that it was for his own good to learn how to behave " in a civilized manner" and that " in this country you can't do that."

In the economic sphere, the Shah authorized just enough development spending to lubricate the machinery of control manned by the *sardar* middlemen, avoiding meaningful development programs that would stir up popular expectations. Finally, he attempted to neutralize the impact of the Baluch within the Iranian political structure with a series of gerrymandering moves. Lumping them together with another, more Persianized ethnic group, the Sistanis, he created a combined province known as Sistan and Baluchistan, which had an officially recorded population of 659,297 in 1978.[3] Nearly one-third of this total was located in Sistan, which meant that the Baluch purportedly numbered roughly 440,000, a figure bitterly ridiculed by Baluch as reflecting less than half of the actual Baluch population in the province. At the same time, the Shah attached ethnically mixed border areas, where the Baluch claim a population of 300,000, to adjacent provinces such as Kerman and Khorasan.* This policy of politically smothering and dividing the Baluch was reinforced by the systematic immigration of Persian settlers, who bought up or confiscated Baluch lands and businesses with the backing of the Persian-manned bureaucracy and gendarmerie. By 1978, Persian immigrants constituted almost 40 percent of the population of 75,000 in the provincial capital of Zahedan. Treated as virtual aliens in their ancestral homeland, an estimated 150,000 Iranian Baluch migrated during the Shah's reign to the Arab sheikhdoms across the Persian Gulf.

As we will see, the Shah's hard-line policies did not completely succeed in crushing separatist activity, which erupted in the 1957–1959 Dad Shah incident and in an Iraqi-assisted insurgency from 1969 to 1973. The Shah became concerned that his continuing troubles with the Baluch would be aggravated by unrest in the Pakistani Baluch areas, especially after the secession of Bangladesh. Moreover, he was obsessed with a geopolitical nightmare: that Moscow would solidify its foothold in Afghanistan and would then synchronize support for the already powerful Baluch nationalist forces in Pakistan with related attempts to intensify Baluch disaffection in Iran. The only way to be sure that his own Baluch problem would not get out of hand, the Shah concluded, was to treat

---

* Reliable data on the Baluch population in Iran does not exist. On the basis of available sources and my field inquiries, I have used an estimate of one million in this book. See chapter nine for a further discussion of this issue.

Pakistani Baluchistan as a virtual Iranian protectorate. Pressures from
the Shah were largely responsible for Bhutto's decision to oust the Baluch state government in 1973 and to use air power as well as ground
forces in crushing the Baluch insurgency. Bhutto told me in a 1977
interview that the Shah "had been very insistent, even threatening, and
he promised us all sorts of economic and military help, much more than
we actually got. He felt strongly that letting the Baluch have provincial
self-government was not only dangerous in itself, for Pakistan, but would
give his Baluch dangerous ideas."

Beginning in early 1973, the Shah asserted repeatedly that he regarded Pakistani Baluchistan as falling within Iran's defense perimeter.
"If Pakistan disintegrates," he told *New York Times* columnist C. L. Sulzberger in April 1973, "another Vietnam situation could develop. We
must see to it that Pakistan doesn't fall to pieces. This would produce a
terrible mess, an Indochina situation of new and larger dimensions. I
dread to think of it." And if it came anyway, Sulzberger asked, if Pakistan
did fall apart? "The least we could do in our own interest," replied the
Shah, "would be some kind of protective reaction in Baluchistan." What
this meant, Sulzberger concluded, was that Iran would "seize it before
anyone else does."[4] In a public declaration during Bhutto's visit a month
later, the Shah declared that what happens in Pakistan "is vitally important to us; and should another event befall that country, we could not
tolerate it. The reason for this is not only our fraternal affection for you
as a Muslim nation, but because of Iranian interests, we would not be able
to tolerate other changes or difficulties in Pakistan....We will not close
our eyes to any secessionist movement—God forbid—in your country."[5]
"What would happen if what remains of Pakistan were to disintegrate?"
he asked a *Newsweek* correspondent in November 1977. "If we don't
assume the security of this region, who will do it?"[6]

An interesting aspect of the Shah's preparations for a possible crisis
in Baluchistan was a joint two-week Field Training Exercise held there by
Iranian Special Forces units and a battalion of U.S. Army Green Berets
near Chah Bahar in March 1978. The Iranian forces were accompanied
by fifteen Baluch who served as guides, interpreters, and cooks. One of
the Americans recalled that the Iranians "seemed very nervous" about
the Baluch and would not let them take part in training sessions conducted by American specialists.

During the last decade of his regime, the Shah came under the
influence of several Western-trained technocrats, especially Jamshid
Amouzegar, who persuaded him that his long-term goals would be
served best by a more positive approach to the Baluch, placing greater
emphasis on economic inducements. In 1972, Teheran was spending

U.S. Green Berets from the 2nd Battalion of the Fifth Special Forces Group, (Fort Bragg, North Carolina) on a field training exercise in Iranian Baluchistan, April 1978

only $750,000 per year on the economic development of Sistan and Baluchistan. Yet it was the poorest of Iran's provinces, with an estimated annual per capita income of $975, less than half of the $2,200 national average for rural areas and less than one-fifth of the overall national average.

Amouzegar, who served initially as the Shah's planning commission chairman and later as prime minister and head of the governing Rastakhiz (Renascence) party, successfully pushed for greatly upgraded development allocations to the province. In 1973, the Shah created the Baluchistan Development Corporation and talked grandly of spending up to $100 million in the Baluch areas during the ensuing five years. Amouzegar also won authority to recruit "reliable" Baluch for key posts in the government bureaucracy and the Rastakhiz party in Sistan and Baluchistan. He was able to sell his liberalization policy partly because rising oil prices in the early 1970s had made more development funds available for the neglected minority provinces. But the Shah was also impressed by the argument that the prospect of ever rising oil revenues could make identification with Iran potentially more attractive to the Baluch than loyalty to the abstract ideal of a Greater Baluchistan or, for that matter, to an economically shaky Pakistan. By giving the Baluch a growing economic stake in Iran's seeming new prosperity, Amouzegar's policy was intended not only to blunt the edge of Baluch disaffection in Iran itself, but also to promote pro-Teheran sentiment among the development-starved Pakistani Baluch.

Amouzegar's choice as secretary of the Rastakhiz party in Baluchistan, Ghulam Reza Hossainborr, the first Baluch to hold this position, frankly described the Shah's liberalization policy as a step toward his broader objective of establishing a regional economic and security sphere "more or less" corresponding to the boundaries of the ancient Persian Empire. It was "inevitable" that Iran would regain most of its lost territories, Hossainborr said, "certainly" including Pakistani Baluchistan, and that the Pakistani and Iranian Baluch areas would then be united as a powerful province of an expanded Iran. "Iran today is the smallest it has ever been," Hossainborr said during an August 1978 interview in Zahedan. "We cannot forget that it used to extend over Afghanistan as well as half of Pakistan. The Indus is the natural boundary between India and Iran. Of course, the Baluch have a distinct identity and want to have relations with other Iranians on the basis of mutual respect, but we cannot say that the Baluch have feelings of a separate nationalism. Iranian culture is the ruler of the Baluch subconscious and they cannot flee from this. They have read Iranian poets and they use Persian when they have something complex or important to say."

Although Amouzegar did not envisage the decentralization of power, Hossainborr said, the premier was committed to a policy of decentralized administration linked to development programs, including expanded education, that would open up widespread new opportunities for the Baluch. Granting that the Baluch in Iran "may be dissatisfied," Hossainborr maintained that "it is not because of their nationalism but simply because they have been neglected by the central government. The government accepts the fact that they have neglected Baluchistan for many years, and it is for this reason that the government of Amouzegar has pledged to do more for Baluchistan. Maybe before they didn't do enough, but now the situation is improving and we hope that this government will pay enough attention to compensate for the past. After ten or twenty years, the degree of development here will be such that no Iranian will think it convenient to live in any country other than Iran. Even after five years, if Mr. Amouzegar rules the country, and if his policies are followed, the Baluch of Iran will certainly want to remain in Iran. They won't want to lose the economic advantages of living in Iran, and we already see that many Pakistani Baluch want to come to Iran."

As it happened, Amouzegar's tenure as prime minister ended just three months later amid the confusion preceding the Shah's downfall, and most of his plans for Baluchistan never got beyond the blueprint stage. Nevertheless, the economic impact of the oil boom unavoidably spilled over into Baluchistan during the 1970s. Already lucrative, the smuggling trade between Afghanistan, Pakistan, Iran, and the Arab sheikhdoms across the Persian Gulf became even more rewarding for the extensive network of Baluch middlemen. More important, while Teheran spent little on programs directly designed to help the Baluch, it embarked on a massive expansion of its military bases, military-related road networks, and administrative infrastructure in Baluchistan, which indirectly stimulated the local economy. Before the oil boom, wages for a construction laborer were ten tumans (US $1.50) a day, but in 1978 they had risen to fifty tumans (US $7.50). "There is definitely money floating around here," said Gurdeep Singh, the Indian consul general in Zahedan. "Look at the road-building, the new cement buildings that are being constructed, the brick factory and the ice factory here in Zahedan, the copper mine near Kerman, the military bases at Chah Bahar and Bandar Abbas, the new radio station and all that. It's bound to have some impact even on these opium-smoking people who drink too much and are too lazy to take full advantage of their new opportunities."

In addition to its economic effects, the oil boom had a significant impact on political consciousness in the Baluch areas, helping to prepare the ground for the nationalist upsurge that was to follow the Shah's overthrow. Instead of alleviating political discontent, as Amouzegar had predicted, the increased economic activity in the province stimulated new demands for development outlays geared more directly to Baluch needs. In Baluch eyes, the Shah deserved no gratitude for building roads and hospitals that were intended mainly to serve the Persian businessmen, soldiers, and civil servants coming to Baluchistan. It galled the Baluch to see millions being spent on the nearby military highway from Zahedan to Chah Bahar, while the government left a dirt road as the only link between Sarawan, with its 90,000 people, and the nearest city, Khash, more than a hundred miles away. Similarly, Baluch repeatedly pointed to the fact that the new military road from Kerman to Chah Bahar deliberately bypassed Baluch settlements that could easily have been included on the route.

Many of the younger Baluch returning from jobs in the Persian Gulf sheikhdoms during the seventies had been exposed to cosmopolitan political currents there for the first time and organized underground nationalist study groups dedicated to "Baluchistan for the Baluch." These returning migrants often brought back transistor radios, which had not been widely used in Baluch villages. As radios gradually became commonplace, more and more Baluch began listening to Baluchi broadcasts on Radio Kabul, All-India Radio, and Radio Quetta, in addition to the ninety-minute daily broadcasts in Baluchi over Radio Zahedan. Confronted with a populace that could no longer be insulated from outside political ideas, the Shah's regime hastily attempted to guide this burgeoning Baluch political awareness into safe channels by stepping up its own Baluchi-language television and radio programming and, at the same time, embarking on a crash program to expand educational facilities.

In contrast to his largely abortive economic efforts, Amouzegar's education program did lay the foundations for rapid growth in the number of schools and teachers in the Baluch areas. According to Iranian government statistics, which were dismissed as inflated by many Baluch, there were a total of 128,274 students of all ages enrolled in Sistan and Baluchistan in the 1978–1979 school year, including 91,315 in kindergartens and elementary schools, 6,815 in high schools, 19,261 in lower technical schools, 4,712 in higher technical and vocational schools, 1,075 in junior colleges, and 230 in teacher-training institutions.[7] Most of these students were concentrated in the urban centers of Zahedan, Iranshahr, Khash, Chah Bahar, Zabol, and Sarawan. The figures represented an enormous increase in enrollment over the previous year. For example, in Zahedan, official statistics showed a 59 percent increase for elementary schools and 42 percent for the teacher-training institutions. In

Khash, technical school enrollment jumped by 152 percent from 57 in 1976–77 to 144 in 1977–1978.[8]

Interviewed in Zahedan, Yusuf Khoshrou-Sefat, the Shah's provincial director of education, bemoaned the shortage of facilities resulting from such rapid expansion and showed me classes held in tents and converted private houses. However, Khoshrou-Sefat, a Persian, acknowledged that many of his new teachers—and students—were Sistanis and Persian immigrants, especially at the high school and junior college level, since "the Baluch are just beginning to come to our schools in significant numbers." Dadullah Daneshi, a young graduate in English literature from the Zahedan Teacher Training College, said that only 6 out of the 16 students in his 1978 graduating class were Baluch. The others were non-Baluch who had qualified for admission as "Baluchistanis" by fulfilling a five-year residence requirement in the province. Initially, Khoshrou-Sefat declared that "at least" 100 of the 450 students at the new University of Baluchistan were Baluch, but it turned out that he meant "Baluchistani" and that only 25 were Baluch. Sixteen high school graduates from the province were among the 62 new entrants to the university from all parts of the country in 1978, he added, and 8 of these were "actual Baluch. But we don't think in these terms. We're all Iranians. It's all the same to me."

As in the case of the economic development generated by the oil boom, the expansion of education during the 1970s failed to win Baluch support for Teheran. The expansion program was not accompanied by political reforms giving the Baluch meaningful local self-rule and was thus not administered in a way that the Baluch regarded as equitable. Most of the Baluch I met in Zahedan, Sarawan, and Khash complained bitterly that it was impossible to get justice from a school system and a bureaucracy run by Persians and their Sistani allies. "There is propaganda on the radio all the time urging us to send our children to be educated," said Ahmed Sheikhzade, a Baluch organizer for the Shah's Rastakhiz party, "but the psychological tensions encountered by Baluch children in dealing with Persian teachers keeps many of them from going." For example, he said, Persians are "very color conscious and Baluch students, whose skin is dark, are often teased as 'blacks' by their Persian teachers, which makes the students very self-conscious." Most of the teachers sent to Baluchistan, Sheikhzade explained, are serving mandatory assignments under various military and quasi-military national service programs and regard both the place and the people with undisguised contempt.

Rashid Mollazai, director of Baluchi programs for Radio Zahedan, stressed that the ban on the use of the Baluchi language made Baluch feel like outsiders, automatically excluded from fair treatment in school admissions and job applications. "As education expands," he declared, "people are becoming more sensitive about being required to learn Persian for admission to college or to get a job. They think of themselves as something other than Persian, and so they feel shut out of the main stream. They easily become discouraged when they encounter the rampant discrimination existing in favor of Persians and Sistanis. The fact is that the Baluch are not wanted in the university or in good jobs—and they know they are not wanted." Even messengers had been brought to Zahedan from Birjan, outside of the province, recalled Mohammed Sepahi, a Baluch employee of a Danish construction firm near the capital. "Persians prefer Persians," he observed, "and our only hope is that as Baluch slowly and painfully squeeze into better jobs, they will give preference to other Baluch and build up a network of Baluch who will help each other and give jobs to new Baluch coming out of the schools. That is how we are beginning to count for just a little bit in the local society."

As the Shah cautiously permitted education to reach the Baluch, Iranian Baluchistan began to look like a miniature version of Pakistani Baluchistan, with the educated unemployed rapidly assuming politically significant proportions. High school and junior college graduates, in particular, had nowhere to go and were starting to think in terms of independence even before the Shah's overthrow opened the way for an unprecedented upsurge of political activity. "If a graduate is not getting a job," said Shah Bakhsh, leader of the 27,000-strong Shah Bakhsh tribe, "then he begins to feel that he should do something for the country to create more opportunities for everyone. He begins to think there may be greater hope if the Baluchis come together."

Nationalism Goes Underground

Until the Shah's overthrow in January 1979, the Baluch nationalist movement in Iran was a relatively insignificant force compared to the movement in Pakistan. Relentlessly pursued by the ubiquitous SAVAK (Sazemane Attelaat Va Amneyate Keshavar, or Organization for Information and Security), its émigré leaders were forced to operate underground from a variety of shifting foreign hideouts and had little continuing contact with their widely scattered supporters inside Iran. Nevertheless, while it never amounted to much in organizational terms, the pre-1979 nationalist movement proved to have great psychological importance. The handful of Baluch activists who braved the Shah's repression kept alive the spirit of resistance to Persian domination and thus directly set the stage for the resurgence of nationalist activity now taking place.

The first martyr to the Baluch cause during Mohammed Reza Pahlavi's reign was Dad Shah, a camel breeder and chieftain of a minor branch of the Mobariki tribe, who was one of the more daring opponents of Persian rule in the inaccessible southeastern corner of Iranian Baluchistan. According to Iranian authorities, he was nothing more than the leader of a "bandit gang" that operated from sanctuaries in the Ahuran mountains, terrorizing rich and poor alike. But according to the Baluch legend that later grew up around his name, Dad Shah started his exploits in the Robin Hood tradition as early as 1944, harassing Iranian police and army outposts and robbing rich Baluch feudal lords to help impoverished nomads.

On March 24, 1957, Dad Shah and a band of some twenty-four men waylaid and killed an American military aid official and his wife, Kevin and Anita Carroll, and an American contractor, Brewster Wilson, who were driving by jeep with two Iranians to the port city of Chah Bahar on the Persian Gulf. It was all a mistake, Dad Shah later explained, since his men thought they were attacking a party of Iranian officials.[9] In American eyes, however, the case had disturbing and sinister aspects that made it a front-page sensation until Dad Shah was killed in a gun battle with Iranian police ten months later. Some reports, suggesting that Carroll and Wilson wanted to size up Chah Bahar as a potential military base, saw a Communist hand in the killings.[10] When early accounts incorrectly indicated that Mrs. Carroll might still be alive, Iranian officials further fanned the fires of American press interest by explaining that she would probably be sold for a handsome profit in the slave markets of Oman or Dubai.[11] Above all, Teheran's seeming inability to ensure the safety of foreign experts raised questions in Washington concerning the stability of the Shah's regime and the advisability of continuing an aid program then costing $50 million a year. In an effort to quiet the uproar, Prime Minister Hussein Alah resigned. The Shah put a price of $10,000 on the head of each member of the Dad Shah gang, dead or alive, and the Pakistan Army and the police joined in the manhunt.

Dad Shah not only eluded his pursuers for ten months until his death but also conducted daredevil running skirmishes with them that made him a legendary figure. Although several dozen nationalist activists reportedly joined him in the hills, his forces never numbered more than forty or fifty. Yet there is general agreement that Dad Shah and his men actively attempted to engage the Shah's forces in combat by staging frequent ambushes and that they fought at least three pitched gun battles with Iranian police contingents. When they were finally cornered, Dad Shah died in battle, refusing to surrender.

"He acted the way a Baluch is supposed to act, bravely and defiantly," explained Mohammed Hussein Hossainborr, an Iranian Baluch student living in the United States. "Everyone saw himself as a potential Dad Shah." Dozens of Dad Shah ballads sprang up among the Baluch in Iran, and a *Le Monde* correspondent found in 1973 that Dad Shah was venerated as "one of the great martyrs of the Baluch movement in Iran."[12] Pakistani Baluch writers elevated him to the stature of a "national leader who raised the flag of revolt."[13] More accurately, an Iranian Baluch nationalist tract later acknowledged that Dad Shah was "a man whose aim in the beginning might not have been the independence of the whole of Baluchistan," but claimed that he had "gradually come to see his role in a larger perspective. During his last days, he gave great sacrifices for the cause of independence, for awakening the Baluch nation and fighting against imperialism."[14]

The nationalist leader who was primarily responsible for making the Dad Shah case a symbol of the Baluch cause was Jumma Khan, a dynamic young Baluch who had roots in both Pakistani and Iranian Baluchistan. He grew up in Turbat, a border town just inside Pakistani Baluchistan but oriented, socially and economically, to the neighboring Iranian Baluch tribes. After working his way through Karachi University, Jumma Khan quickly became a celebrity among both Pakistani and Iranian Baluch as a producer and announcer of Baluchi programs on Radio Karachi and as president of the leading Baluch literary group, the Baluch Academy. His political debut came when Pakistan captured Dad Shah's brother, Ahmed Shah, in late 1957. It was Jumma Khan who saw a nationalist issue in Pakistan's agreement to turn Ahmed Shah over to Iran as a gesture of Central Treaty Organization (CENTO) solidarity, despite the lack of an extradition treaty between the two countries. Denouncing the move to extradite Ahmed Shah as a violation of human rights, Jumma Khan organized a vigorous Baluch protest movement that quickly took on broader nationalist overtones. The Dad Shah case marked the first time that a Baluch leader had attempted to rally nationalist sentiment in both Pakistan and Iran around an issue of common concern under the banner of Greater Baluchistan.

Dismissed from his Radio Karachi post as a result of his nationalist activity, Jumma Khan shifted his operations in 1961 to Dubai, where he worked as a theater manager and quietly began to set up underground links in nearby Iranian Baluchistan. He was soon joined by a small group of leading Iranian Baluch political exiles, and in 1964 Jumma Khan and other exiles launched an organization known as the Baluchistan Liberation Front.* The new organization scored its biggest success when it attracted the support of one of the best-known tribal chieftains in Iranian Baluchistan, Mir Abdi Khan of the Sardarzai tribe. Permitted to leave Iran in 1965 for the ostensible purpose of making a pilgrimage to Mecca, Mir Abdi Khan never went back. Instead, for the next three years, he made Baluchi-language broadcasts beamed from Dubai to Iranian Baluchistan and regularly toured the Persian Gulf sheikhdoms, rallying Baluch émigrés and migrant workers to the Greater Baluchistan standard. Several lesser tribal notables followed his lead; one of them, Mir Mauladad, organized attacks on Iranian army units in the name of the Front. But it was Mir Abdi Khan's identification with the movement that gave it an aura of legitimacy previously lacking, not only in Iranian Baluchistan itself but also in the eyes of its sympathizers and supporters outside Iran, especially in the Arab world.

Although Mir Abdi Khan received some funds from his tribesmen in the Dashtiari and Bahu tribal areas, and Jumma Khan was also backed in a minor way by wealthy Baluch émigrés, the Front depended mainly on clandestine support from a variety of radical Arab sources. In one of its early manifestos, the Front made a bid for Arab support by endorsing the controversial thesis of some Arab and Baluch scholars that the Baluch have ethnic links to the early Arabs (see chapter two). The manifesto declared that "we consider ourselves a part of the great Arab nation, and we are wholeheartedly with our Arab brethren in their struggle against imperialism, colonialism and Zionism." The Front specifically supported Iraqi claims to the Shatt-al-Arab estuary and the Arab-populated Khuzistan area of Iran, as well as "the just rights of Palestinian Arabs over Palestine." It expressed confidence that "freedom-loving people the world over, and our Arab brothers in particular, will become more enthusiastic in helping us in our struggle for freedom."[15]

Initially, the only open Arab support that Jumma Khan received was from Iraq and from Yasser Arafat's wing of the Palestine Liberation Organization, which made him a member of its central advisory committee. Later, Syria and Egypt permitted him to open offices, and the Syrians even gave him quasi-diplomatic status during 1965 and 1966 as the representative of a provisional Baluchistan government-in-exile. Arab support was cautious and circumscribed, however, because Arab objectives differed in Iran and Pakistan. While they were happy to support the Baluch movement in Iran as a means of harassing their enemy the Shah, most Arab governments were unwilling to associate themselves with the

---

* Despite the similarity in name, this group was not related to the Baluch People's Liberation Front, discussed in chapter five.

Greater Baluchistan concept, which implied support for Baluch dissidents in Pakistan, a friendly state.[16] Pakistani pressure on Syria for the extradition of Jumma Khan eventually became so intense that he fled from Damascus in 1968 to escape arrest and ended up in Baghdad.

Unlike other Arab states, Iraq had compelling reasons to give priority to its support for the Baluch cause. Deeply embroiled in 1968 in their feud with the Shah, who was backing Kurdish rebels opposed to the Baghdad government, Iraqi leaders saw the Baluch as natural allies in their conflict with Teheran. The Iraqi Baathist regime subsidized Jumma Khan, Mir Abdi Khan, and other leaders linked with the Front for the next five years, and Baghdad became the headquarters for intensified radio broadcasting and insurgent activity in Iranian Baluchistan.

Politically, the Front attracted considerable attention during the 1968–1973 period. Shah Bakhsh, the Iranian Baluch tribal leader, recalled that "at least seventy or eighty" unemployed, educated Baluch went underground and joined Jumma Khan in the late 1960s. In military terms, however, Iraqi help to the Baluch turned out to be relatively insignificant. Most accounts indicated that Baghdad saw Baluch guerrilla activity as a mere diversion intended to tie down some of the Shah's forces in eastern Iran. Shah Bakhsh estimated that "four or five hundred" fighting men from Dad Shah's Mobariki tribe, Mir Abdi Khan's Sardarzais, and the Gamshadzais went for arms and training in Iraq, together with some of the seventy-odd educated nationalists. Baghdad was able to smuggle men and weapons into Iranian Baluchistan, he said, by sending "fishing vessels" from hidden bases along the wild Qatar coast across to Chah Bahar and other Baluch-controlled ports on the Iranian side of the Gulf of Oman. Ashraf Sarbazi, who was a Baluchi announcer on Radio Zahedan at the time, said that the largest single guerrilla force sent into Iran consisted of about a hundred men, who attacked military outposts in Mir Abdi Khan's home territory.

The Front's field commander inside Iran was a fiery Mobariki youth named Rahim Zardkoui, who continued to maintain a group of some seventy-five highly politicized tribal guerrillas after Iraqi support ended, using hideouts in the Ahuran mountains of southern Baluchistan, Dad Shah's old stronghold. With the exception of the Zardkoui group, however, the Front did not accomplish much in organizational terms during the "Baghdad period."

Seeking to account for their failure to win broader rank-and-file support, nationalist leaders generally pointed at first to the lack of education and political consciousness in the Iranian Baluch areas. But a more basic explanation, they conceded, was that the Shah had successfully pursued his policy of co-opting many of the more influential Iranian

Baluch tribal chieftains, in marked contrast to the situation in Pakistan, where Islamabad had attempted to crush the *sardari* system and the most prominent *sardars* had become leaders of the nationalist movement. Mir Abdi Khan was a lonely exception that proved the rule. From the start, the Shah was able to blunt the edge of Iraqi-supported insurgent activity by inducing cooperative *sardars* to serve as informers. "The ordinary Baluch people were sympathetic to the insurgents," said Ashraf Sarbazi, "but they were afraid to join them and were subject to a great deal of pressure from the government and some of the *sardars* if they helped them." Sarbazi was uniquely situated to gauge local support, he observed wryly, because he was broadcasting government propaganda against Iraq and was repeatedly threatened with death by irate tribesmen.

The crowning blow to Jumma Khan came in 1973 when Mir Abdi Khan succumbed to the Shah's blandishments. Uprooted from his tribal environment, the sixty-five-year-old Sardarzai chieftain had become increasingly dissolute. When the Shah's agents offered to provide him with a harem, a lifetime pension, and a handsome house in Teheran, he agreed to retire from politics—adding insult to injury, in the eyes of his erstwhile colleagues, by praising the Shah in a Radio Teheran broadcast. Iraqi help was gradually tapering off, in any case, and in March 1975, Baghdad and Teheran signed a peace agreement in which Iran promised to stop its support of the Kurds in exchange for Iraq's termination of its help to the Baluch and the Khuzistani Arabs. Fearful that some of their Iraqi "friends" might turn them over to SAVAK, disillusioned Front leaders hastily dispersed after the 1975 truce, most of them fleeing to Persian Gulf sheikhdoms. SAVAK eventually found and killed two well-known Front leaders, Abdus Samad Barakzai and Musa Khan Lashari, but Jumma Khan eluded the Shah's net and reportedly turned up in Baghdad again soon after the Shah's overthrow.

The Front's alliance with Iraq had a lasting impact on Iranian Baluch attitudes in two significant respects. First, it instilled a distrust of Iraqi intentions that is likely to affect the nature and extent of any future Baluch collaboration with Baghdad against the Khomeini regime and its successors. But more important, the alliance sharply underlined the differences between Communist and nationalist approaches to the future of Baluchistan. Iraq had close ties with the Soviet Union during the 1968–1973 period, and it was Soviet military equipment that Iraq was giving to the Baluch. Baghdad served, accordingly, as a base of operations for Iranian Communist factions opposed to the Shah, including Communist groups in the non-Persian minority areas. Iraqi leaders attempted to hold Communist and non-Communist elements together in a united anti-Teheran campaign. But this proved to be a particularly difficult task in the minority areas, since the Communists, reflecting Soviet policy, explicitly favored the retention of a "united, socialist, federal" Iran.

As early as 1952, the Moscow-oriented Tudeh party in Iran had defined a policy toward the "national question" directly emulating the Soviet model. While the Baluch and other minority nationalities were accorded the residual right of self-determination, "progressives" in all parts of Iran were enjoined to work together for the overthrow of feudalism and imperialist-controlled reaction in Teheran.[17] This policy automatically alienated most politicized Baluch, who favored ultimate independence. Nevertheless, there were a handful of Tudeh sympathizers among the Iranian Baluch, some of whom joined a Tudeh-sponsored group in Baghdad known as the National Front of the Iranian People. Led by former Iranian army general Mahmoud Panahiyan, an Azerbaijani Turk, this group championed the grievances not only of the Baluch but of the Azerbaijanis, the Kurds, and the Khuzistani Arabs. It published its own journal, *Rah-e-Ittehad* (Path of Unity), in Arabic, Kurdish, Persian, Turkish, and Baluchi, and conducted its own radio broadcasting in these languages.

With considerable difficulty, Iraqi leaders were able to persuade Panahiyan's National Front and Jumma Khan's Baluchistan Liberation Front to concentrate their fire on Teheran, avoiding attacks on each other. But the differences between the two groups were fundamental. In its political program, the Baluch branch of Panahiyan's coalition, which called itself the Democratic party of Baluchistan, advocated a "national democratic government" in Baluchistan that would be a provincial component of a "federal, socialist" Iran. Demanding a redemarcation of provincial boundaries in Iran on a linguistic basis and the right to use Baluchi as a medium of instruction in the schools, the program pointedly avoided saying whether the party's goals should be pursued peacefully or through military struggle.[18] By contrast, Jumma Khan's Front declared that "the only way of liberating Baluchistan is through the armed struggle of the masses" and rejected the idea of "compromise and political solutions. We do not believe in the so-called stage-by-stage pursuit of independence, i.e., first to struggle for linguistic, cultural, and political rights as a part of Iran, and then, afterwards, to struggle for independence. Our experience is that an oppressed people prepares itself and struggles for a cause only once. If they get something, even if it is minimal, they become contented and satisfied."[19]

Hampered by their policy on the independence issue, the Communists were even less successful in rallying the Baluch during the 1968–1973 period than Jumma Khan's Front. K. B. Nizamani, the Pakistani Baluch leftist who helped to organize the Democratic party under Iraqi auspices, recalled that the party's first and only conference, held in "a border village inside Iran" in February 1972, was "restricted to fifteen selected delegates as a result of various problems confronted by all democrats at that time." Eight years later, however, the Tudeh party had not changed its policy on the independence issue. Nuroddin Kianuri, the party's first secretary, told an interviewer in January 1980 that the party "has always supported the demands of the minority nationalities for self-government, but only within the framework of a unified Iran, giving strict priority to a political solution instead of an armed struggle."[20]

When I visited Iranian Baluchistan in August 1978, I was struck by the lack of support for the Tudeh party, despite the obvious strength of Marxist-Leninist sentiment among politically conscious youth. I was also surprised to find that anti-Teheran sentiment was not sharply focused on the personage of the Shah. While bitterly resentful of Persian domination in a generalized sense and critical of SAVAK in particular, most of the Iranian Baluch I met did not openly express the intense hatred for the Shah that I had encountered among opposition elements in the Persian heartland of Iran. This was partly explained by the prevailing atmosphere of repression. But I also sensed that I had arrived on the scene at a moment of unusual confusion and anxiety, when the possibility of a Khomeini-led revolution was just beginning to loom on the horizon. Throughout the country, religious tensions were building up between the majority Shiites and the minority Sunnis,* and the Sunni Baluch saw the Shah, with his secular emphasis, as a shield of protection against potential Shiite religious oppression.

During the course of my 1978 visits to Zahedan, Khash, and Sarawan, I was able to engage in meaningful conversations with fifteen highly articulate Baluch from varying backgrounds. Given their pervasive fears of SAVAK, however, it was extraordinarily difficult at first to win their confidence. It seemed to make little difference whether we talked in hushed tones in coffee houses and hotel rooms or in the privacy of jeeps and trucks, roaring over desert and mountain roads. I found a cautious willingness to talk in generalities about Baluch grievances relating to school admissions and job discrimination. When I asked about underground political activity or about attitudes toward independence,

* Sunnis acknowledge the first four caliphs to be the rightful successors of the Prophet Mohammed and look to the Sunnah, or traditional Koranic law, as the authoritative guide to the theory and practice of Islam. Shiites regard Ali, Mohammed's son-in-law, and his descendants as the inheritors of the Prophet's spiritual authority and have their own school of law, the Jaafari.

however, I was invariably greeted by terror-stricken silence and a degree of alarm that I had not found among Pakistani Baluch. It took three long conversations over a ten-day period before one of my informants told me of the coming "revolution." Unbeknownst to SAVAK, he said, secret visits had been paid to Baluchistan during mid-1978 by representatives of various anti-Shah groups, notably the Marxist Fedayeen-e-Khalq (Those Who Sacrifice for the People) and Paykar (Battle) factions, and the Mujahideen-e-Khalq (Crusaders for the People), which styles itself as Islamic Socialist.

Among the younger Baluch I met, the Marxist Fedayeen and Paykar appeared to have the most support, though none of these Persian-dominated leftist groups, I was told, really understood Baluch aspirations. As for the Tudeh, there was general agreement that it could not claim to be progressive, since it represented Soviet "great power chauvinism," just as the Shah's Iran had symbolized "American imperialism." The majority of these younger Baluch were clearly thinking about forming new organizations under Baluch control that would have closer links with Pakistani Baluch groups than with any political factions in Teheran and would work, in one way or another, for eventual independence. By contrast, among Baluch of the older generation, I found a more cynical appraisal of the future. Nothing would change, in their view, even if the Shah were overthrown, because one set of Persians would simply replace another in Teheran and there would always be Baluch quislings to play their game.

On the issue of independence, I found the generation gap among Iranian Baluch particularly striking. A twenty-eight-year-old personnel officer for a European firm declared that "there is an awakening now taking place among the Baluch, even among illiterate people. There is very deep anger that we do not have equal opportunity in benefiting from the economic development taking place in our own homeland. The Baluch should be treated on a par with others. Otherwise, we will go out of Iran." A young teacher who sat silently through day after day of discussion finally volunteered quietly that "every area of Iranian Baluchistan except for the Sarhad in the north would be sympathetic to a struggle for independent Baluchistan, and many would join it, if our Pakistani friends give us adequate help and leadership." He named Sarbaz, Sarawan, Chah Bahar, and Rask as areas that are still relatively immune to Teheran's control and have been most influenced by politically minded Baluch returning from the Persian Gulf. A thirty-four-year-old government employee in the communications field acknowledged that "the younger generation is very unhappy about the position of the Baluch and is thinking the situation over. The idea of independence is in their minds." But even as he said this, he added anxiously, "While we don't know about the future, for the present, I can't even think of it—I dare not—it's impossible."

Reflecting the frankly skeptical attitude of the few older tribal leaders I was able to meet, Shah Bakhsh said that while the Iranian Baluch "might have some sympathy for their brethren in Pakistan, it is unlikely that we will join them because to talk of an independent Baluchistan means that we are talking about the Russians coming here. The main objective of Russia is to get a way to Hormuz, and so the government knows that it has to keep the Baluch satisfied. They will do more for us economically, I am sure." Similarly, Mir Amin Barakzai, son of Dost Mohammed, the Baluch martyr who led the struggle against Reza Shah in 1928, said he doubted that the independence movement would succeed because it would need financial and military support that could only come from Moscow. Now that "every Baluch has a radio set," he said, "our people know that the way of life in Russia is not favorable for religion, and you must remember that our tribal people here are very conservative in their customs and their religious beliefs."

In mid-1978, the Iranian Baluch were leaderless, disorganized, and politically quiescent. They were keenly watching unfolding events in Teheran but played a relatively marginal role in the tumultuous final months of the anti-Shah struggle. Beneath the surface, however, Baluch nationalist sentiment was becoming increasingly volatile. The underground nationalist activity that had persisted during the Pahlavi years had prepared the ground, psychologically, for a relatively rapid nationalist resurgence during the post-Shah period.

After the Shah

The collapse of the Shah's regime led to an almost complete breakdown of central authority in Iranian Baluchistan, as well as in the other outlying non-Persian areas of Iran. For the first time in half a century, the Baluch suddenly found themselves free to carry on open political activity. This new freedom quickly produced a sharp struggle between the conservative Hezbe Ittehad-al-Muslimin (Islamic Unity party), organized by leading religious dignitaries, and a cluster of leftist and nationalist groups representing the young, politicized Baluch intelligentsia.

Although the Islamic Unity party embraced tribal *sardars* and other vested interests in the local power structure, its guiding spirit was the foremost Iranian Baluch *moulavi* (Muslim divine), Abdol Aziz Mollazadeh, and its strength came principally from a network of some 400 lesser *moulavis* scattered throughout Iranian Baluchistan. Mollazadeh, sixty, was the highest-ranking judge in the powerful system of religious courts that governs the application of Islamic law to the everyday lives of the Baluch. He was also one of the few public personalities well known throughout the Baluch areas as a result of his weekly Baluchi-language lectures on religion over Radio Zahedan.

The Muslim clergy in Baluchistan were largely ignored by the Shah, who relied on cooperative *sardars* as his middlemen in administering the Baluch areas. Nevertheless, at the grassroots level, the power of the *moulavis* had steadily increased during the Shah's regime. Faced with the ever-growing presence of Shiite Persian overlords, many Baluch, who belong to the orthodox Sunni sect of Islam, had turned to their Sunni faith to reinforce their sense of Baluch identity. Moreover, in the southern Baluch areas, the *moulavis* had stepped in to fill the leadership vacuum created by the Shah's destruction of the power of the *hakoms* (local chieftains) and by his failure to replace their authority with an effective centralized administration.[21]

In December 1978, the prospect of a Teheran regime dominated by Shiite clerics galvanized the Baluch Sunni *moulavis* into unprecedented political activity. Shiite influence was a clear threat to the religious freedom of the Baluch and to the *moulavis'* control over their elaborate hierarchy of Islamic courts and schools. At the same time, as Mollazadeh was quick to perceive, the *moulavis* had an opportunity to bolster their local power by assuming the intermediary role in dealing with Teheran that the *sardars* had played under the Shah. Even though Ayatollah Ruhollah Khomeini and his palace guard were Shiites, they were also fellow-clerics, Mollazadeh reasoned, and they might conceivably turn out to be more accommodating on religious issues than the Shah's Western-trained technocrats. By the time Khomeini had formally assumed power, Mollazadeh had organized the Islamic Unity party, which promptly emerged as the principal spokesman for Baluch interests during the confused early months of the new regime.

In contrast to Izza-al-din Husaini, the fire-breathing Kurdish Sunni leader who espouses a militant brand of nationalism, Mollazadeh has attempted to pursue conciliatory tactics toward Teheran. He has explicitly criticized Husaini for "excessive zeal in his actions."[22] Greeting the new regime with studied moderation, he declared that "we will give our full support to the new government, so long as there is no disrespectful behavior toward our Sunni religion and so long as our national rights are respected." By national rights, he said he meant freedom for the Baluch to practice Sunni Islam without interference, to use the hitherto-banned Baluchi language in the schools, and to make the "maximum use of local talent" in the provincial administration, including the police and military

Moulavi Abdul Aziz Mollazadeh, leader of the Islamic Unity Party

Karim Bakhsh Saidi, former member from Baluchistan of the Iranian Majlis (Parliament), who made unsuccessful overtures to the United States for support in 1979 and 1980

Amanullah Barakzai, leader of the Baluch Pesh Marga (Baluch Volunteer Force) in Iranian Baluchistan

forces stationed in Sistan and Baluchistan. When he led a Baluch delegation to meet with Khomeini in March 1979, Mollazadeh did not press
for a written agreement spelling out specific concessions, as the Kurds
did, deciding instead to trust in informal guarantees given by the Ayatollah.[23] Returning from Teheran, he reported that Khomeini had promised to clear government appointments in Sistan and Baluchistan
through the Islamic Unity party and had agreed that the projected national constitution would treat Shiite and Sunni Islam on a par. He called
on the Baluch to vote for the new Islamic Republic in the April referendum. "All your national and religious wishes have been accepted," he
declared, "and will continue to be accepted in the future. There is no
cause for anxiety whatsoever."[24]

Despite Mollazadeh's conciliatory posture, the Islamic Unity party,
together with other Baluch groups, soon became embroiled in intermittent conflict with Teheran that was still continuing in mid-1981. Angered
by the initial appointment of a Persian, Tadollah Keshtkaran, as provincial governor-general, Baluch leaders persuaded Teheran in April
1979 to replace him with a Baluch mathematics professor from Baluchistan University, Danesh Naroui. Within three months, however, Naroui
quit in disgust, complaining that Teheran refused to let him exercise his
powers and had boxed him in with Khomeini-controlled Persian subordi-
nates. Naroui's successor, Habib Jaririe, a Persian, was regarded by Baluch of all shades as condescending and ethnically prejudiced against the
Baluch. More important, by late summer, the early drafts of the proposed constitution revealed that Khomeini's promised concessions to the
Baluch and other minorities had failed to materialize.

Article 13 made Shiism the state religion. Article 15 required the
study of Persian as the official language and its exclusive use as the
medium of instruction in the schools. In addition to banning the use of
Baluchi as a medium of education, Article 15 prohibited both the teaching of Baluchi as a second language and its use in textbooks, except for
those presenting Baluch literature. The only significant concession on
the language issue was permission to publish Baluchi newspapers and
magazines. Ruling out meaningful regional autonomy, Article 100 and
related provisions stated that major decisions by provincial "advisory
councils" would be subject to a central government veto. Moreover, the
members of these councils were not to be elected but were to be appointed by various Baluch religious and tribal groups.

Commenting on the draft constitution in an interview with a Teheran newspaper, Mollazadeh demanded that the provincial councils be
given stronger and more clearly defined powers. "We are not seces-
sionists," he declared. "And it is not in our interests to be independent

in all fields. Our goal is to see that the Baluch make their own decisions in the cultural and political fields, instead of being forced to accept decisions made in Teheran. At the very least, we want our provincial councils to choose our own governor general, our own governor, and our own administrators (although not our military officials). That is what the Baluch mean by autonomy."[25]

By September 1979, sentiment against Khomeini's "betrayal" had grown so intense that a split developed in the Islamic Unity party. In direct defiance of Mollazadeh's radio pleas for restraint, a rebel group led by a nationalist *moulavi* in Iranshahr, Mohammed Nazar, organized protest demonstrations throughout the province. In addition to their disenchantment over the constitution, Baluch leaders charged that Khomeini was deliberately arousing conflict between the Sunni Baluch and their Shiite neighbors, the Sistanis, giving job preference to Sistanis and even arming Sistanis with guns taken away from Baluch. Armed clashes soon became commonplace between Baluch activists and Sistanis, who were often allied with Khomeini's *pasdarans* (revolutionary guards).

When a national referendum on the constitution was held in early December, 200 Baluch set fire to the ballot boxes in Iranshahr, stormed Governor-General Jaririe's palace there, abducted Jaririe, and held him prisoner for three days until Mollazadeh intervened. Even Mollazadeh, however, called on the Baluch to boycott the referendum. As more and more *pasdarans* began patrolling the province, tensions sharpened, erupting in serious violence in Zahedan in late December in which twenty-four Baluch, Sistanis, and *pasdarans* were killed and some eighty injured. Teheran was able to quell the week-long disturbances only after it declared a state of emergency and stationed the Eighty-eighth Armored Division in the streets of Zahedan.

Alarmed by the December explosion, Khomeini attempted to appease his Baluch critics by agreeing to a constitutional amendment specifically empowering the Sunni minorities to operate their own Sunni court systems, despite the designation of Shiism as the state religion. This gesture won Mollazadeh's endorsement of Baluch participation in the presidential election in late January. Mollazadeh gradually reached an uneasy truce with Teheran, but anti-Khomeini sentiment steadily mounted among the Baluch public during 1980, leading to a growing polarization between forces supporting the Islamic Unity party and a loose coalition of embattled leftist and nationalist elements. Popular dissatisfaction was heightened by the chaotic economic conditions developing throughout Iran and the decline of the rial in relationship to Pakistani and United Arab Emirates currencies, which made smuggling less profitable than it had been during the Shah's regime.

The most significant rallying point for leftist and nationalist opinion was the Sazman-e Demokratik-e Mardom-e Baluchistan (Baluchistan People's Democratic Organization, or BPDO), which brought together Baluch adherents of the Fedayeen-e-Khalq and Paykar factions, as well as an assortment of freewheeling intellectuals. In a manifesto setting forth its objectives, the BPDO directly attacked the new constitution. It demanded the election of regional assemblies with control over law and order, education, local civil service appointments, including the selection of a provincial governor, and the exploitation of the oil, uranium, and other natural resources believed to exist in Baluchistan. At the same time, it stressed that self-rule was not a prelude to independence and pledged to "struggle against all manifestations of secessionism in the country." In the eyes of many BPDO members, this strong stand on the independence issue was a tactical ploy designed to forestall government repression. But it also reflected the influence of Fedayeen and Paykar sympathizers, who shared the Tudeh view that Baluch "progressives" should make common cause with like-minded elements in other parts of Iran.

The BPDO was linked with a short-lived monthly in Baluchi, *Makran*, named after the Arabian Sea coastal area of Baluchistan (see Figure 2). The new journal was started by one of the group's more influential covert supporters, Khalidad Arya, a sixty-year-old Baluch intellectual who has held a variety of minor Iranian government civil service posts. *Makran* was nominally dedicated to the revival of Baluchi and the promotion of Baluch literary and cultural activity. Its inaugural issue listed numerous cases in which Baluch had been punished by the Shah's regime for possessing Baluchi books and periodicals published in Pakistan. "Even those who dared to read the Holy Koran in their mother tongue," the journal alleged, "were hounded by the informers of the Pahlavi regime, arrested, and tortured." It called for the exclusive use of Baluchi as the language of government offices, schools, and radio broadcasting in Baluch-majority areas.[26]

Seeking to forestall charges of separatism, *Makran* consistently referred to the Baluch as one of the "peoples of Iran." However, its pages had unmistakable overtones of Baluch nationalism. The inaugural issue published the full text of the BPDO manifesto. It also published several poems containing thinly veiled appeals for independence and a page of "useful slogans," among them "Our unity is our power" and "Our mouths have been unlocked after fifty years." Proclaiming that *Makran* "belongs to all Baluch," including those living in Pakistan, Afghanistan, the Soviet Union, and the Persian Gulf sheikhdoms as well as Iran, Arya's inaugural editorial declared that "all of us are fully aware of the problems and difficulties faced by our oppressed people. Their grief is our grief. Let us tell the world the story of our tragedy."[27]

Ironically, Arya gave lavish praise to the new regime for permitting the minorities to publish in their mother tongues. He termed this policy "a gift by the Iranian Revolution to the peoples of Iran." As soon as his first issue reached the eyes of Teheran officials, however, *Makran* was promptly suppressed. Similarly, the authorities cracked down during 1980 on the three other publications that had been launched by Baluch intellectuals: *Mahtak* (Monthly Dispatch), a literary journal; *Graand* (Majesty), an organ of hard-core Fedayeen and Paykar opinion; and *Roshanal* (Light), the voice of militant nationalism. All three of these publications went underground and now appear irregularly. Given the lack of education in Iranian Baluchistan, the potential audience for such publications and the membership base for groups such as the BPDO is limited to some 350 Baluch college graduates and another 5,000-odd high school graduates. The BPDO claims only 200 members and "several thousand" actively involved sympathizers. Now underground, it has faced growing repression, and one of its leaders, Rahmat Hossainborr, suffered serious leg injuries during a police raid on his Iranshahr home. A loosely affiliated, more openly nationalist group, the Kanoon Siasi-Farhangi-Khalq Baluch (Baluch People's Political and Cultural Center) burst onto the scene in a fury of activity during 1979 but has also been driven underground. For six months, until evicted by the army, it used the former SAVAK office in Zahedan as its headquarters. This lively but poorly organized group, which centers around the educated unemployed, also embraces Baluch students currently attending high schools, junior colleges, and the University of Baluchistan and has loose ties with the Baluch Students Organization in Pakistan.

In addition to ideologically sensitized groups organized by urban intellectuals, there were several potentially significant guerrilla groups operating in the tribal fastnesses of Iranian Baluchistan during 1980. Like Dad Shah's followers, most of these groups were simply fighting to make it hot for their Persian rulers, in the hope of driving them out of Baluchistan. Beyond that immediate goal, their nationalist objectives were hazy, although the Baluchistan Liberation Front, led by Rahim Zardkoui until his death in a clash with *pasdarans*, represented what was left of Jumma Khan's Liberation Front and continued to espouse independence. Another group, the Baluch Pesh Marga (Baluch Volunteer Force), organized by a Sarawan aristocrat with nationalist leanings, Amanullah Barakzai, was committed more vaguely to "freedom for the Baluch people."

Barakzai, fifty-six, is a powerful personality who started out as a vocal nationalist during the 1960s but later made his peace with the Shah. A direct descendant of Dost Mohammed, who led the Baluch struggle against Reza Shah, he is one of the leading figures in the politically influential Barakzai tribe, which has traditionally been allied with the Sardarzais and Saidis in a coalition against the Mobarikis and Lasharis. The Baluch Pesh Marga and a related movement, Vahdat Baluch (United Baluch), seek to bridge this ancient rivalry and to bring urban nationalists together with tribally based guerrillas. However, Barakzai is distrusted by many intellectuals as a result of his accommodation with the Shah.

While tribal loyalties are still strong in Iranian Baluchistan, the political importance of the tribal chieftains was greatly eroded by five decades of Pahlavi rule. In southern Baluchistan, as we have seen, Teheran virtually crippled the *hakom* system, and in the north, the *sardars* who served as the Shah's agents lost much of their luster in the eyes of their tribesmen. The *hakoms* and *sardars* still continue to have loyal followers, including many who will lay down their lives for them in accordance with Baluch tradition, but the tribal chieftains are no longer the only power brokers who count in the Iranian Baluch areas. Like the *sardars* in Pakistan who allied themselves with urban nationalists in the 1950s and 1960s, the Iranian Baluch tribal chieftains are beginning to look for broader alliances in the 1980s in order to make the most of their remaining power.

Many of the tribal chieftains who aligned themselves initially with the Islamic Unity party became disillusioned as they found themselves shut off from the spoils of power by the *moulavis* and as they watched Mollazadeh, flattered by growing attention from Teheran, gradually working out a *modus vivendi* during 1980 with the Khomeini regime. Searching for a way to outflank Mollazadeh, some of these disgruntled *sardars* attempted to do business with Teheran independently, with limited success, while others supported efforts to gain Baluch autonomy or independence through military struggle. Amanullah Barakzai's movement drew some tribal support, and tribal leaders in the Chah Bahar area formed a potent partnership in 1979 with a Fedayeen-sponsored guerrilla group, the Baluch Sarmarchar (Those Ready to Offer Their Lives).

Several of the *sardars* who collaborated most closely with the Shah, notably Karim Bakhsh Saidi, a former member of the Shah's Majlis (parliament), approached the United States and other non-Communist sources on several occasions in late 1979 and early 1980, offering to organize guerrilla activities against Teheran with U.S. assistance. In the short run, they said, such activities would be helpful to former premier Shahpour Bakhtiar and others seeking to unseat Khomeini. Even if Khomeini could not be unseated, they argued, "destabilization" of his regime would be desirable in any event, especially if the United States should decide at some later stage to support an independent Baluchistan.

It would be logistically easy to smuggle arms into Baluchistan, they contended, since the United States has military links with Oman, just across the Strait of Hormuz, and many of the dock hands and other workers in Chah Bahar harbor are Baluch nationalist sympathizers. I have detailed knowledge about one of these approaches, which occurred in January 1980, from several sources who were directly involved. A group of Iranian Baluch *sardars* went to Karachi and asked a Pakistani Baluch nationalist leader for help in contacting the U.S. government. This overture was conveyed to U.S. officials by a Pakistani intermediary but, so far as I have been able to determine, was categorically rejected.

During the Iran-Iraq war, Radio Teheran and leading Iranian newspapers warned repeatedly that Washington and Baghdad were arming a group of Iranian Baluch *sardars* for a revolt to be staged in cooperation with Sultan Qabus Ibn Sa'id of Oman and his army, which consists partly of Baluch mercenaries.[28] These charges were not backed up by specific evidence and were denied by American officials. There were indications that the Iranian *sardars* were continuing to seek American help for anti-Khomeini guerrilla operations, but these approaches did not have the blessing of the principal Baluch nationalist leaders. In addition, coordination between the Iranian *sardars* and the Baluch nationalist elements in Pakistan was extremely loose in the early part of 1981.

Iraq and the Arab Connection

An explosive and imponderable factor likely to affect the Baluch movement in Iran is the possibility of renewed Arab support for the Baluch as a response to the militant Shiite regime in Teheran. As we have seen, Iraq gave support to Jumma Khan's Liberation Front as a weapon against the Shah until the 1975 truce between Baghdad and Teheran. The Yasser Arafat wing of the PLO backed the Liberation Front, and the more militant George Habash wing of the PLO trained a small group of Pakistani guerrillas in 1973.

Soon after the Shah's overthrow, Iraq once again began to express support for the Baluch and other non-Persian minorities in Iran, calling on Teheran to grant them greater autonomy. Moreover, for the first time, the Baluch movement began to attract significant interest among conservatives in the Arab world, who were outraged by Khomeini's revival of Persian expansionist claims in the Persian Gulf and by his calculated attempts to inflame Shia-Sunni tensions in the Persian Gulf sheikhdoms. Conservative Arab interest increased after the Soviet invasion of Afghanistan, which heightened Arab fears that Moscow would seek to exploit Baluch nationalism for its own purposes.

The impact of the Soviet invasion on Arab thinking was exemplified in the writings of Riyad Najib Al-Rayyes, a commentator in the influential, Saudi-backed Paris weekly *Al-Mostakbal* (The Future). Writing on Baluchistan prior to the invasion in September 1979, Al-Rayyes, a Lebanese, expressed warm sympathy for the Baluch and supported the view that they were ethnically Arab in origin. But he concluded that "their revolution is close to being defeated because nobody is ready to support it. Even Moscow does not seem enthusiastic about this revolution." While stressing that "the situation in Baluchistan concerns the Arabs, especially those of the Arabian peninsula and the Gulf," he was guarded in alluding to the possibility of Arab support for Baluch independence, observing vaguely that "the future is liable to force the Arabs to follow different policies toward Baluchistan."[29] By contrast, in February 1980, six weeks after the Soviet invasion, he argued passionately and explicitly that Arab countries should support

> an independent Baluch nation. First, because the Baluch movement is a movement of Arabs, whose Arab history goes back centuries and would fill volumes of books. Second, if the Arabs do not protect the Baluch movement, it will definitely succumb to Soviet influence. Instead of having a new Arab nation, a Communist Marxist nation will take its place, and the Arabs would have lost their chance to assert the Arab heritage of the Baluch.

The Khomeini regime, he warned, is

> threatening every political system in the Gulf, and Moscow is getting closer to the Strait of Hormuz....The establishment of a Baluch nation would positively secure the political systems in the Gulf, and it would enhance and strengthen the Arab presence in the Gulf area by protecting it from the continuous flow of immigration from India, Korea and other places....By helping Baluch leaders, the Gulf states will be protecting the Arabian Gulf from Persian and Asian expansion.[30]

Dismissing arguments that help for the Baluch would divide Pakistan, an Islamic country, Al-Rayyes declared that "the establishment of an Arab nation, with its Arab heritage and history, is more important than saving an already-divided Islamic country ruled by military leaders and suffering from political instability, which makes it vulnerable to every threat from outside."[31]

The most comprehensive statement of the case for Arab sponsorship of an independent Baluchistan is a 310-page book by an Iraqi, Ma'n

Shana al-Ajli Al-Hakkami, published in Bahrain in 1979, which was
circulated clandestinely in several Arab countries during 1980. Titled
Baluchistan: Land of the Arabs, it recites detailed historical evidence to
establish the Arab origins of the Baluch. This version of Baluch history
partially coincides with that of some Pakistani Baluch writers, since it
accepts the view that the original Baluch tribes came from Aleppo, in
what is now Syria. However, Al-Hakkami argues that these tribes were
originally Arabs, descended from the Prophet Mohammed's uncle, Amir
Hamza, who were forced to flee from Medina to Aleppo. Thus, he
disputes the view expressed by other Baluch writers that the original
tribes were Babylonians or linked with Aryans in Asia Minor. Moreover,
he emphasizes that the majority of Baluch migrated from Aleppo to the
Arabian peninsula through southern and western Iraq and then sailed
from Oman across the "Arabian Gulf" to the Makran coast of southern
Baluchistan. Once in Baluchistan, he maintains, they were able to keep
in contact with their fellow Arabs across the Gulf, receiving periodic
infusions of Arab cultural influence from the Arab invaders who continually swept through Iran and Baluchistan. Throughout history, he
points out, the Baluch consistently sided with Arab armies in their struggles against Persians.[32]

While bemoaning the Baluch "loss" of the Arabic language, Al-
Hakkami attempts to demonstrate that they have retained many other
elements of their Arab cultural and religious identity, especially in the
Makran coastal areas. He appeals to the Baluch in Pakistan and Iran for
"an awakening of the Arabic spirit," contending that "the unification of
Iranian and Pakistani Baluchistan should be accomplished through their
common Arabic heritage." This awakening, he says, can only come if the
Baluch "master the language of their ancestors and use the Arabic language in every aspect of their lives. I would like to stress to the Baluch
people that the Arabic language should be the nucleus of their future
bond, whether social, cultural or political." In an oblique swipe at the
Baluchi language, he states that Arabic "is particularly valuable and
important for the Baluch people, since the twentieth century has proven
to be the least fit for any form of tribal society, with all of its social,
economic and cultural complexities."

Al-Hakkami reserves special venom for Persian historians and Western orientalists who have sought to establish either the Persian ethnic
origins of the Baluch, or Baluch ethnic distinctiveness, by "drawing a
special historical picture. All of these writings have been intended to
cover up the real ethnic background of the Baluch people, since the main
fear of the enemies of the Arabs was, and still is, that when the Baluch

people recognize their true ethnic background, they will form a united political front with the rest of the Arab countries."[33]

Although Al-Hakkami is an Iraqi, it is not clear whether his book was subsidized by Baghdad or by a wealthy young Baluch sheikh in Bahrain, Mohammed Bin Hassan Al-Mohammed, who claims credit for sponsoring its publication. Interviewed in Bahrain in March 1980, Sheikh Mohammed, a pudgy, affable twenty-eight-year-old businessman and a leader of the Baluch tribe known as the Hoots, presented the book to me as the "handbook and Bible, you might say" of his newly formed Islamic Arab Front for the Liberation of Baluchistan. His principal mission, the sheikh said, is to unite the 350,000 Baluch living in the Persian Gulf sheikhdoms. However, this must go hand in hand with efforts to enlist broad Arab support for the Baluch cause, he added, which makes it necessary to fly back and forth regularly between Bahrain and other Arab countries, especially Saudi Arabia, Syria, and Jordan. A licensed pilot who took his flying lessons in England and owns his own planes, Sheikh Mohammed looks like any other Bahrain sheikh, sporting a traditional Arab headdress, albeit with a mod touch in the form of a bright, red-checked scarf. Arabic is the only language he can speak or write, but he declared fervently that "all of the Baluch living here are very proud to be Baluch. We never forget our cousins across the water, and our feelings are with them in their struggles."

The Hoots, some 28,000 strong, have been centered in Bahrain and surrounding areas since 1782, the sheikh explained, having fled there to escape the depredations of the Persian shahs. Until then, Bahrain had been a Persian colony, but the arriving Hoots and other Baluch tribes joined with the locally dominant Al-Khalifa Arabs, expelled the Persians, and installed the Al-Khalifa dynasty, which still controls Bahrain today. Many Baluch intermarried with the Arabs and became part of the Bahrain power elite. The managing director of the Bank of Bahrain and Kuwait, Ismail Baluch, boasted to a reporter in London that he is worth $70 million.[34] Sheikh Mohammed's aunt is married to the present ruler of Bahrain, Isa Bin Sulman Al-Khalifa. When his father died in 1978, the sheikh, who heads the Al-Mohammed branch of the Hoots, inherited control of a thriving furniture-importing concern and extensive real estate interests. He shares leadership of his tribe with two cousins, Mir Murad Barakat of the Fujaira Oasis and Sheikh Sayeed Bin Rashid of Muscat.

In addition to the Hoots, three other Baluch tribes migrated to the Gulf from Iran centuries ago. These "old Baluch" elements have absorbed Arab culture, the sheikh said, while the "new Baluch," who have come in recent decades as migrant laborers from Pakistan and Iran, continue to speak Baluchi. Nevertheless, he insisted, the old Baluch still retain close links with affiliated branches of their own tribes that did not migrate to the Gulf sheikhdoms and with other kindred tribes living in the coastal areas of Baluchistan. Flatly declaring that "the most important leaders of the Iranian tribes are in the Gulf, especially coastal tribes like the Hoots," the sheikh declared that "all of the Baluch in this part of the world are very interconnected. We are all nationalists, we all look up to the Baluch leaders in Pakistan as our senior leaders, and nationalism is growing all the time." This affinity is especially true among the migrant workers, he added, since they are "far from home, which makes them particularly conscious of their roots. Their feelings naturally affect us old Baluch. I find the younger people coming to me. So far, no one else has organized them, and if we work for the good of all Baluch, they will support us, as their traditional leaders, rather than the Communists, who are active here, of course." Like Al-Hakkami, he argued that all Baluch should learn Arabic, but with somewhat less certitude.

Asked why Arab leaders have been hesitant to support the Baluch nationalist movement, the sheikh responded that "they are divided, because they disagree on what it would mean. Some of them agree with us that an independent Baluchistan is the best way to save the Gulf area from communism, but others are afraid that Moscow would ultimately control Baluchistan if it once became independent. Some are reluctant to have a head-on conflict with Iran and Pakistan. But it's time for them to help us. Khomeini is going to spoil the Gulf, and he is only temporary, anyway. Sooner or later Iran will go to the left. Why doesn't the United States use its influence with the Arab countries? Through your allies, you should help us to form a free Baluchistan. This is the best way to stabilize this area." Then he quickly added that an independent Baluchistan should "not be linked to either the U.S. or the Soviet Union. We want to be independent because we are working for the interest of our own people." Too often, he said, American policy has been "egocentric. You are losing support everywhere because of your attitude. For example, you are not interested in the Gulf for its own sake, but merely as a place to get oil. Why should I convince my people to be killed for America?"

Except for the sheikh's efforts and the influence of *Nedae Baluchistan*, an irregularly published London-based publication he has helped to finance (see chapter seven), there was little evidence of organized nationalist activity among the Gulf Baluch in 1980. Nor were there signs of significant Arab support for such activity. The sheikh's identification with Al-Hakkami's book led some observers to view him as a front man for Iraq, but his open appeal for American help cast doubt on this theory and suggested that his Arab encouragement, if any, has come from U.S.-oriented elements in Saudi Arabia and Jordan.

Despite their fears of Khomeini, the Arab rulers of the Persian Gulf sheikhdoms were notably ambivalent about the Baluch cause. Initially, the sheikh received qualified encouragement from the Sunni-dominated Bahrain government, which was alarmed by Khomeini's overt attempts to incite the Shia majority in Bahrain. A well-knit bloc of Sunni Baluch no doubt appeared to offer a useful counterweight to Teheran. Subsequently, however, when Khomeini adopted a more restrained approach to the Gulf, the Bahrain authorities put the sheikh under wraps.

Initially, when the Iran-Iraq war broke out in 1980, many Baluch leaders expected Iraq and its sympathizers in the Gulf to embrace the Baluch cause as a means of putting pressure on Teheran. Iraq did intensify its verbal support for greater Baluch autonomy in Iran but did not define what "autonomy" meant and gave only token financial support to Baluch nationalist groups in Iran and the Gulf. As in the case of its earlier decision to phase out support for the Baluch in 1973, Baghdad was reluctant to alienate Pakistan. Moreover, Iraqi leaders pleaded that their resources were limited and that it was all they could do to keep their own forces on the Shatt-al-Arab front well supplied.

Looking ahead, Arab support for the Baluch is likely to be closely linked with the fluctuating relations between Teheran and Arab capitals, especially those in the Gulf, just as it has been in earlier decades. Should conflict between Iraq and Iran become chronic, the possibility of Arab backing for an independent Baluchistan could grow, especially if internal economic and political conditions in Pakistan should continue to deteriorate. Significantly, in conversations with Sheikh Mohammed and Arab sources, including Iraqi diplomats, it was clear that they were preoccupied with developments in Pakistan as well as in Iran. They recognized that the growth of Baluch nationalism would make it increasingly difficult to give aid to the Iranian Baluch that would not spill over into Pakistani Baluchistan, and they were well aware that the Iranian Baluch movement was a relatively weak adjunct of the more developed nationalist movement in Pakistan. As of early 1981, Sheikh Mohammed had met on at least one occasion with Ataullah Mengal, and there were increasing Iraqi contacts with Pakistani and Iranian Baluch leaders alike as the war with Iran dragged on.

Pakistani Baluch leaders were cautiously receptive to the idea of Arab support for an independent Baluchistan during my conversations with them, but not on the terms suggested by Al-Hakkami and Sheikh Mohammed. "We are Aryans, like the Kurds!" exploded Mengal. "We are not Semites! If we give up Baluchi, as they ask, how can we call ourselves Baluch? We can be friends with the Arabs, perhaps close friends, although some of their present rulers are very reactionary. Certainly Baluchistan has much in common with the Gulf states especially. We have historical ties, and they are physically close to our tribes in Iran, very interconnected. We might want to form a special union with some of them. We could have a special relationship with them that could be very valuable to us, since they are very rich, without being threatening to us, since they are, after all, quite small. If the Arabs would allow us maneuverability, this might not be a bad idea after all. But we cannot give up our language and our identity!"

Like Mengal, Khair Bux Marri dismissed the idea of substituting Arabic for Baluchi, but he appeared ready to finesse the issue of whether the Baluch are Semites or Aryans. "If they think we are Arabs, we need not argue about our history," he mused. "What is important to us is our freedom. If we were to form a union with them, would they try to absorb us? Would they try to force some of their reactionary ideas on us? We are, after all, inspired by progressive and socialist ideals, which are essential for the development of a poor country." Marri did not rule out the idea of future links with one or more Arab states, observing that "there are a number of Arab states, and no one Arab state would necessarily be paramount if we were to join an Arab union." But he added that "most of their present leaders are reactionary, and in any case we are too weak now to talk about joining with others. We should try to buy time in which to strengthen ourselves so that we can hold our own in association with stronger partners."

Communism and Nationalism in Baluchistan

7

Given the widespread assumption that Moscow has its eye on Baluchistan, it is surprising to find that there have never been effective Soviet-oriented Communist organizations in the Baluch areas of either Pakistan or Iran. This is primarily because Soviet policy has consistently stopped short of supporting the concept of an independent Greater Baluchistan. Many Baluch regard the Soviet Union as more sympathetic to Third World aspirations than the capitalist and "imperialist" West and continue to look hopefully to Moscow as a potential supporter of their cause. But this pro-Soviet sentiment has not yet been translated into a strong Communist organizational base.

While defining the Baluch as a separate nationality and upholding their inherent right of secession, Soviet ideologues have until now advised against invoking this right, calling on their Baluch sympathizers to work with other "progressives" for overall Communist victories in Pakistan and Iran as a whole. Moreover, in addition to laboring under this doctrinal burden, Baluch Communists have been hampered by ethnic frictions with the Pakistani and Iranian Communist leadership. The faction-ridden Pakistani Communist movement has been controlled since its inception by urban, middle-class leaders who migrated from areas now in India at the time of partition and lack local roots in any of the ethnic regions now constituting Pakistan. Similarly, as we have seen, the Tudeh party in Iran is Persian-dominated and has alienated potential Baluch supporters by pushing for a loose federalism rather than for Baluch independence.

Even the Afghan Communists have been somewhat suspect in Baluch Communist eyes. For all of its expressions of sympathy with Baluch grievances, the Pushtun-dominated Afghan Communist movement has been cool to the idea of Baluch independence, promising only that the Baluch would be given autonomy within the larger framework of a Pushtunistan or a Greater Afghanistan.

Soviet Policy Toward Baluch Nationalism

The multiethnic Soviet Union employs a cynical form of ideological sleight of hand to justify strong centralized control of its diverse constituent republics while making a ceremonial bow to their separate national identities. On the one hand, communist nationality doctrine affirms the right of every nation to self-determination, including the right of secession; on the other, it stipulates that only the proletariat, whose will is embodied in the communist party, can decide whether it is in the interests of a particular nation to exercise that right on a given occasion. This doctrinal flexibility has been peculiarly suited to shifting Communist tactical priorities in the multiethnic South Asian environment.

Even before independence, the Communists in undivided India were well aware of the relevance of Soviet nationality doctrine to the Indian scene. The draft program of the nascent Indian Communist party declared in 1930 that only an "Indian Federal Soviet Republic would be capable of insuring to national minorities their right to self-determination, including that of complete separation."[1] Later, when the Hindu-Muslim conflict dominated Indian political life, Communist theoreticians turned to Soviet nationality doctrine in formulating their response to the Muslim League's demand for a separate Muslim state to be known as Pakistan. This demand was anathema to the Hindu-dominated Congress party led by Gandhi and Nehru, and its religious rationale initially made the proposal repugnant to the Communists. Seeking to maintain their popularity among Muslims, however, Indian Communist party leaders decided to support "what is just and right" in the Muslim League's demand. "The rational kernel of the Pakistan demand," wrote the party's leading theoretician on nationality, G. Adhikari, is that "wherever people of the Muslim faith living together in a territorial unit form a nationality...they certainly have the right to autonomous state existence just like other nationalities in India."[2]

In its memorandum to the British Cabinet Mission in April 1946, the Indian Communist party called on Britain to turn over power not to the provisional central government headed by Nehru, but to seventeen sovereign regional constituent assemblies, each to be empowered to decide whether or not to join the projected new Indian Union "or remain out and form a separate, sovereign state by themselves, or join another Indian Union." Four of these assemblies were to have been in Muslim-majority areas that later on became part of Pakistan—among them Baluchistan—while the other thirteen were in areas that later constituted the Indian Union.[3]

Despite the nominal allowance made for the formation of "separate, sovereign" states, the memorandum had the practical effect of supporting the Muslim League by envisaging "another Indian Union." By all indications, Moscow encouraged Communist support for the creation of Pakistan, believing that India would be "weak and disorganized, and would eventually be fragmented in the process of achieving independence."[4] In the immediate aftermath of the 1947 partition, the Indian Communist party continued to operate on the premise that India would fall apart, espousing separatist policies in Andhra and other ethnic minority regions. Fearing that the new Indian government would adopt anti-Soviet policies, the Soviet Union encouraged these separatist policies. Within less than five years, however, Moscow concluded that the Nehru government was an established fact and that India's neutralist policies would not be hostile to Soviet interests. In 1953, Moscow formally signaled its acceptance of the Indian state by decreeing that "though for India, too, the principle of self-determination means and naturally includes the right of separation, it is inexpedient for Indian nationalities to exercise the right."[5]

In the case of Pakistan, Soviet ideologues were initially less explicit, and as late as 1964, Yuri Gankovsky, a leading Soviet writer on nationality problems, asserted that "the dismemberment of India into two dominions along religious lines did not solve the national problem of Pakistan." To be sure, he conceded, "the slogan of Pakistan, albeit in an indirect, deformed way, expressed the striving for national autonomy and self-determination" of the two homogeneous Muslim regions in the subcontinent, Baluchistan and the Pushtun-dominated Northwest Frontier Province, as well as of "the Muslim parts of the Bengali, Punjabi and Sindhi peoples." But after the partition, he said, reactionary landowners, theologians, and businessmen had distorted the original intention of Mohammed Ali Jinnah and the other Muslim League founders, who had "emphasized that the areas encompassed in Pakistan would be autonomous and sovereign." Gankovsky did not directly challenge Pakistan's legitimacy or its continued right to exist, but he presented detailed historical analysis to show that it consisted of five distinct nationalities whose right to autonomy had yet to be recognized in the Pakistani state as it was then constituted.[6]

In contrast to Moscow's increasingly explicit support for Indian nationalism, Soviet policy toward Pakistan has been more ambivalent. Soviet writings have strongly advised the Baluch and other ethnic minorities against exercising their right of separation but have continued to emphasize the multinational character of Pakistan and have thus implicitly kept the separatist option open. The underlying premise of Soviet policy has been that Pakistan's chronic political instability offers fertile soil for a synchronized Communist takeover of the entire country. Rather than support uncoordinated separatist movements in the Baluch, Sindhi, and Pushtun areas without regard for the future of the Punjab, Moscow has argued, Communists should work for the conversion of the whole country into a loose multinational federation under their leadership. In effect, Moscow has treated separatism as a weapon of last resort, to be used only if and when hopes for an overall Communist victory in Pakistan must be abandoned. Similarly, as in the case of India, Moscow has attuned its evolving doctrine on the "national question" to its foreign policy priorities in Pakistan. Separatism has been consciously soft-pedaled as part of a Soviet diplomatic offensive to counter Chinese and U.S. influence in Islamabad. By implication, however, Moscow has continued to suggest that it is ready to invoke the separatist option if Islamabad should stray too far into the Sino-American orbit.

Soviet writings have treated Baluch nationalism as a nascent but growing phenomenon. The Baluch, Gankovsky wrote in his 1964 work *The Peoples of Pakistan: An Ethnic History,* "are the only one of Pakistan's major peoples who had not consolidated into a bourgeois nation by the time the colonialists left the Indo-Pakistan subcontinent." Baluchistan's economic dependence and backwardness were even greater than in other areas of British India during the colonial period, which had "a negative effect on the ethnic processes at work in the country, curbing the development of capitalist relations and arresting the rise of bourgeois-society classes and social strata." British economic neglect of Baluchistan drove many Baluch into Sind and other provinces in search of work. "This territorial dispersion did and does make the Baluch national consolidation exceedingly difficult." Nevertheless, he concluded, despite these handicaps, "the rise of the Baluchi nation is under way.... The national consolidation of the Baluchis is still on the move in our day.... The Baluchi proletariat is growing and the bourgeoisie and intelligentsia are taking shape. The birth of Baluchi national consciousness is in evidence."[7]

Parenthetically, it should be noted that when the English-language edition was published in 1971, *The Peoples of Pakistan* had been considerably toned down in keeping with a Soviet diplomatic offensive to curtail the growth of Chinese influence then taking place in Pakistan and to capitalize, if possible, on the coolness that had developed between Islamabad and Washington following the 1965 Indo-Pakistani war. The concluding chapter completely omitted the operative paragraphs in the 1964 edition that explained that the partition of the subcontinent along religious lines "did not solve the national problem in Pakistan."

Gankovsky's 1964 study marked the first extensive public scholarly Soviet treatment of the Baluch, with the exception of an economic treatise several years earlier by another author, M. G. Pikulin.[8] In 1960, Pikulin had written an article on the Baluch in Pakistan in which he concluded that the idea of a Greater Baluchistan uniting the *Pakistani*

Baluch is "a pressing issue." While expressing sympathy for Baluch self-determination, he was deliberately vague about whether it required separation from Pakistan and the creation of an independent state linking Pakistani and Iranian Baluch.[9] Similarly, Gankovsky's 1964 study, which was a historical tome focusing mainly on the preindependence period, did not offer specific policy advice to the nationalities in Pakistan. It pointedly avoided the debate then developing within Pakistani Communist ranks over the right of secession. By 1967, however, in a book devoted to postindependence "national movements," Gankovsky made clear that Moscow was opposed to separatist activity.

In his 1967 book, Gankovsky praised the "democratic movement" in Baluchistan for concentrating on the economic grievances of peasants and workers while also seeking the administrative unification of the Baluch areas into a single provincial unit which would enjoy "complete autonomy." At the same time, he directed vitriolic attacks at the "openly separatist position" of the Khan of Kalat and his uncle, Sultan Ibrahim Khan, who wanted to create an independent Baluchistan as a means of perpetuating their feudal privileges. "Imperialism and internal reaction do everything possible to sow suspicion and hatred among ethnic communities of multinational liberated states," Gankovsky concluded, "and to make their cooperative struggles for social progress impossible." He called for "incessant work" by all "progressive, patriotic forces interested in consolidating the independence and unity of their countries to prevent the spread of separatist tendencies and moods."[10]

In a 1973 book devoted entirely to the Baluch, Beknazar Ibragimov, a Gankovsky disciple, explicitly advised the Baluch against seeking independence. "The problems confronting all of the national regions of Pakistan cannot be solved on a narrowly nationalistic basis," he declared, "but require resolution on an all-Pakistan scale. This means that the national-democratic movement of the Baluchis can attain its objectives only in conjunction with all of the national and democratic forces of the country."[11] Belittling the "stubborn attitude" of those Baluch leaders who supported guerrilla activity during the 1960s, he praised the leaders of the Baluch "democratic movement who understood that the Baluch were not in a position to stand up to the military force of the government, which relied on monopolistic capital, imperialism and Maoism." He spoke contemptuously of the "weakness" of the guerrilla forces, their lack of coordination, and their shortages of supplies.[12]

Ibragimov pointed to the "major changes" that had contributed to the "integration of the Baluch into a nation" during the 1947–1970 period. Economic contacts with the more developed regions of Pakistan had disrupted the traditional economic and social structure, he said, leading to the growth of landless agricultural labor and a small but significant Baluch working class. The "Baluch national intelligentsia" had also grown progressively stronger, he added, and an "important turning point" in the Baluch struggle had come in the late 1960s, when the "national movement of the Baluchis became an indispensable part of the entire democratic movement in the country." Nevertheless, he threw up his hands at the magnitude of the social and economic problems confronting leaders of the Baluch Communist movement, pointing in particular to "inadequate organization and political literacy of the working class, the diversity of the economy, and the continuing influence of patriarchal and feudal-clerical circles." These problems would defy solution "for many decades," he said, adding that "strong nationalist traits still remain in the Baluchi movement, and this is a real danger for its successful development."[13]

In a 1977 review of nationality issues in Asia, a panel of Soviet specialists clearly ruled out Communist support for separatist movements in Pakistan, India, and Malaysia, pointing to these three cases as examples of "very unstable" multinational states marked by the absence of a "clearly-established ruling nation." By attempting to assert their dominance, the "larger and stronger nations" in these states, such as the Punjabis in Pakistan, invariably provoke a "narrowly nationalist particularism" on the part of the smaller nations. But along with the "incessant activity" of the centrifugal forces, centripetal forces are also "growing and becoming stronger," the panel concluded, reflecting the "growth of the supra-national community" in each of these countries and "the growing consciousness among the masses of the need to strengthen all-national unity."[14]

Soviet writers have been conspicuously silent on the issue of Baluch nationalism since the Soviet occupation of Afghanistan. However, Foreign Minister Andrei Gromyko made a thinly veiled threat that Moscow would seek to dismember Pakistan if Islamabad "becomes a springboard for aggression against Afghanistan." Speaking at a New Delhi banquet on February 12, 1980, Gromyko warned that "if Pakistan continues to serve as a puppet of imperialism in the future, it will jeopardize its existence and its integrity as an independent state."

Communist Strength in Baluchistan

Soviet unwillingness to support the Baluch aspiration for independence has cast a continuing pall over Communist organizing efforts in Baluchistan. "At first, in the 1930s, our prospects looked extremely promising," recalled K. B. Nizamani, who served as secretary of the Sind-Baluchistan branch of the Indian Communist party from 1935 to 1941. The party had recruited Ghaus Bux Bizenjo, then a rising young political activist, and Mohammed Hussain Unqa, one of the most popular Baluch poets of the day. As the independence of the subcontinent approached, however, Bizenjo, Unqa, and other Baluch "progressives" thought increasingly in terms of an independent Baluchistan. The Communist decision in 1941 to support the Pakistan movement "had a very bad effect, a very demoralizing effect, cutting the ground out from under us before we could really get started," Nizamani said.

In the decade preceding the 1947 partition of the subcontinent, the Indian Communist party's stand in support of the Pakistan movement reflected the marginal position of Baluch and Pushtun comrades in party councils and a corresponding dominance of party leaders from other parts of the subcontinent that has persisted since the creation of the Pakistan Communist party following partition. Both the Baluch and Pushtun regions were homogeneous Muslim areas where there was little fear of Hindu domination and little interest in the Pakistan cause. The Muslim League was not a dominant force in these areas, drawing its principal support from the Muslim-minority provinces that were destined to remain in India. Similarly, the Muslim Communist leadership was also concentrated in the Muslim-minority provinces, especially the populous Ganges Valley state of Uttar Pradesh, which happened to be the major center of political life under the British Raj.

After partition, many of the wealthier, better-educated Muslims in the Muslim-minority provinces migrated to Pakistan, where they assumed powerful positions in the bureaucratic and business worlds. As allies of the dominant Punjabis, these *mahajirs* (refugees) or "Hindustanis" became political targets of the minority Baluch, Pushtuns, and Sindhis. The Communist leaders who migrated to Pakistan were also suspect as *mahajirs* in the eyes of many of their locally rooted party comrades, but this did not prevent them from promptly asserting their claims to leadership of the new Pakistan Communist party.

Looking back on the aftermath of partition, Nizamani wrote in 1979 that

> since the areas constituting the western part of Pakistan did not have an effective Communist organization, the Pakistan Communist Party fell largely under the control of Punjabis and newly-arriving Hindustanis who had no understanding of the most acute contradictions in the country. From the very first day Pakistan was formed, the primary contradiction in the country was between the dictatorship of the ruling class and the suppression of the rights of the smaller nationalities. But since the majority of the so-called Communists were Pun-

jabis or Hindustanis, they considered this a secondary or minor con-
tradiction.[15]

When Communist organizers came to Baluchistan, Nizamani recalled, they were looking for industrial workers and landless agricultural
laborers who could be rallied on the basis of conventional Marxist-
Leninist class appeals. Instead, they confronted a nomadic tribal society
and generally hurried back to Karachi, concentrating their efforts on the
migrant Baluch factory workers there. Nizamani cited, in particular, an
organizer named Azizullah, who threw up his hands after discovering on
several visits to Quetta in 1951 and 1952 that Baluch activists were primarily interested in talking about their "national" grievances. Azizullah
did persuade Sher Mohammed Marri to start the short-lived Mazloom
(Workers) party, but he devoted most of his attention to Pushtun students and other non-Baluch recruits.

By 1954, Nizamani was convinced that a conventional Marxist-
Leninist approach could not win Baluch support without the added
emotional appeal of the independence issue. He turned for help to his
influential friend Prince Abdul Karim, who had staged the unsuccessful
1948 revolt against accession to Pakistan in which Nizamani had participated. Together, they attempted to organize a Baluch Marxist party
dedicated to an independent Baluchistan. Abdul Karim was still serving
a prison term for his revolt, but in March 1954, he was able to smuggle
out a letter he had prepared for Nizamani's use in organizing the
projected underground movement. The letter said that "in order to get
out of a situation in which we are treated like Red Indians, and to find
a place among the independent nations, we Baluch should unite in a
single organization." Authorizing Nizamani to contact other Baluch on
his behalf, Abdul Karim said that "the nation can achieve its independence only under the leadership of an organization formed with a Marxist outlook. We have failed in the past because of the lack of a scientific
ideology."

The proposed party never got off the ground, Nizamani lamented,
because he was unable to raise funds for organizational work, least of all
from his former comrades within the Communist party of Pakistan, who
disapproved of his emphasis on the independence issue. In the Baluch
areas "there was not a semblance of a party organization from which to
draw cadres, though there was a great deal of sympathy among some
intellectuals," he explained. "We would have had to start from scratch."
When Abdul Karim emerged from prison a year later, he had lost his
appetite for underground activity and founded an open, legal party, the
Ustoman Gal (People's party), which hewed to the Communist line that

Baluchistan should have autonomy, but within Pakistan. Nevertheless, Abdul Karim's flirtation with the idea of an autonomous Baluch national-communist party committed to independence makes an interesting historical footnote, since he is still a respected figure in Baluchistan, with his royal lineage as one of Nasir Khan's heirs, and could conceivably re-emerge at some future stage.

With the exception of Nizamani's abortive 1954 attempt, there has been no serious effort to alter the Pakistan Communist party's position on Baluch independence, which has consigned the party to continuing oblivion in the Baluch areas. Acknowledging that the Communists lost out during the 1960s to the Pararis, who combined nationalism with a vague Marxism-Leninism, Aijaz Ahmed, a Communist-oriented intellectual, said that "of course, many progressive elements supported the Baluch side, and almost all progressive Baluch forces participated in the fight at some time or other. That is precisely what makes the error so poignant." Since the guerrillas had survived by hiding out in remote, unpopulated areas, they were "unable to transform or politicize the masses. Ten years or more of guerrilla warfare has had little radicalizing impact on the masses." In an allusion to Khair Bux Marri and Ataullah Mengal, Ahmed declared that the "only appreciable result" of the insurgency had been to "prop up the leading *sardars* of the insurrection as the leaders of Baluchistan today. The *sardars* have retained their feudal power and have gained political legitimacy in addition."[16]

In a definitive, previously unpublished "strategy document" adopted at their second congress on May 1, 1976, Communist party leaders declared that "the question of national rights has not been solved in Pakistan." However, it warned party members

to guard against the two erroneous lines found on this question in the country. The first line denies the existence of nationalities, thus strengthening the exploitation of the oppressed nationalities. The second line equates the struggle for national rights with the struggle for national states, leading to the breakup of the country into penny pockets which again, like the first line, serves the interests of reaction and imperialism as it divides the democratic struggle.

Referring only obliquely to the insurgency then raging, the third item in a list of seven priority political tasks called on party members to "participate in the just struggle of the people of Baluchistan," but enjoined them, at the same time, to "unite and connect the struggle in Baluchistan with the other democratic issues in the country." Imperialism and its agents "are trying to cut off the struggle of the Baluch people from the general anti-imperialist struggle in the country," it cautioned, "by propagating that the Baluch people are struggling for separation." Elsewhere, the "strategy document" stressed that the party's struggle for national rights includes "the right of self-determination, so that national barriers may be broken and class consciousness may develop." Communist party leaders made a gesture to Baluch leftists by declaring that "if the struggle develops faster in some sectors or some areas, that specific contingent of the overall democratic forces will be of great help in throwing back the enemy all along the line and bringing nearer the emancipation of the whole of Pakistan."[17]

The 1976 congress was actually the first ever held by the Communists in Pakistan; the first congress cited in the "strategy document" turns out to have been the 1948 congress of the Indian Communist party in Calcutta, which took place just after partition and was attended by delegates from Pakistan.

In contrast to the more liberal environment enjoyed by the Communist party of India, the Communist party of Pakistan has faced severe repression from the start. This harassment has aggravated built-in leadership rivalries and ideologically based factional tensions. The ranking refugee leader in the immediate aftermath of partition, Sajjad Zaheer, died in prison after his arrest for complicity in a 1952 left-wing coup attempt known as the Rawalpindi conspiracy case. Another dynamic refugee leader, Hassan Nasir, who was rapidly taking Zaheer's place, was tortured to death in prison in 1961 at the age of twenty-eight, throwing the party into a state of confusion from which it has never recovered. The nominal leader since Nasir's death, Imam Ali Nazish, is a reclusive ideologue who has failed to emerge as a commanding figure.

Attempting to play down his *mahajir* heritage, Nazish has dropped his last name, Imrohi, which reflects his origins in Imroha, a town in Uttar Pradesh state in India. Nonetheless, he personifies the refugee character of the party leadership. Leftist rivals dismiss his organization as a "*matarawa* (chickpea) communist party," likening it to the lowliest of the foodgrains used in Pakistan. In the absence of anything better, the Soviet Union has indicated its preference for Nazish's group as the closest thing to an "official" Communist party in Pakistan. Moscow clashed with Nazish openly only for a brief period in the early 1970s, when the party refused to go along completely with Soviet support of the Bhutto regime. However, Soviet representatives have also shown intermittent interest in some of the thirteen other groups vying for leadership of the Left in Pakistan and have given strong support to Bhutto's Pakistan People's party, especially since his execution.

Significantly, none of these dissident communist factions have a consequential organization in Baluchistan. The two most important of the thirteen rivals to the official organization are based in other areas: the Mazdoor-Kisan (Worker-Peasant) party, led by Afzal Bangash, which has a strong organization in the Pushtun region, and Rasul Bux Palejo's Awami Tehriq (People's League) in Sind. Bangash is an on-again, off-again Soviet partisan who has been operating out of Kabul and London since early 1980. When he attempted to unify some of the smaller leftist factions under his leadership in 1978, the leadership roster of his new leftist alliance failed to include a single Baluch. Palejo, a onetime Maoist, is basically a Sindhi nationalist, but he works closely with Baluch student and labor union factions in Sind.

It should be emphasized that despite the lack of a unified, tightly knit Communist movement in Baluchistan, the Soviet Union has enjoyed, more often than not, a favorable image among the Baluch. Soviet support of the Bhutto regime during the insurgency and the 1979 Russian invasion of Afghanistan have tarnished, but not fundamentally altered, this image. In Baluch eyes, Washington has been consistently and directly identified with the repression of the Baluch by successive Islamabad regimes through its military and economic aid, while Moscow, which has been arrayed against every Pakistani regime except Bhutto's, represents a potentially liberating alternative. In addition, the Baluch, like many Third World peoples, tend to identify the Soviet Union as a friend of the underprivileged, in contrast to the United States, with its multinational corporations, which is seen as a source of support for exploitative local capitalists. As for the Afghan invasion, Akber Y. Mustikhan, one of the leading Baluch businessmen, explained that most Baluch regard the descriptions of Soviet atrocities that appear in the Western press as "greatly exaggerated. They are reluctant to believe that the Russians, whom they don't know firsthand, could be worse than the Punjabis, whom they do know all too well. We talk to them of freedom, but they say, 'What freedom do we have to lose? We never had freedom like the Afghans.'"

Pointing to Pakistani and Western demands for free elections in Soviet-occupied Afghanistan, a London-based Baluch nationalist publication asked whether "these Punjabi politicians and foreigners would be willing to have free elections in occupied Baluchistan under the supervision of an impartial international organization."[18] British correspondent David Housego of the *Financial Times,* visiting Baluchistan in early 1980, reported that "a journalist's notebook is rapidly filled with the rhetoric of a people who feel bitter at having been cheated of self-government by successive Pakistani regimes, and who are now tempted to see in the Russians potential allies for their cause.... What would be the reaction if the Russians were to descend on the province? 'We would welcome them, of course,' says a senior tribal *sardar* with breathtaking abandon. His companion goes one further: 'We would ask them why they did not come earlier.'"[19]

As a result of this readiness to give Moscow the benefit of the doubt, there has always been a goodly scattering of active pro-Soviet "progressives" in Baluchistan linked with assorted leftist factions in Karachi and Lahore. Some of these factions are staunchly pro-Soviet, but most are freewheeling Marxist-Leninist groups with a vaguely Soviet-inclined program. In the 1960s, it should be noted, there were also a few pro-Chinese groups, but Peking's identification with Islamabad, and later the normalization of Sino-U.S. relations, have put these elements on the defensive in the Baluch areas. In one of its rare references to the Baluch issue, Peking showed little sympathy for Baluch aspirations, charging in 1980 that Moscow was "fomenting trouble among the Baluchis and other ethnic minorities in Pakistan and Iran in preparation for the dismemberment of the two countries."[20]

Many of the pro-Soviet activists in Baluchistan have played a key role in energizing left-oriented political groups, including the Ustoman Gal in the 1950s, the Baluch Ustoman Gal in the early 1960s, and more recently the National Awami party and the Baluch Students Organization. To cite an example, during his student years in the early 1970s, Khair Jan Baluch, former president of the BSO, kept in "fairly close touch" with Communist functionaries in Karachi. While the BSO "gives priority to its nationalist aims," he said, "it has played a role in the practical political field as a sort of communist party in Baluchistan, since there has been no effective Communist organization as such. We supported socialism and the role of Russia on many issues. For example, we joined them in supporting India in Bangladesh and in condemning the role of the Pakistan Army in Bangladesh." This kind of support is transitory, however, as the case of Khair Jan shows. By 1980, he had gone into business and was no longer active in leftist politics, though he still expressed vague pro-Soviet sympathies.

One of the more durable personalities in Baluch leftist circles has been K. B. Nizamani, who went into political exile in London in 1974, but who has continued to work actively to promote his own special, Soviet-oriented brand of Baluch nationalism. Using the pseudonym Karim Baluch, Nizamani, a sharp-witted, engaging political adventurer, publishes the monthly newspaper *Nedae Baluchistan* (Voice of Baluchistan), which claims some 3,500 subscribers, primarily Baluch migrant workers in the Arab sheikhdoms of the Persian Gulf. He has focused his efforts on the Gulf, Nizamani said, because the Baluch there have become "more cosmopolitan politically, more politically conscious" than many of the Baluch living under repressive regimes in Pakistan and Iran.

Although his paper is banned by the Zia and Khomeini regimes, copies are smuggled into Pakistan and Iran and are then reproduced for underground use by his sympathizers. Given the absence of Communist support for Baluch nationalist aspirations, Nizamani added, *Nedae Baluchistan,* which mixes its nationalism with the "anti-imperialist" approach to global issues popular among Baluch youth, "has been filling a void in Pakistan, virtually serving as a political tendency, a political grouping or incipient party." His sympathizers are not comfortable with the "*mahajir*-dominated" Communist party of Pakistan and its occasional "opportunist" Baluch allies, such as Ghaus Bux Bizenjo. Instead, they work closely with independent Baluch leftist elements linked with the Marxist Sindhi nationalist Rasul Bux Palejo.

Nizamani's checkered political history has aroused understandable suspicions that there may be a hidden Soviet hand behind his present role. According to his own account, he studied in Moscow in 1934 and 1935 and spent nearly ten years in the Sind-Baluchistan branch of the Communist party before quitting as a result of its refusal to support Baluch independence. Still, he remained sympathetic toward the Soviet Union and worked in the information department of the Soviet embassy in Karachi until 1969. Fearing arrest after Bhutto began to crack down on Baluch activists, Nizamani went to Baghdad early in 1972, where he joined a group of émigré Baluch who were working with Iraqi encouragement to organize a Baluch uprising in Iran. The Iraqis were using the Baluch as one of their weapons against the Shah in retaliation for his support of the Kurdish rebellion. When Iraq and Iran made their peace, the Iraqis abandoned the Baluch as part of the bargain. Nizamani subsequently took refuge in London with his family and is now a British citizen.[21]

Although he expresses disillusionment with Moscow for its "opportunist, great-power attitude" and its indifference to the Baluch and other "smaller nations," Nizamani speaks more in sadness than in anger about the Russians. His newspaper, known until 1980 as *People's Front,* rarely wanders very far from the Soviet line except on issues relating directly to the Baluch. Even on the issue of independence, the paper equivocated in its early issues, hewing to the demand for a "socialist, federal" Pakistan made by the Pakistani Communists and most other Pakistani leftist groups. It was not until early 1979 that *People's Front* came out for sovereign independence. On the issue of the Afghan revolution, Nizamani has hailed with equal enthusiasm the Nur Mohammed Taraki coup of April 1978 and the advent of the Soviet-installed Babrak Karmal regime in December 1979.[22]

Nizamani's shift on the independence issue came in April 1979, just after Khomeini had taken power and Iraq had begun to reactivate its support for Kurdish, Khuzistani Arab, and Baluch rebels in Iran. This coincidence of timing has stirred speculation that his paper is financed by Baghdad. To complete the picture, however, it should be noted that in May 1979 he was invited as a government guest to Kabul, where he was received royally by both President Taraki and Prime Minister Hafizullah Amin. Nizamani himself laughed off suggestions that he receives Iraqi, Afghan, or Soviet financing, saying only that his shoestring operations are covered by contributions from wealthy Baluch in the Gulf, among them Sheikh Mohammed Bin Hassan Al-Mohammed, whose activities were discussed in chapter six.

My own impression, based on six conversations spanning the period from 1975 to 1981 as well as other inquiries, is that Nizamani is an independent Baluch nationalist who keeps his operations going by picking up help from Communist and non-Communist sources alike in a spirit of cheerfully unabashed opportunism. Ideologically speaking, however, his sympathies have remained consistently and frankly pro-Soviet, despite his continuing dissatisfaction with Moscow's attitude toward Baluchistan. He has never flirted with Maoism, Titoism, or other heresies and is not attracted to the kind of national-communist approach espoused by Khair Bux Marri or the Baluch People's Liberation Front. Should Moscow ever decide to support an independent Baluchistan, producing a polarization in the independence movement between nationalist and pro-Soviet elements, *Nedae Baluchistan* would in all likelihood be in the forefront of the pro-Soviet parade.

As one of the earliest recruits to the Baluch Communist movement in the 1930s, Nizamani presents a poignant figure four decades later, still struggling to reconcile his nationalism with his Moscow-oriented world view. Examined from one perspective, his experience illustrates the dispersion and fragmentation of the pro-Soviet forces in Baluchistan. Viewed from another, it serves as a reminder that Moscow has extensive latent Baluch support that it might well be able to convert into an effective Communist party should it embark on a separatist course in Baluchistan.

In the aftermath of the Soviet occupation of Afghanistan, unsubstantiated press reports have periodically emanated from Washington, Islamabad, and elsewhere stating that Moscow is training "thousands" of Baluch agents. I have no independent evidence to verify these reports, which have not been confirmed by American or Pakistani officials. However, Pakistani intelligence sources state that a dozen or more Baluch students have attended Lumumba University on Soviet scholarships during the past decade. An interesting variation on this theme has come from Inayatullah Baloch, a nationalist scholar at Heidelberg University's South Asian Institute. Moscow's "secret weapon" in Baluchistan, Baloch writes, is the existence of some 13,000 Soviet citizens of Baluch ancestry "who can be called upon to form part of a communist vanguard in Baluchistan if and when required."[23]

This is a provocative line of speculation, especially with respect to Iranian Baluchistan, since the Baluch tribes now living in the Merv area of Soviet Turkmenistan originally came from Iranian Baluchistan and southwestern Afghanistan. However, some of these tribes migrated to the Soviet Union nearly a century ago, and the most recent migrants came between 1918 and 1928. Eden Naby, a Harvard specialist on Soviet Central Asia, contends that their Baluch identity has been considerably diluted over the years. She specifically disputes Baloch's assertion that Moscow has encouraged the use of the Baluchi language and states that the Baluch in the Soviet Union have been forced to live together with Turkmens in collective farms where they have lost their tribal ties. "Given the small number of Baluch in the Soviet Union, their rapid assimilation into surrounding populations and the lack of Baluchi-language cultural facilities," she writes, "the Soviet Baluch role in future Baluch movements appears likely to be minimal."[24]

The Afghan Communists and Baluchistan

In contrast to the Soviet Union, which has emphasized the achievement of Baluch rights within Pakistan, Afghanistan has traditionally encouraged Baluch ambitions for some form of liberation from Islamabad. For their part, however, Baluch nationalists have always had mixed feelings concerning Afghan interest in their cause. This ambivalence is rooted in the well-founded belief that Afghan leaders, who are primarily Pushtuns, do not actually favor an independent Baluch state but rather the ultimate incorporation of Baluchistan into a Greater Afghanistan or an Afghan-controlled Pushtunistan.

As we have seen in chapter two, Afghanistan's seventeenth-century founder, Ahmad Shah Durrani, ruled over the Baluch state of Kalat as a tributary for fourteen years. Leaning on this slender historical reed, Kabul has periodically included Baluchistan in its sweeping irredentist claims to areas east of the Durand line. In its vaguely defined demand for Pushtunistan, Kabul has generally implied that the proposed state would embrace only Pushtun areas of Pakistan. But some maps have depicted

Baluchistan, in its entirety, as Southern Pushtunistan. While Afghan Communist leaders have made cosmetic gestures to the Baluch as a separate nationality, in keeping with Marxist-Leninist precepts on the "national question," their approach to the Baluch issue, in practice, has betrayed the same Pushtun bias shown by other Afghan leaders.

In their approach to the manipulation of Pushtun and Baluch separatism, the Khalq (People) and Parcham (Banner) factions of the Afghan Communist movement have followed radically different policies, reflecting the broader tactical differences that have divided the two groups. Khalq, led by Taraki and Amin, was initially committed to a "people's democracy" line, which ruled out united fronts with "bourgeois nationalist" leaders, while Parcham followed a Soviet-dictated "national democracy" line. Thus, Khalq refused to join Parcham in supporting the non-Communist Mohammed Daud regime, notwithstanding strong Soviet support for Daud, insisting that to do so would be a betrayal of Marxist-Leninist principles. Similarly, Khalq opposed the Parcham policy of collaborating with "bourgeois nationalists" in Pakistan such as National Awami party leaders Abdul Wali Khan and Ghaus Bux Bizenjo. Instead, Khalq favored efforts to build up Communist cadres under its aegis or to establish cooperative links with existing Communist factions.

Pointing to the fact that Wali Khan and most of his fellow NAP leaders in the Pakistani Pushtun areas were relatively big landholders, Khalq aligned itself with Afzal Bangash, leader of a Pushtun tenant-farmer movement linked with a Pakistani Communist faction mentioned earlier, the Mazdoor-Kisan (Worker-Peasant) party. Parcham, by contrast, worked mainly with a leftist NAP faction led by Ajmal Khattak. So far as can be determined, neither Khalq nor Parcham paid much attention to the Baluch areas until after their 1977 merger and the advent of the Khalq-dominated People's Democratic party regime in Kabul in 1978.

The significance of this Khalq-Parcham divergence is that Parcham followed a flexible line attuned to Soviet regional objectives, which called for efforts to achieve Pushtun and Baluch rights within Pakistan, while the Khalq policy foreshadowed what was to become a Greater Afghanistan approach. Strictly speaking, Wali Khan and his venerated father, Abdul Ghaffar Khan, leader of the anti-British Redshirt movement, had never indicated clearly whether their concept of Pushtunistan meant an autonomous Pushtun state within Pakistan, an Afghan-linked Pushtun state, or an independent Pushtun state. Like Afghan leaders, they had demanded only that the Pakistani Pushtuns be given the right of self-determination. As a practical matter, however, Wali Khan had made it increasingly clear that he was prepared to come to terms with

Islamabad if agreement could be reached on guarantees of regional autonomy.

In its first published program, the Khalq declared in April 1966 that the Durand line had been imposed upon Afghanistan "against the wishes of its people, and as a result, a part of the territory of the country was detached from its body." Since the Durand line serves as the de facto boundary of Afghanistan with both the Baluch and Pushtun areas of Pakistan, this declaration clearly implied that Baluchistan was part of the lost territory. However, the manifesto said only that "in accordance with their belief in the right of self-determination, the people of Afghanistan support the liberation movement of the people of Pushtunistan."[25]

Once in power, the Khalq-dominated People's Democratic party of Afghanistan (PDPA) continued to keep its Greater Afghanistan option open, treating the issue of Pushtun and Baluch aspirations with calculated ambiguity. In his first declaration of party principles, President Nur Mohammed Taraki called for "the solution of the national issue of the Pushtun and Baluch people," which gave cosmetic recognition to a separate Baluch identity but lumped Pushtun and Baluch aspirations together in a single "national issue."[26] Taraki denied the validity of the Durand line, as past Afghan regimes had done, declaring that Pushtun and Baluch grievances had to be redressed in the light of the "historical background." At the same time, he stressed that Afghanistan and Pakistan should settle their differences "through understanding and peaceful political talks," pointedly avoiding strident rhetoric in support of Pushtun and Baluch rights.[27]

The vagueness of his language left open the possibility that the new Communist regime, prodded by Moscow, might accept a solution of the dispute within the Pakistan framework. However, it soon became clear that there were significant differences on this issue between Taraki, the Khalq's elder statesman, and Hafizullah Amin, a strong Pushtun nationalist and an advocate of a Pushtun-controlled Greater Afghanistan, who controlled the party organization, including its cadres in the armed forces. Taraki had become leader of the PDPA, created by the merger of Khalq and Parcham, because he was more acceptable to Parcham. He had emerged as president after the 1978 coup, with Amin as foreign minister and Parcham leader Babrak Karmal as vice-president. But Amin gradually pushed Taraki and Karmal aside, and as his power grew, so did the stridency of his appeals to Pushtun and Baluch separatist feeling.

As soon as Amin became prime minister in March 1979, his Greater Afghanistan rhetoric began to intensify, reaching a climax in the July to September period, when the Kabul regime convened a series of meetings of Pushtun tribal notables from border areas where rebel activity was raging. His speeches were replete with imagery depicting Afghanistan as reaching from the Oxus River, which marks the northern boundary with the Soviet Union, to the Abasin (the Pushtu word for the Indus River in Pakistan). The Indus presently serves as the border between Pakistan's Punjab state and the Pushtun-majority Northwest Frontier Province, but it once marked the easternmost limits of the Afghan empire prior to the British Raj.

Addressing a meeting of Charmang and Bajaur tribal leaders on July 29, 1979, Amin declared that "all the nationalities from the Oxus to the Abasin are brothers from one homeland.... In Kabul, the roaring waves of the Abasin are mingled in revolutionary cascades with the waves of the Oxus. The waves of bravery of the Pushtuns and Baluchis of the whole region are reflected in the revolutionary emotions of the toilers here."[28] "Our revolution is revered and welcomed from the Oxus to the Abasin," he said on August 20, "from the mountains of Pamir to the beaches of Gwadar in Baluchistan."[29]

In a speech on September 20, 1979, he recited the names of several Afghan cities and made allusions, in the same breath, to Baluchistan; to Attock, the historic fort on the Indus symbolizing the high point of nineteenth-century Afghan expansion; and to Peshawar, once governed by an Afghan viceroy but now the capital of the Northwest Frontier Province. Amin hailed the

> great love of the toilers and laborers for their country, whether they are in Peshawar, Herat, Kandahar, Badakshan, Baluchistan, or Kabul.... Our sincere and honest brotherhood with the Pushtuns and Baluchis has been sanctified by history. They have been one body in the course of history and have lived together like one brother. Now the waves of their love and brotherhood extend from the Oxus to Attock, and they want to live side by side, embrace each other, and demonstrate this great love to the world at large.[30]

In two off-the-record interviews on June 6 and August 10, 1978, Amin spoke passionately about the injustice of the Durand line, which "tore us apart," assuring me that "we will do our historical duty when the time is right, when we have consolidated our revolution. The Pushtun and Baluch national movements are very dear to us." When I attempted to pin him down on the issue of an independent Baluchistan, however, he would say only that "time will decide the proper correlation between the Pushtun and Baluch nationalities." Later, Amin revealed his Greater Afghanistan sentiments more explicitly in an off-the-record interview with Feroz Ahmad, editor of the leftist *Pakistan Forum*. Dismissing Ahmad's contention that the Pushtuns in Pakistan were becoming economically integrated with the rest of the country, Amin declared that "the class struggle will solve all of these problems." Ahmad quotes Amin as saying that the Afghan leaders who acquiesced in the creation of a Pakistani state in 1947 based on the Durand line were "not patriotic. If they had been patriotic, this problem would have been solved a long time ago, and today there would have been one country."

During his visit to Kabul in early 1979 at the invitation of the Communist government, K. B. Nizamani, the pro-Soviet Baluch nationalist described earlier, received the impression that Amin envisaged autonomous status for the Baluch within a Greater Afghanistan. When the Khalq had first come to power, Nizamani observed, Baluch nationalists had seized hopefully on a number of straws in the wind suggesting that the Khalq might support Baluch independence. One such indication was the fact that the Baluch were treated on a par with the Pushtuns in Taraki's statements. Another was the inauguration of a government monthly in Baluchi, *Soub* (Victory). Baluch hopes reached a high point when the Taraki regime decided to rename the annual Pushtunistan Day celebration traditionally held in Kabul as Pushtunistan and Baluchistan Day and to give equal billing to Pushtun leaders and to Mir Hazar Ramkhani, leader of the Baluch People's Liberation Front. In conversation with Amin, however, Nizamani became skeptical about his intentions. Amin told Nizamani that he envisaged a federal constitution for Afghanistan patterned after the Soviet constitution, in which the Pushtun and Baluch areas of Afghanistan would be among the "national" units. The implication was that such a restructuring would facilitate the eventual incorporation of the adjacent Pushtun and Baluch areas of Pakistan into the "homeland."

The Baluch image of the Khalq regime was also affected by tensions that developed between Amin and the Afghan Baluch tribes. Despite the fact that it introduced the Baluchi language in the schools for the first time and promoted Baluch cultural activity in other ways, the Khalq government alienated many of the Baluch tribes by seeking to circumvent the established tribal leadership structure in carrying out its reform programs. An estimated 10,000 of the 90,000 Baluch living in Afghanistan migrated to adjacent areas of Iran during the Khalq regime. Some 500 to 700 of these Afghan Baluch carried on anti-Kabul resistance activity from bases in Iran. However, this group operated independently from the Islamic fundamentalist resistance organizations based in Pakistan, which are regarded as instruments of the "anti-Baluch" Zia Ul-Haq regime in Islamabad.

Significantly, Amin wanted Communist factions in the Pakistani Pushtun areas to become affiliates of the Khalq party. This policy contributed to a split in the Mazdoor-Kisan party between its veteran leader,

Afzal Bangash, who insisted on the continued autonomy of the party, and rebels who formed a new splinter group with links to the Khalq. Amin's plan to extend the Khalq organization into Pakistan was just getting started at the time of his death and had not yet involved the Baluch areas.

Although it is difficult to establish firmly, my own belief is that Amin's strong Pushtun nationalist commitment was one of the underlying factors that led the Soviet Union to decide on his removal. It was bad enough, in Soviet eyes, that he resisted KGB efforts to get control over the armed forces and the secret police and that he refused to heed Soviet counsels of restraint in handling the anticommunist tribal rebellion. Beyond this, what must have made his continued leadership of Afghanistan seem intolerable to Moscow was his refusal to follow Soviet dictates in dealing with Iran and Pakistan. While Moscow soft-pedaled its criticism of Khomeini after he took power, Amin continued to attack him, combining traditional Pushtun anti-Persian invective with Marxist-Leninist denunciations of the "obscurantist theocracy" in Teheran. More important, while Moscow wanted to play down the Pushtun and Baluch issues until it had a secure foothold in Kabul, Amin consciously used those issues to fortify his nationalist standing with his followers.

Viktor Lessiovsky, a special assistant to U.N. Secretary General Kurt Waldheim and long regarded as a top KGB operative, told me in early 1980 that "we were, quite seriously, afraid that he would get us involved in difficulties we did not want to get involved in. He was continually asking us to help equip them for actions across the border, in order to 'liberate' their territory, and we were continually trying to restrain him."

To some extent, Lessiovsky may have been engaging in "disinformation" as part of a Soviet effort to justify Amin's removal. Nevertheless, it is clear that Babrak Karmal promptly softened Kabul's rhetoric on the Pushtun and Baluch issues following his installation by the Russians in December 1979. In his first address to the Afghan people on January 1, 1980, Karmal made only a passing reference to "the right of the Pushtun and Baluch brethren to express their will and to decide for themselves about their own future destiny."[31] He reaffirmed past Afghan denials of the validity of the Durand line at his first press conference a week later, declaring that "there exists no border at all due to historical reasons. It is an open area."[32] Subsequently, a *Kabul Times* editorial deplored the "Machiavellian" use of the "Pushtunistan" issue by the Daud regime as a means of diverting attention from internal discontent, adding that "what lukewarm support of the Pushtun and Baluchi tribes the past Afghan governments have enjoyed was lost during the period of the sanguinary Amin and his rogue band."[33]

Asked in late February 1980, whether the Pushtuns and Baluch would be mobilized to counteract Pakistani support of the anticommunist rebels in Afghanistan, Karmal replied that "the national issue of the Pushtun and Baluchi nationalities in Pakistan is entirely their own. If the Pushtuns, Baluchis, or Sindhis are not satisfied with their regime, it is up to them to take any action. It is also quite clear that we have always nurtured warm fraternal sentiments toward Pushtuns and Baluchis, due to the common historical bonds binding us, but their problem is theirs."[34]

By mentioning the Sindhis together with the Pushtuns and Baluch, Karmal signaled that Kabul had shifted from a Greater Afghanistan line to one more in tune with Soviet policies on Pakistan. With the advent of the Parcham regime, Kabul gradually became a base of operations for Soviet-oriented leftist leaders operating in all parts of Pakistan, with the notable exception of Baluchistan. Imam Ali Nazish, secretary of the Pakistan Communist party, directed his campaign for a "socialist, federal" Pakistan from a Kabul headquarters. Nazish worked closely with Zulfiqar Ali Bhutto's oldest son, Murtaza, and several other leaders of the left wing of Bhutto's Pakistan People's party who announced plans to form a paramilitary People's Liberation Army. Karmal's old ally in the Pakistani Pushtun areas, Ajmal Khattak, was also restored to prominence after a period of eclipse during the Khalq regime. For the first time in a generation, Communist leaders in the Pushtun areas of Pakistan worked together in 1980 as part of a broader partnership with Kabul and with Communist units in other parts of Pakistan.

Given the strength of Pushtun opposition to the Soviet presence in Afghanistan, Khattak and other Pushtun Communist leaders have stressed economic appeals in 1980 much more heavily than the appeals to Pushtun solidarity with Kabul used in earlier years. This was a viable strategy in the Pushtun areas, where there are class-conscious tenant farmers in the fertile Peshawar Valley and small but significant pockets of industrial workers. By contrast, in Baluchistan the class struggle had not yet arrived. Communist leaders still confronted the same shortage of cultivable land and the same undeveloped, nomadic society that they had faced in the 1930s. Nationalism was still the horse to ride there, but the Communists were not ready to ride it.

There were some signs of a possible change brewing in mid-1980, notably Bizenjo's proposal, cited in chapter four, for an opposition platform demanding the right of secession for nationalities in Pakistan if Islamabad violated their constitutional autonomy guarantees. Did Bizenjo put this proposal forward on his own, seeking to keep in step with militant Baluch opinion, or was he reflecting a new climate in Moscow and in Pakistani Communist circles on the issue of an independent Baluchistan? The latter possibility was suggested by persistent rumors that Nazish had issued a secret party circular authorizing Communists to pursue the "piecemeal liberation" of Pakistan if the "liberation movement" developed more rapidly in some parts of the country than in others. Moreover, there have been increasing indications of Soviet efforts behind the scenes to stimulate indigenous Communist organizations in both Pakistani and Iranian Baluchistan.

In any event, Moscow would have to choose between two equally challenging alternatives if it should decide, at this late stage, to support Baluch independence. One would be a crash program to convert its extensive latent support in Baluchistan into a well-knit Communist machine. Another option, implying more limited goals, would be to support one or more of the Baluch nationalist leaders, recognizing full well that they might prove to be unusually obstreperous clients.

The View from Islamabad and Teheran

8

In attempting to assess the potential of the Baluch nationalist movement, this book has focused until now on how the Baluch feel and what Baluch leaders have done in past years to lay the foundations for future action. Let us now examine underlying Pakistani and Iranian attitudes toward the Baluch challenge before turning to a more detailed discussion of the prospects for compromise.

In the eyes of Pakistani and Iranian leaders, Baluch demands for regional autonomy constitute, at best, a thinly disguised form of blackmail designed to extort a disproportionate share of the benefits of economic progress or, at worst, a prelude to eventual secession. Not surprisingly, the dominant Punjabis in Pakistan, comprising 58 percent of the population, find it infuriating that a Baluch minority of less than 4 percent should seek to assert proprietary claims over Baluchistan, which represents 42 percent of the land area of the country. Similarly, in Iran, where the Baluch constitute at most 2 percent of the population, the ruling Persians, who make up 52 percent, ridicule the proposition that the Baluch have any special rights in Baluchistan. The idea of demarcating provincial units in accordance with historic ethnic homelands is anathema to the ideologues of Pakistani and Iranian nationalism. In both cases, a succession of authoritarian regimes, operating through highly centralized constitutional systems, have sought to minimize or obliterate regional identities in order to pursue modernization programs addressed to the overall needs and growth potential of their respective countries.

Discussing the Pakistani case, political scientist Robert G. Wirsing has pointed to the "awesome asymmetry" of a situation in which such a small minority demands recognition of special interests that conflict directly with the ambitions of such a powerfully entrenched majority. Militarily, as he observes, Baluchistan has become a strategic buffer of "incalculable importance" for the rest of Pakistan, especially in the wake of the Soviet invasion of Afghanistan.* In the context of their economic

---

* The military importance of Baluchistan was also underlined by reports in 1981 that Islamabad was preparing to use a site in the remote Chagai district for its first nuclear weapons test.

priorities, Pakistani planners are bound to view the sparsely settled expanses of Baluchistan as a safety valve for surplus population. Punjabi, Pathan, and Sindhi settlement of Baluch areas is "certain" to increase, he believes, "under the weight of one of the world's highest population growth rates." In a period of growing energy scarcity and spiraling energy costs, exploitation of Baluchistan's natural gas, coal, and mineral resources has become an increasingly crucial link in Pakistan's overall development effort. In contrast to the plight of forgotten minorities in some countries, Wirsing concludes, the problem confronted by the Baluch "is not that, having control of so little, they may be neglected by an indifferent majority. It is that, having control of so much, they are highly visible obstructions in the way of the majority's progress and are likely to be swept aside."[1]

Zia's Velvet Glove

In conversations on July 29, 1978, and March 8, 1980, General Zia Ul-Haq distinguished between Baluchistan, which he regards as important, and the "Baluch problem," which he believes has been greatly exaggerated by foreign observers. Referring to Baluchistan as "the most sensitive area of Pakistan," he warned that "if the Russians come there, it will be by naked aggression, and that is the only 'Baluch problem' we have to worry about." Given the military importance of Baluchistan, he declared, "we obviously cannot think of it as having something in particular to do with the Baluch. They have a provincial population equal to one third of the population of one city in the Punjab, Lahore. They have coal, gas, and oil that the whole country needs. We are one country, and the Baluch are part of our country. They can go anywhere to work. Why do you Americans and other foreigners make so much of this? Many countries have problems like this and they deal with them in the necessary way. People don't talk about their breaking up. Look at the Irish, Welsh, and Scotch in Britain. Look at Canada. Look at your own country. It may be a crude example, but take the case of your South Carolina. It is a depressed state, while California is a developed state. What would you think if the demand should be raised that Carolina should have the' same status as California?"

On the critical autonomy issue, Zia made clear that he has little sympathy for the concept of a "multinational" Pakistan in which Baluch, Pushtuns, Sindhis, and Punjabis are entitled to local self-rule. "I simply cannot understand this type of thinking," he said earnestly, pausing to reflect on the matter. "We want to build a strong country, a unified country. Why should we talk in these small-minded terms? We should talk in terms of one Pakistan, one united, Islamic Pakistan." If circumstances should ever permit, he commented at one point in our 1978 conversation, he would "ideally" like to break up the existing provinces and replace them with fifty-three small provinces, erasing ethnic identities from the map of Pakistan altogether. President Ayub Khan's One Unit concept was a valid one, he stated, and it was "unfortunate for the country" that Yahya Khan had "surrendered to pressures," and created the existing provinces. Nevertheless, "what is done is done," he emphasized, and for the sake of national unity he would adhere to the constitution adopted in 1973, which defines a "very liberal" type of federation in which the provinces enjoy "much more power than they do in the United States or in most federations."

Zia said flatly that he would "not consider for one moment" proposals by Baluch leaders for amendments to the 1973 constitution that would rule out central intervention to dismiss an elected state regime. "We won't go beyond the 1973 constitution," Zia declared. "There was a national consensus on this constitution, more of a consensus than we have ever had before. We would be opening a Pandora's box if we were to admit the possibility of changing it by one iota." Given Pakistan's record of political instability, Zia added, it would be "suicidal" for Islamabad to relinquish its right to intervene in politically disturbed provinces. Indeed, if there is a need to alter the constitution, he went on, "it would be in the direction of strengthening it rather than weakening it." For example, he speculated, "it might be appropriate" for Pakistan to emulate the Turkish constitution, which explicitly empowers the army to take over political power when it deems such intervention necessary in the national interest.

Until taking power from Zulfiqar Ali Bhutto in July 1977, Zia reflected, "I had never met a politician, and I must confess that I am continually amazed at the way they think." He questioned the meaning of the 1970 elections held by Bhutto, in which Ghaus Bux Bizenjo, Ataullah Mengal, and Khair Bux Marri emerged as the pre-eminent leaders of the Baluch. These elections were "based on emotional grounds, on ethnic appeals, on the politics of negation," he explained, "rather than on reason and national considerations." Thus, they produced " a certain group of leaders who had a particular trend of mind" and were not representative of the Baluch as a whole. Even so, Zia maintained, Bhutto and the Baluch leaders both deserved a share of the blame for the confrontation that led to the 1973–1977 insurgency. "It was the first time they had ever had power," he said of Bizenjo, Mengal, and Marri, "and they took the bit in their teeth, even though Bhutto was holding the reins. They did childish things, saying that the police must

President Zia Ul-Haq of Pakistan
greets a Baluch elder
on a 1980 visit to Baluchistan

be from Baluchistan, giving out arms openly to their friends, trying to put all powers in the hands of local officials. National interests were forgotten and they had only regional interests in mind. But it should have been handled politically. You can't solve a problem like that through military means. They played into his hands, they gave him the grounds for doing what he did, and he took advantage of it. It wasn't the constitution that was at fault. If something isn't implemented properly, you shouldn't blame the system."

When he released Bizenjo, Mengal, and Marri from prison in 1977, Zia initially accorded them recognition as the legitimate spokesmen for the Baluch by holding a series of meetings with them to discuss mutually agreed machinery for the administration of amnesty and postinsurgency rehabilitation programs. As indicated in chapter four, however, these discussions broke down in 1978 when the three Baluch leaders, charging that the projected machinery would be Punjabi-controlled, insisted on the replacement of Raja Ahmad Khan, the Punjabi chief secretary who presided over the Baluchistan state government. Zia angrily refused to remove Khan. Instead, he attempted to appease the Baluch by appointing a suave, non-Punjabi military intellectual, Lt. Gen. Rahimuddin Khan, as the provincial governor in place of an unpopular, blunt Punjabi officer, Lt. Gen. Ghulam Mohammed. The new governor proved to be less abrasive than the old, but the Baluch "triumvirate" maintained that the real power in Baluchistan still rested with the Punjabi bureaucrats.

Since the rupture of the 1978 talks, Zia has gradually written off hopes for a reconciliation with Bizenjo, Mengal, and Marri and has looked for other Baluch leaders whom he considers to be "more sensible, more levelheaded, and less emotional, around whom a new consensus can emerge." As an example of such leaders, he cited Doda Khan Zarakzai, leader of the cohesive but numerically small Zarakzai tribe, who "has as much support as Mengal." Zarakzai is one of a handful of Baluch adherents of the Muslim League who have cooperated with successive Islamabad regimes. Once powerful as the party that founded Pakistan, the League was renovated by Ayub Khan as his political vehicle but became virtually inoperative during the seventies and has never had a significant following in Baluchistan except among non-Baluch.

Zia stressed that Baluchistan has a "significant" number of non-Baluch. While sidestepping the controversy over the proportion of non-Baluch in the provincial population, he said that the Pushtuns and other minorities "would continue to play an important role in the province." Zia's most effective allies in Baluchistan are among the Pushtuns, notably the powerful, landowning Jogezai family. However, the Baluchistan branch of Bhutto's former People's party is Pushtun-dominated and has been bitterly anti-Zia.

Despite Zia's refusal to hold new elections and his failure to work out a *modus vivendi* with Bizenjo, Mengal, and Marri, he sharply contrasted his own approach to the Baluch with Bhutto's "needlessly provocative" policies and said that he would be careful to avoid comparable assaults on Baluch pride. "All that these people want is sympathetic consideration," he said. "We have no grudge against them." Even Bizenjo, Mengal, and Marri, he added, had been "unnecessarily built up as having anti-Pakistan secessionist tendencies." As a result of his policy of "non-provocative" firmness, Zia contended, "what you people call the 'Baluch problem' will gradually subside." Thus, he recalled, he had shrugged it off when Akbar Bukti, leader of the Bukti tribe, had made inflammatory statements "that were secessionist in tenor and could have justified serious measures." Similarly, he had ordered army units in Baluchistan to maintain a low profile in Baluch villages, though "we will not consider, for one moment, demands that have been made for the withdrawal of the army from the interior of Baluchistan. The army has to be housed somewhere, you know. We have had cantonments in Baluchistan since the British days, and we need them there now more than ever, with the Russians breathing down our necks." When funds became available from the United States or other sources, he added, Pakistan would build new airfields at Sibi and elsewhere in the Baluch areas bordering Afghanistan.

Bhutto's Chess Game

In depicting his approach to the Baluch as a more benevolent one than his predecessor's, Zia flatly contradicted Bhutto's own version of the historical record. Shortly before his execution, Bhutto told the supreme court that Zia, as army chief of staff, had consistently blocked his efforts to wind down the 1973–1977 insurgency. Zia displayed an "almost paranoid" attitude toward the Baluch, Bhutto alleged, bitterly opposing proposals for troop withdrawals and for the release of the imprisoned Baluch leaders. "He used to argue very emotionally in meetings," recalled Bhutto, "saying that the army had given its blood against the Baluch traitors and would fight to the finish until the enemy was crushed. He repeatedly spoke of the Baluch leaders as traitors who had never wanted Pakistan in the first place." Blaming Zia for the mid-1977 breakdown of negotiations on a coalition government that provided the pretext for the army's coup, Bhutto said that the principal stumbling block in his discussions with opposition leaders was the issue of releasing the Baluch leaders and other political prisoners, on which the army was adamant. "I was willing to do this, as I had been for some time," Bhutto stated, "but the army wouldn't hear of it." Yet ironically, Bhutto observed in his submission to the supreme court, Zia promptly did an about-face on this issue after taking power "for the blatantly obvious political purpose of presenting himself as a liberator."[2]

Bhutto's allegations against Zia were broadly consistent with the tenor of statements that he made to me during conversations on December 15, 1974, and January 21, 1977. Against the background of earlier off-the-record exchanges in which we had discussed the army's political role in Pakistan, he confided in our 1974 conversation that he still faced a "delicate situation" in handling his generals but thought he would eventually be able to bring them under full control. While heatedly defending his dismissal of the Baluch state regime and his imprisonment of the Baluch leaders, Bhutto was somewhat defensive in responding to my questions about the counterinsurgency operations then in progress. He clearly implied that the army had embarked on a much bigger and more freewheeling campaign than he had sanctioned or envisioned. Similarly, in our 1977 talk, he spoke lightly of letting the generals "play their games in Baluchistan, though it's really all over, completely over."

Despite their differences, Zia and Bhutto shared broadly similar views with respect to the desirability of a unitary constitutional system for Pakistan. Bhutto would have endorsed Zia's categorical rejection of Baluch demands for a loose federalism. Since I had written a book dealing with India's problems as a multilingual state,[3] Bhutto used me as a sounding board, on several occasions, for some of his own reflections on the difficulties posed by Pakistan's ethnic diversity. One of those occasions was a conversation in Dacca on March 23, 1971, just four days before the Pakistan Army launched the brutal repression of the Bengalis that provoked the Bangladesh independence struggle. Bhutto said that he saw little chance of holding Pakistan together, blaming Sheikh Mujibur Rahman, the Bengali leader, for "a reckless attitude, typical of the unthinking emotionalism of these Bengalis that makes it impossible to talk reason to them." But he mused that a separation "might not be an undivided disaster, after all, because we are a very unwieldy country now, and the only way to keep together would be to have a type of loose constitutional arrangement that would provide a dangerous precedent for West Pakistan, where the Baluch would demand the same thing. We might be better off with a smaller but more manageable and more compact Pakistan. We would still be one of the bigger countries in the world." Clearly expecting to be the leader of such a truncated Pakistan, Bhutto said that the ethnic differences in West Pakistan were "not a small thing, but we are geographically contiguous and I can manage it. I know them and I can handle them. Baluchistan can never be Bangladesh."

When we met in December 1974, Bhutto recalled this conversation. He volunteered that he was "more convinced than ever that we have the basis for a more viable country now" and expounded at length on his plans for dealing with the rebellious Baluch. The idea of a confederation was " a ridiculous one for a country that wants to count for something in the world," he declared. "It would never work, and the smart ones know it. Bizenjo knows it very well; he's the smartest. It's a slogan. There was nothing wrong with our constitution. It wasn't Bizenjo's fault that we had to step in last year. The others pushed him." What role had the Shah played in his 1973 decision to dismiss the Baluch regime? "The Shah wanted us to take strong action, of course," Bhutto replied. "It was a convenient way to please him, but we knew what we were doing. We knew what we wanted."

In our 1977 conversation, Bhutto stressed that his approach to the Baluch differed completely from that of his predecessors, Ayub Khan and Yahya Khan, who had been correct in branding the *sardari* system a "medieval hangover," but who had erred in attempting to uproot it purely through military means. "I recognize that the *sardari* system is a symbol of their identity for many Baluch," Bhutto said. "You can't get rid of it overnight without putting something in its place, something substantial in the form of economic modernization. This is what we have been trying to do, and the *sardars* realize they are done for if we can do it, if we can get roads in, schools in, hospitals in. That is why they are opposing us. They know that if we destroy the *sardari* system, we will destroy Baluch identity, or at least begin the process of destruction." When I noted that most of the *sardars* were on his side and that Bizenjo, Mengal, and Marri professed to be in favor of land reforms, he scolded me for "talking in clichés. You know it's all a charade. We will deal with 'our' *sardars* when we don't need them any more. As for the 'progressive' Mr. Mengal and Mr. Marri, they are hypocrites. They have never really given up their power as *sardars,* and they will do so only when we force them to accept modernization."

In retrospect, one of the most significant aspects of my exchanges with Bhutto concerning the Baluch was that he did not depict the Baluch leaders as inevitably committed to secession. "Some of them have romantic notions," he said in 1977. "They don't know what they want, like Marri. But most of them are just bargaining with us, like Bizenjo and perhaps Mengal. Well, we are ready to bargain, but we're not willing to submit to blackmail." Many Pakistanis deeply resent "these blackmail tactics, these threats," he said, because "they can't forget that the Baluch leaders never wanted to be a part of Pakistan in the first place. There is a feeling of deep distrust, a feeling that if we give them an inch, they will move, bit by bit, toward secession. I don't agree; I think we have to bargain, but we won't submit to blackmail."

Bhutto's abrupt flip-flop from a soft line to a hard line in dealing with the Baluch epitomized the opportunism that marked so much of his career. In agreeing to the establishment of the first Baluch-controlled state government, headed by a popularly based Baluch leader, Bizenjo, Bhutto went far beyond what any other Pakistani leader before or since has done in seeking to work out a *modus vivendi* with the Baluch. He felt that he had a tacit understanding with Bizenjo that would preserve his own control, and he saw the Baluch as allies in his efforts to counter the power of the army. When he concluded that Bizenjo could not control the situation, Bhutto reversed course, calculating that he had more to gain politically from pursuing the repressive policies favored by the army. As it happened, however, this calculation proved to be his undoing, since his five-year embroilment in Baluchistan imposed crippling economic and political stresses on his regime that set the stage for Zia's takeover.

As a member of the Sindhi minority, Bhutto did not share what he called the "majoritarian complex" of his Punjabi allies. To him, the Baluch, like the Punjabis, were simply pawns on his personal political chessboard. By contrast, as he observed, many Punjabi and *mahajir* leaders "subconsciously equate 'Pakistan' with their own ethnic group and believe that the only way to preserve Pakistan is to dominate or absorb others. Remember, the feelings of distrust are very deep, going back to the conflicts before partition."

In the minds of Mohammed Ali Jinnah and the other Muslim League leaders in undivided India who fought for the creation of Pakistan, a new Islamic state was a sacred imperative to forestall oppression by the overwhelming Hindu majority in the subcontinent. The Muslim Leaguers saw themselves as the heirs to the noble tradition of the Moghul Empire and guardians of its cultural as well as its religious legacy. In this perspective, Baluch and Pushtun leaders who refused to support partition and gave direct or indirect help to the Hindu-dominated Congress party were nothing less than traitors to their Islamic heritage. Baluch and Pushtun leaders, citing various statements by Jinnah, have sought to prove that he would have favored a loose federation. In support of this view, they point to the original formulation of the Pakistan concept in the League's 1940 Lahore Resolution, which envisaged a loosely defined confederation (see chapter nine).[4] However, this contention is heatedly rejected by most *mahajirs* and their Punjabi allies, who identify Jinnah's "ideology of Pakistan" with a unitary state.

The contention that Baluch leaders want regional autonomy as a prelude to secession invariably emerged as a central theme in my conversations with Punjabi leaders. "It should not be surprising that we should look with some caution toward the behavior of leaders who were opposed to the original concept of Pakistan," commented Riaz Husain, a justice of the Pakistan supreme court who served as a U.N. delegate from Pakistan in 1979. "After all, as soon as he became president of Bangladesh, Sheikh Mujibur Rahman confessed that he had been working for independence since 1956. We don't understand why you Americans should raise questions about our constitution. When other countries suppress separatists, no one objects. There are other multiethnic countries in the world, you know. Look at the Philippines! Look at Nagaland! Look at Switzerland, or the USSR, or the United States itself! There is nothing defective about the constitution of Pakistan!"

Grievances voiced by the Baluch "should be objectively investigated and remedied," said Justice Husain, "and Baluchistan should, of course, be developed, since it is quite backward. But we will not be blackmailed, and we will not depart from national priorities." He laughed off Baluch complaints that it was unfair for 80 percent of the natural gas obtained from the Sui fields, in Baluchistan, to be used by industries in the Punjab and Sind. On the contrary, he declared, "it would be very unfair to the Punjab if special arrangements should be made for the use of Sui gas in Baluchistan whether or not there is commercial justification for it. If we are one country, then does it matter who uses a given product? Should we charge them a special tax for the wheat and rice that we send to them?" In any event, he added, corruption had made it difficult to promote industrialization in Baluchistan, since "if a permit for a factory is given to a Baluch, he will more often than not sell it to a Punjabi for his own private gain."

As for Baluch objections to Punjabi settlement of farm land in Baluchistan, Justice Husain countered that the Baluch "have traditionally disdained farming, and they had not farmed the land themselves, so what could they expect?" Similarly, he dismissed charges that the Baluch are underrepresented in civil service and military posts. The Baluch had been given "more than their share" of the civil service quota, he maintained, "but they didn't qualify."

"You Can't Trust Them"

Talking with Iranian leaders, I encountered attitudes toward the Baluch issue strikingly similar to those expressed in Islamabad. The late Prime Minister Amir Abbas Hoveida, interviewed in January 1977, observed that "there are not very many of them, are there? But they happen to live in a strategic part of the country. Should we let them use this accident of geography and history to provoke us into devoting precious resources to develop that wretched part of the country? Why not move them elsewhere, where development is more rational?"

Echoing the Shah's preoccupation with Soviet manipulation of Baluch nationalism, discussed in chapter six, Hoveida exclaimed that "if it were not for the Soviet Union and its friends in Iraq, we would not give such inflated importance to such a small part of our population." In a similar vein, Foreign Minister Mahmud Khalatbary, who had served as director general of the Central Treaty Organization, recalled that "in CENTO, we always assumed that the Baluch would attempt to create their own independent state some day, with Soviet support, so it was desirable to keep them as politically weak, disunited, and backward as possible."

One of those most directly concerned with the Shah's policy toward the Baluch was Manuchehr Zelli, who served as Iranian ambassador to Pakistan from 1973 to 1978 and had just returned to assume the post of undersecretary of state for political affairs when I interviewed him in Teheran. "The Baluch tribal leaders are used to having their own way," said Zelli in August 1978, "and it will take a long time to erase these attitudes left over from history and get them to become part of our countries. It's at least a twenty-five-year problem. In both countries, it will take strong, guided governments to lead the Baluch out of their difficulties." I asked him what he thought of Ghaus Bux Bizenjo's argument that a hard-line approach would only stiffen Baluch resistance to integration in Pakistan and Iran and that concessions to demands for regional autonomy would strengthen the hands of Baluch moderates. "You can't trust the Baluch leaders," he declared. "They will say anything that suits them at a particular time, but their ultimate objective is independence. They will only take advantage of weakness and concessions in order to move toward this ultimate objective."

In Pakistan and Iran alike, the specter of an independent Baluchistan tends to discourage development expenditures that are not directly related to military needs. This linkage was explicitly articulated by Mohammed Islami, the governor general of Iranian Baluchistan. Interviewed with four of his aides in Zahedan in August 1978, Islami said that the province had been "unstable in the past, and we should wait to see what happens before we make excessive financial commitments here." In any event, he said, "it would be a mistake to look on the development of Baluchistan as a particular economic challenge in and of itself. No, we should look at the province in terms of the whole nation, concentrating on how we can reform the social habits of the people while improving their welfare. We must see how we can unite this area with other, more developed areas in such a way as to advance the country as a whole. For example, it may be of no use to have educated people here, given the backwardness of the area, but we can use them in other parts of the country."

As indicated in chapter six, the Persian-dominated Khomeini regime pursued a more liberal approach toward the Baluch during early 1979 but subsequently displayed attitudes similar to those evidenced by the Shah and his aides. The only significant difference is that the new government points to the possibility of American, as well as Soviet, support for Baluch independence. "The Baluch?" said former foreign minister Ibrahim Yazdi, answering a question following a 1979 appearance in New York. "Why do you ask about the Baluch? If the superpowers would stop interfering, this would not be a problem for us."

The Independence Issue: Problems and Prospects   9

With each passing year, the angry stalemate between Baluch leaders and the Pakistani and Iranian governments continues to deepen. The Baluch nationalist struggle is steadily growing in intensity as hopes for a political settlement wane. At the same time, as the preceding analysis shows, the nationalist forces have not yet achieved a degree of unity and discipline comparable to such tightly organized guerrilla movements as the Polisario in the Sahara.[1] In the absence of large-scale foreign support, the Baluch movement appears unlikely to prevail over two determined central governments equipped with modern weaponry, and the prospects for such foreign help, or for direct foreign intervention, remained murky in early 1981.

Whether or not there is foreign involvement, the Baluch issue seems certain to trigger an ugly cycle of intermittent bloodshed and destruction unless some basis for compromise can be found between the Pakistani and Iranian governments, on the one hand, and Baluch nationalist leaders on the other. This chapter will explore the critical economic and political factors that are likely to govern the attitudes of the two sides toward possible negotiations on a political settlement: What has been accomplished, to date, in the economic development of the Baluch areas? What is the basis for Baluch charges of economic neglect and exploitation? Would an independent Baluchistan be economically viable? How secure are the political and cultural foundations of Baluch nationalism? Is compromise still possible, and if so, on what terms?

The Development Debate

By any yardstick, Baluchistan is clearly Pakistan's most impoverished province. In 1976, its per capita income was only $54 per year, compared to $80 for the Punjab, $78 for the Sind, and $60 for the Northwest Frontier.[2] Its literacy rate is only 6 to 9 percent, while the national average is 16 percent.[3] Life expectancy in rural Baluchistan was only forty-two years in 1977, as against a national average of sixty.[4]

Surveying the record of previous Pakistani regimes in overcoming this poverty, the Zia government presented a gloomy judgment. "By and large," concluded a 1980 Information Ministry review,

> it has been the general practice of the previous governments to
> hurriedly draw up a panel of development schemes sector-wise, sup-
> ported by guess estimates of costs, and to launch them without un-
> dertaking proper studies. As a result, a number of schemes used to
> drag on for years without achieving the targets. And when, at long
> last, some schemes reached a stage of fruition, these were found to
> be faulty and economically unsound or completed at tremendous
> expense to the state with enormous leakages through corrupt prac-
> tices.

When the first provincial government was formed in 1972, the review
said, "it was hoped that progressive programs would be launched to
better the lot of the people." But then came the insurgency, which the
report described as "a serious deterioration of the law and order situation." It was only after Zia stepped in to restore order in July 1977, the
study concluded, that the work of economic development could seriously
begin.[5]

At first glance, it might be assumed that Baluch nationalists would
applaud this negative appraisal of the pre-1977 Pakistani record, while
reserving judgment with respect to Zia's claim that a "new dawn" has now
broken for Baluchistan. But in reality, the nationalist perspective is an
altogether different one. In Baluch eyes, what previous regimes have
done in Baluchistan has been too much, not too little, because it has been
exploitative in character. To the extent that development efforts have
taken place at all, in this view, outside interests, backed by the Islamabad
bureaucracy, have been getting the lion's share of the profits from the
state's resources, which are rapidly being depleted without any lasting
benefit to Baluchistan itself.

As indicated earlier, natural gas has been the most significant focus
of controversy. The Sui gas fields (see Figure 3), discovered in 1953, in
the Bukti tribal area of Baluchistan, have recoverable reserves estimated
at nearly 9 trillion cubic feet and were producing more than 400 million
cubic feet a day in 1980. Originally developed by British firms, the fields
are now controlled by the central government. Sui gas provides more
than 80 percent of Pakistan's total gas production and saves an estimated
$275 million per year in foreign exchange. Yet royalties to the Ba-
luchistan state treasury from Sui gas production totaled only $1.23 mil-
lion during 1979–1980.[6] The royalty rate in 1981 was 12.5 percent of the
well-head price, as against the 45 percent rate enjoyed by the petroleum-
producing provinces of Canada, and the well-head price was $0.06 per
1,000 cubic feet, as against $1.90 in Canada.[7]

All of the gas produced from the Sui fields has been piped either northward to the Punjab and the Northwest Frontier Province or southward to the Sind. Similarly, when another gas field with reserves half as big as those at Sui was discovered at nearby Pirkoh in 1977, Pakistani officials promptly announced plans for piping it to already developed industrial centers in the Punjab and the Sind, ignoring Baluchistan altogether. As the Baluch observed, they are caught in a vicious circle in which industrialization plans have been delayed pending plans for a gas pipeline, while pipeline plans have been delayed until a commercial demand is demonstrated.

Next to natural gas, the most important mineral resource so far developed in Baluchistan is coal. Discovered during the British period, the ten principal Baluchistan mines, all of them now owned by non-Baluch operators, yielded an estimated annual value of $25 million in 1980. As in the case of gas, most of the coal produced goes to fuel industries elsewhere. Coal is scarce and expensive in Quetta, despite the city's proximity to the mines. Moreover, "we don't see any of the profits from these mines invested in Baluchistan," wrote Mir Khuda Bux Marri, the Baluch historian, who became chief justice of the Baluchistan High Court during the Zia regime.* "They take the money to the Punjab and to Karachi. Very little of it comes back to us even for the improvement of the mines, which are old and technologically obsolete." As Justice Marri noted, many of the mines still use open kerosene lamps instead of safety lamps, and there were 394 mine accidents in Baluchistan between 1973 and 1977, one of the highest rates in the world.[8]

In contrast to the coal industry, the marble-quarrying monopoly in Baluchistan is held by a Baluch entrepreneur, Nabi Bux Zehri, who has supported successive Islamabad regimes politically in exchange for government licenses and credits. There are also several lesser Baluch businessmen who have achieved their success largely through political cooperation with Islamabad, as well as one Baluch multimillionaire, Akber Y. Mustikhan, discussed in chapter five, who supports the nationalist movement. For the most part, however, the leading private entrepreneurs in Baluchistan in 1980 were non-Baluch. Nationalist leaders complain that

* Justice Marri was dismissed by General Zia Ul-Haq in March 1981 after Marri issued a stay of execution of a Baluch student leader charged with attempting to murder an Omani military officer who was recruiting Baluch as mercenaries for the Omani army. (For an account of this case, see Lawrence Lifschultz, "A Fundamental Debate," *Far Eastern Economic Review*, 13 March 1981, pp. 21–22). Marri's insistence on judicial independence touched off Zia's promulgation of a Constitutional Order that bypassed judicial authority and led to the resignation of four other state High Court judges and three justices of the Pakistani supreme court.

even Baluch businessmen show little interest in developing the province. Zehri, for example, set up his marble-carving factory in Karachi, where he lives, rather than in Baluchistan. Shortly before Bhutto dismissed their regime in 1973, Bizenjo and Mengal had announced plans to make marble a state government monopoly and to shift carving operations to several new factories in the Baluch hinterlands.

One of the principal grievances voiced by Baluch nationalists is that even in the few local mines and industries, outsiders get the best jobs. *Jabal,* the organ of the Baluch People's Liberation Front, alleged that of forty employees at the Goonga barite mine near Khuzdar in 1975, fifteen non-Baluch workers received wages three times higher than the Baluch workers there.[9] It is difficult to authenticate such charges, which are legion, or to judge the rejoinders, which generally cite the lack of appropriately trained manpower among the nomadic Baluch.

However, there is general agreement that the Baluch are grossly underrepresented in civil service jobs and thus have little or no say in the governmental decisions that shape their economic lives. According to official figures, of 830 higher civil service posts in Baluchistan, only 181 were held by Baluch in 1979, and almost all of those were minor posts. There was one Baluch among the twenty state officials holding the rank of departmental secretary, and one Baluch enjoyed the rank of director. There were no Baluch among the four local commissioners, and only one among the sixteen deputy commissioners. The inspector-general of police and his four deputies were non-Baluch, as were 70 percent of the police force.[10] Nationalist leaders contend that even these figures are misleading because many of those enumerated as Baluch are actually "Baluchistani" Pushtuns.

In any event, the Zia government, acknowledging Baluch complaints of underrepresentation in civil service posts, promised in 1980 that it would make Baluch representation in federally controlled bureaucratic posts commensurate with the 3.9 percent Baluch share of the national population. The economic review cited earlier said that "over 350" Baluch had been recruited for government jobs since the army takeover and that "the process will be continued on a recurring basis."[11] So far as can be determined, there are only a few dozen Baluch in the armed forces, mostly detribalized Baluch from Karachi. Stephen Cohen, who studied the army in 1980, said there were "very few" Sindhis or Baluch in its ranks.[12]

Pakistani officials point to a $1.97-billion Special Development Plan for Baluchistan unveiled in late 1980 as evidence that the Zia regime is more sensitive to Baluch concerns than were its predecessors. The plan envisages $765 million in road construction, much of it designed to link Baluchistan with neighboring provinces; $147 million in railroad construction; a $300-million copper-mining project at Saindak in the northwest corner of the state, near the Iranian border; a $200-million iron mine at Chagai; a $67-million, 210-mile natural gas pipeline from the Sui fields to Quetta; and a variety of smaller projects embracing education, dams, irrigation, and rural electrification. Out of the $1.97 billion total, $472 million would be required in foreign exchange, including $250 million for the Saindak project and $33 million for the Quetta gas pipeline. When Zia visited Washington in late 1980, he presented the plan to World Bank president Robert McNamara, requesting the bank's help. However, in early 1981, the fate of the Saindak project and the Quetta gas pipeline remained uncertain. Most of the other projects were still in the planning stage and did not yet figure in Islamabad's announced budgetary allocations.

The most ambitious of the projects in the Special Plan is the $300-million Saindak copper-mining venture. In the first stage of this project alone, officials said, more than 1,000 mining jobs will be created, and these will go primarily to local Baluch. Nationalist leaders point out, however, that the first stage is only the tip of the iceberg. Once the mine is built, they maintain, ancillary smelting and processing facilities could create at least 9,000 more jobs. The nationalists want assurances that these smelting and processing facilities will be set up in Baluchistan rather than in established industrial centers. Cost-conscious Islamabad planners object that local facilities would necessitate the construction of new townships and other costly infrastructural investments in order to make the desolate Saindak area suitable for industrial activity. But in the nationalist perspective, most of the profits expected to result from Saindak should rightfully flow back to Baluchistan rather than to other more developed parts of Pakistan.

According to a U.N.-assisted study, the Saindak ore deposits are likely to yield not only 412 million tons of copper, but also gold, silver, pyrite, and magnetite with an overall potential value of at least $4 billion. Steel billets can be manufactured from the magnetite and pyrite deposits, the study said, and sulfuric acid can be obtained as a by-product of the copper-smelting process. Islamabad hopes to start operations at Saindak in 1983, which could mean a production level of 22 million tons of finished blister copper per year by 1993. That level of production would bring in an estimated $92 million annually in foreign exchange, assuming a $1 per pound copper price and a $70 per ton price for sulfuric acid.[13] But in early 1981, Islamabad had not yet found adequate private foreign investment capital, and Saindak's prospects depended on a favorable response from the World Bank or assistance from private investors backed by the bank's International Finance Corporation.

Officials of the American Smelting and Refining Company (ASARCO) dismissed the U.N. study as "extremely over-optimistic." Pointing to the low grade (0.4 percent) of the Saindak deposits and the high production costs likely to result from the isolated location of the mine, ASARCO sources questioned the profitability of the Saindak venture and said that its revenues would probably not exceed $60 million per year at a $1 copper price. However, these sources said that U.S. Geological Survey aerial studies had revealed the existence of "significant" copper prospects in the vast belt to the west and north of Saindak reaching as far as the Sar Cheshmeh area of Iran, where the Shah's regime had found high-grade (2 percent) copper deposits (see Figure 3). ASARCO exploration manager R. L. Brown said that the Saindak–Sar Cheshmeh belt was "one of the five or six most promising unexplored copper areas in the world, from a strictly geological point of view, leaving politics aside." Most of this area is in Baluchistan, though Sar Cheshmeh itself is not.

The emphasis on road construction in the Special Plan is consistent with Islamabad's past approach to Baluchistan. Despite the Zia government's disparaging assessment of the economic achievements of previous regimes, there has clearly been significant progress over the past three decades in the construction of new road networks in Baluchistan. The Bhutto regime, in particular, pointed with pride to its record in road-building, blaming the lack of roads in the province on the desire of the *sardars* "to keep their feudal preserves closed to commerce and the traffic in men and ideas that would threaten their power." By 1976, said a Bhutto white paper, the army had built 562 miles of new roads, including a key link from Sibi to Maiwand, which cut down what had been a 340-mile journey to 65 miles.[14]

While grudgingly acknowledging the economic impact of Islamabad's road construction, Baluch nationalists argue that the location of many of the new roads was not determined in accordance with economic priorities. Instead, they say, the army put its roads where they were needed to penetrate to inaccessible guerrilla strongholds. In the case of the Marri area, nationalist spokesmen concede that Islamabad had an economic objective in seeking to build roads that would open up oil exploration activity. However, they contend that Islamabad's oil development program typifies the exploitative character of its economic approach to Baluchistan, since the resulting profits would go mainly to Pakistani government coffers and to foreign oil companies rather than to the Baluchistan treasury. To the leaders of the Baluch People's Liberation Front, the fact that they were able to hold up the construction of thirty-six miles of oil-related road-building for nearly five years was one of the more notable achievements of their guerrilla struggle. Conversely, to the Bhutto regime, the army's success in ultimately getting the roads finished was a momentous breakthrough that would permit the eventual resumption of the oil exploration activities abandoned during the 1973–1977 insurgency. In its 1980 economic review, the Zia government, taking credit for the army's previous road-building efforts in Baluchistan, promised to give priority to a long-pending Karachi–Quetta road, as well as to another major new highway designed to integrate Baluchistan with the Punjab.[15]

In addition to its impressive record of road construction under extremely difficult logistical conditions, Islamabad can also point to significant achievements in electrification and in the expansion of educational facilities. In 1972, the total electric power generation capacity in Quetta and a surrounding thirty-square-mile area was 17.5 million watts and in the remainder of Baluchistan only 15 million. By 1976, a 25-million-watt gas turbine had been installed in Quetta and the power-generating capacity in the rest of the province had increased to 40 million watts. Similarly, in September 1949, there were 186 primary schools, 23 secondary schools, and 60 adult education centers in the entire province, serving only 18,500 students. By 1978, there were 2,848 educational institutions of all types in Baluchistan, with 1.6 million students. These included 2,372 primary schools, 426 secondary schools, 19 junior colleges, 9 colleges, 5 technical colleges, and Baluchistan University.

Pakistan's approach to the expansion of education in Baluchistan contrasts markedly with the Shah's deliberate attempt to prevent the politicization of the Iranian Baluch by keeping educational facilities at a minimum. In most other spheres of economic development, however, Islamabad and Teheran pursued broadly similar economic policies toward Baluchistan, neglecting many critical areas, such as water development, while giving disproportionate attention to others, notably road construction, for military reasons. Ironically, under its aid program, Teheran provided funds for a cement factory and two textile mills in Pakistani Baluchistan, which surpassed what it spent on comparable industrial development ventures in the Iranian Baluch areas.

Prime Minister Amouzegar's ambitious programs for Baluchistan in Iran's fifth five-year plan, discussed in chapter six, proved to be only paper programs, as his economic spokesman, Ahmed Mesbah, frankly acknowledged in a 1977 Teheran interview. Until 1976, Mesbah said, "little had been spent in Baluchistan, I am sorry to say, but now the province is receiving attention, primarily because we have increasingly recognized its strategic importance." When I asked about projected timetables for the steel mills, textile mills, railroad networks, and irrigation programs highlighted in the five-year plan, Mesbah replied that "we have much to do elsewhere, and these things won't get off the ground for some years." He stressed repeatedly that Baluchistan was the "poorest and least populated" part of Iran, with "very backward people, nomads and that sort of thing." Budgetary decisions concerning the future of Baluchistan were "under review," he explained, and would be incorporated in the projected sixth national five-year plan, to be unveiled in March 1978. But the sixth plan was suspended indefinitely and later scrapped amid the confusion of the Shah's last months, and as of early 1981, the Khomeini regime had not yet settled down to systematic economic planning.

Would Independence Be Viable?

In both Pakistan and Iran, Baluch nationalist demands for autonomy rest, in large part, on two closely linked economic premises. One is that the small size of their population makes it all but impossible for the Baluch to achieve economic justice within the framework of unitary constitutional systems dominated by substantially larger population groups. The other is that Baluchistan has an adequate natural resource base to support either autonomy or sovereign independence and does not require largesse from the Punjabis or the Persians in order to overcome its economic backwardness.

The first of these premises, involving as it does subjective value judgments, is inherently beyond the range of objective appraisal. Suffice it to say that Baluchistan receives much less favorable treatment in certain significant spheres (e.g., petroleum royalties) than provincial units in many other federations and that Baluch nationalists thus have little difficulty in giving credibility to their charges of injustice.

As for the second premise, the exploration of Baluchistan's resource potential has not yet been extensive enough to establish definitively the extent to which an independent state would be economically viable. Even under the most optimistic assumptions, it is clear that the development of this resource potential would require substantial foreign assistance. In nationalist eyes, however, there is already more than sufficient evidence of a resource base to make the concept of an independent state extremely attractive.

According to officials in Islamabad and Teheran, who downgrade the economic potential of an independent Baluch state, Baluchistan has been receiving development outlays in recent years much in excess of the level justified by its population and will continue to require comparable infusions of outside assistance for some time to come. Thus, in Pakistan, the National Finance Commission recommended in 1970 that Baluchistan receive a 3.9 percent share of national tax allocations on the basis of its population, as against 57.9 percent for the Punjab, 21.6 percent for the Sind, and 16.6 percent for the Northwest Frontier Province. On the basis of its population alone, noted a subsequent Bhutto government report, Baluchistan would have been entitled to receive only $8.7 million during the 1975–1976 fiscal year. Nevertheless, the report said, Islamabad adopted what was to become a well-established preferential policy toward Baluchistan, taking into account its "underdeveloped state." In 1975–1976, the report stated, Islamabad also gave Baluchistan special subventions totaling $5 million.[16] In the following year, the central government, stepping up its development programs in the province, not only gave Baluchistan $19 million in subventions over and above its population entitlement but also picked up a provincial budgetary deficit of $11.9 million.[17] By 1978–1979, the Zia regime reported, the level of special subventions had risen to $24.8 million and the annual budgetary deficit covered by Islamabad had reached $28.2 million.[18]

Confronted with these figures, Ataullah Mengal exclaimed that "first they annex us militarily! They impose unfair ground rules upon us, denying us our inheritance, our rightful control over our resources and the level of revenues from them that we rightfully deserve! Then they have the effrontery to adopt a patronizing attitude, treating us as if we are wards!"

In the kind of confederation envisaged by Mengal, Islamabad would have greatly reduced powers of taxation. Each of Pakistan's four provinces would have to raise most of its own revenues, which would vary in accordance with their respective population size and natural resources. "This would be fair to all," said Mengal. "The Punjab would have substantial revenue from the income taxes imposed on such a large population. We would obtain relatively little from income taxes, but we could live and develop by earning what we deserve from the exploitation of our natural resources, and even if this should prove to be less than fully sufficient in the early years, we would prefer this to living on the terms imposed by others." During his tenure as chief minister of Baluchistan in 1971–1972, Mengal charged, Sui gas was being sold by the Pakistani government to industries outside of Baluchistan at "one of the cheapest rates in the world." Mengal said that "if we raised the price, together with the royalty rate, we could obtain at least $35 million per year, without disrupting existing markets in the slightest."

As an example of another major source of income already in existence or on the horizon, Mengal cited projections that the Saindak copper deposits could yield $100 million yearly in foreign exchange within a decade, dismissing the doubts expressed by ASARCO officials. He also pointed to the Gadani ship repair yard, which has provided some $50 million in revenues yearly for the central government and only $15 million for the provincial government, "a most unfair arrangement, which would be reversed in a confederation." Looking ahead, however, Mengal stressed that "we could not rely on existing sources of income, and it would be necessary to move quickly into new areas of development." If a confederation should prove possible, he said, some of this new development would be undertaken in cooperation with Islamabad. He spoke of "joint institutions" in which costs, risks, and benefits would be "equitably shared, taking into account, of course, our sovereignty over the resources concerned." Alternatively, if independence should prove necessary, "we would have to obtain capital from private and public foreign sources on our own."

When I expressed skepticism with respect to the economic viability of an independent Baluchistan, Mengal replied that "the arithmetic is really very favorable, once you stop to consider it carefully. Remember that low population density can be an advantage, and don't forget that there is enormous wealth simply waiting to be exploited." For example, he said, despite Baluchistan's 750-mile coastline and an abundance of king-size shrimp in the Arabian Sea, Islamabad has done little to foster the growth of a modern fishing industry. "Enormous revenues could be obtained rather quickly, with relatively little investment" through the creation of government-owned fisheries. Above all, he declared, "the real key to our future prosperity lies in the fact that we have very substantial mineral reserves in addition to those already surveyed. If we are masters of our own destiny, we will see that proper studies are conducted. But there is already little doubt that we have iron, we have uranium, we even have oil, and none of these are being seriously exploited. Even the copper around and beyond Saindak has not been tackled seriously. They are dragging their feet. They don't want us to know the full extent of our riches."

The nationalist conviction that Baluchistan contains vast, untapped natural wealth and would thus be viable as an autonomous or independent state has deep roots in Baluch folklore. "We have a saying here," said the late Khan of Kalat, "that a Baluch child may be born without socks on his feet, but when he grows up, every step he takes is on gold." In a characteristic statement of an often-heard theme, *Jabal* declared that

In Islamabad's calculations, Baluchistan is a vast estate for plunder, an arid desert floating on oil and minerals. A large part of their political strategy is dictated by the desire to extract this treasure for the benefit of the Pakistani bureaucratic bourgeoisie and foreign imperialist interests.... The Pakistani oligarchy needs Baluchistan's oil and minerals to overcome the severe economic crisis gripping the whole country.[19]

To some extent, it appears to be true that Baluchistan has substantial unexploited mineral resources, but the geological evidence available to date suggests that nationalist hopes may be greatly exaggerated. Even in the Saindak–Sar Cheshmeh copper belt, definitive information with respect to the extent of such resources must await a wide range of costly surveys. Moreover, even in the event of promising discoveries, the disproportionately high cost of extracting and transporting mineral deposits located in the inaccessible, undeveloped interior regions of Baluchistan could delay or discourage their exploitation.

Experts agree that Baluchistan has iron ore deposits totaling some ten million tons at Nokandi and proven reserves of at least thirteen million tons in the Chagai district. Some experts believe that the potential reserves at Chagai exceed one hundred million tons. Geologists also agree that there are large deposits of metallurgical-grade fluorite in the Kalat district and chromite at Muslimbagh, as well as the potential for expanding the existing production of limestone, magnetite, marble, sulfur, and barite. An American scholar who investigated Baluchistan's economic potential highlighted the abundant supplies of limestone throughout eastern Baluchistan. Citing as an example deposits in the northern Sarawan district, where proximity to coal and to rail transportation would facilitate establishment of a cement-manufacturing industry, he argued that the full-scale exploitation of Baluchistan's limestone deposits could give a big boost to a variety of construction activity.[20]

Scattered gold deposits have been discovered in various parts of Baluchistan, including those at Saindak, but it remains to be seen whether these are worth $5 billion or more, as some experts claim. Similarly, there is no expert consensus with respect to the uranium deposits discovered in the Dera Ghazi Khan district, which the Karachi newspaper *Dawn* has described as "extensive."[21] Dera Ghazi Khan, it should be noted, is now part of the Punjab province, and claims of a Baluch majority in the district are hotly contested.

In the case of petroleum reserves, geologists minimize the prospects in central Baluchistan, where there is a history of volcanic activity, but have long expressed keen interest in the eastern and western portions of the province. "For centuries," observed the *Financial Times* of London in a review of Pakistani oil prospects, "Baluchi tribesmen have found oil seepages coming out of the ground good enough to light their oil lamps. But the source of these seepages has eluded early oilmen—indeed, even now, its complex underground geological structures make Pakistan a notoriously difficult place to drill for oil."[22]

Surveying the prospects in Baluchistan, the Pakistan government's Oil and Gas Development Corporation reported in 1978 that four wells out of ten drilled in the province had been successful, a significantly higher ratio than the international average of one in ten.[23] Two of these were the natural gas discoveries at Sui and Pirkoh cited earlier. Another was a gas discovery at Jhandran. The fourth, at Dhodak, was located just over the border in the Punjab, but was part of a grouping of geological structures extending for a considerable distance into Baluchistan. The report pointed to a vast area enclosed by Bambore, Pirkoh, and Dhodak (see Figure 3) as "forming a golden triangle in which the future petroleum prospecting efforts of the country should be concentrated."[24]

By a strange quirk of fate, Amoco had just launched seismic survey and drilling operations at assorted sites in the mountainous part of the Marri area when the insurgency broke out in 1973. Aerial surveys had suggested the existence of "a magnificent, huge structure" in the Bambore-Jhandran-Tadri area, said J. C. Van Wagner, former director of Amoco's operations in Pakistan. By early 1976, however, the American company had pulled out of Baluchistan, despite its gas discovery at Jhandran. "There could very well be a multimillion-barrel deposit there," Van Wagner declared. "We just don't know because we did not feel that the amount of expenditure involved to find out in that difficult, mountainous terrain made sense for us in the light of our options elsewhere." In the case of the Jhandran discovery, he said, Amoco was particularly bothered by what it regarded as the low price for gas fixed by the Pakistani government.

Van Wagner denied that guerrilla attacks on its activities in Baluchistan were a "major or decisive factor" in Amoco's decision to abandon its wells at Jhandran and Tadri. This assertion was consistent with official statements in Islamabad designed to reassure other companies that the Pakistan Army could be relied upon to protect oil-drilling activities in other disturbed parts of the country. Van Wagner did not dispute a *Jabal* account of clashes between guerrilla units and the army during seismic surveys at the Tadri site in February 1975 and later during summer drilling operations.[25] However, he insisted that the only casualties were Pakistani soldiers assigned to protect the Amoco team and that only four soldiers had been killed, one in February and three in August. Van Wagner denied *Jabal*'s claims that a British engineer on the Amoco staff was killed at Jhandran and that three Americans were killed when a seismic survey patrol was ambushed near Bambore in February 1976, shortly before the cancellation of exploration activity there. "Amoco knew that to extract and transport crude oil it would need a completely stable infrastructure of roads, pipelines, electricity, housing, and water supplies," declared *Jabal,* echoing Van Wagner's explanation. That infrastructure did not exist, nor was there any prospect that it would exist in the foreseeable future in view of the Liberation Front's activities. "This is why Amoco left Baluchistan. They were unwilling to increase their investments in an area where the entire might of the Pakistan Army could not guarantee their safety."[26]

Undeterred by Amoco's withdrawal, the army finally succeeded in opening up a key sixteen-mile road link between the town of Temple Dera and the Bambore site in 1978, and the Oil and Gas Development Corporation took over the Bambore concession that same year. An agreement between Islamabad and Gulf was reached in 1978 for exploration at nearby Sibi.

Outside the Bambore-Pirkoh-Dhodak golden triangle, petroleum prospects are also regarded as favorable in parts of western Baluchistan, especially at Ras Koh in the Chagai district, where there are hopes for natural gas, and at Meshkuth, near the Pangjur oasis (see Figure 3). An American firm, Murphy Oil, holds a 10,500-square-mile concession area near the Iranian border that overlaps the Kharan and Makran districts, but Islamabad was fearful of political disturbances and asked the company to postpone exploration in January 1979. Marathon has two offshore concessions that are valid until 1984, but the company stopped exploration there in 1980 after drilling two dry holes that were only "moderately encouraging."

One of the more colorful arguments voiced by nationalists of all shades is that the Shah's Iran, in league with "imperialist interests," prevented the full-scale exploitation of Pakistani Baluchistan's petroleum resources. "The oil springs on the Pakistan side are located in the same oil belt that connects with Iran," wrote the late Khan of Kalat. "They are at a lower level. Thus, if all the oil supplies available in Pakistani Baluchistan are exploited, Iran will invariably have to face the danger of going dry. Meanwhile, the Anglo-American monopoly through world petroleum control continues undisturbed."[27] This theme was echoed by *Jabal,* which charged that "a sizable oil strike could slowly drain Iran's oil reserves, and her aid has been a form of blackmail of Pakistan, forcing her not to declare any oil find without Iran's permission."[28]

Geologists ridicule the idea of a geological linkage between the golden triangle petroleum zone in eastern Baluchistan and any petroleum deposits that may exist in distant Iranian Baluchistan. However, they agree that the Murphy concession area in the northwest corner of Pakistani Baluchistan is geologically related to adjacent border areas of Iranian Baluchistan. Similarly, a clear geological link exists between the Saindak copper site and the nearby copper deposits in Iranian Baluchistan, revealed by U.S. Geological Survey studies.

At periodic intervals, the Shah's planners invited foreign geologists and economic consultants to survey the economic potential of Baluchistan, but the findings of these surveys were closely guarded. For example, most of the report presented by the Italian firm Italconsult after an extensive survey in 1961 and 1962 was treated as confidential, with the exception of several portions relating to water development. The report of a French consulting firm in 1978 was also kept under wraps. An informed Iranian source said that the Italian study had led to the Sar Cheshmeh copper discovery and had also suggested the probability of uranium deposits of undetermined magnitude north of Chah Bahar and west of Zahedan. So far as can be determined, the Shah did little to develop copper, uranium, or other mineral resources in Baluchistan, fearing that to do so would only whet the Baluch appetite for independence.

The portions of the Italconsult report dealing with water development demonstrated in exhaustive detail how Teheran could expand the capillary water supply system in Baluchistan. In addition to the agricultural implications of such expanded water facilities, the report said, increased water supplies, together with "plentiful" existing supplies of limestone and other local raw materials, would make possible the establishment of cement factories, slaked lime factories, solid and hollow brick factories, hydraulic lime factories, and brick and tile kilns.[29]

Studies in Pakistan have also pointed to the development of water resources as the key to unlocking the economic potential of the Baluch areas. Citing a variety of favorable geological factors, M. B. Pithawalla, a Pakistani expert, concluded as early as 1952 that it was technically feasible to capture underground water resources in most parts of Baluchistan.[30] Pithawalla saw no quick fixes in one or two "magnificent barrages" or giant, multipurpose dams. Instead, he recommended a diversified program to drain rivers, develop smaller storage dams, and implement thirty-seven already projected irrigation schemes. No action was taken on his proposals, but another five-year, $25-million study of ground water resources was initiated in 1977 with foreign help. When the regime led by Bizenjo and Mengal controlled Baluchistan in 1972, ambitious plans for the installation of tubewells were outlined, only to be shelved following the outbreak of the insurgency. Bhutto later announced a program for 6,000 tubewells, including 1,185 to be built with a U.N. Development Programme grant. It was this program that became embroiled in conspicuous corruption and mismanagement, as the Zia government's economic review conceded, though many tubewells were nonetheless installed, especially on farms belonging to Baluch, Punjabis, and Pushtuns who supported the Zia regime.

Baluch nationalists and Islamabad technocrats alike emphasize the interdependence of agricultural and industrial development in Baluchistan. Thus, experts suggest, a 177-mile gas pipeline winding its way from the Sui fields through the Kohlu, Maiwand, and Kahan valleys in the Marri area and the Dera Bukti, Loti, and Singsila valleys in the Bukti area could open up an extensive network of electric power stations along the way. According to Chief Justice Mir Khuda Bux Marri, such a pipeline would facilitate the electrification of 9,000 square miles in the Marri and Bukti areas and possibly an additional million acres in the adjacent Kachhi area, setting the stage for greatly stepped-up irrigation activity as well as "all sorts of small industries." However, Marri, a moderate who has avoided identification with nationalist groups, warned against

> a repetition of the past pattern, in which development has been undertaken to provide opportunities for outside interests. The exploitation of our resources by outsiders is creating a sense of frustration which, if not checked in time, may lead to undesirable consequences. Conversely, Baluchistan will no longer be a "problem" the day that its educated and patriotic sons and daughters get their due opportunity to participate in the socio-political and economic spheres.[31]

The Demographic Muddle

Apart from the issue of Baluchistan's natural resource potential, which cannot be definitively resolved in the absence of further geological studies, nationalist leaders have inherited a variety of complex demographic and sociocultural problems that would affect the economic and political viability of an independent Baluch state.

By far the most serious of these problems is the widespread dispersion of the Baluch population. Not only is the ancestral Baluch homeland divided territorially among three countries, Pakistan, Iran, and Afghanistan; in addition, many Baluch have been compelled by the lack of development in Baluchistan itself to seek work elsewhere, most of them in other parts of Pakistan and Iran, but some in places as far away as the Persian Gulf sheikhdoms and East Africa.[32] Many of the Baluch who live in Pakistan were forced to migrate from Baluchistan to the Sind and the Punjab after losing their flocks and homes during the 1973–1977 insurgency. Most evidence indicates that there are now nearly as many Pakistani Baluch living outside the Pakistani province of Baluchistan as within it.

There is a vast discrepancy between various nationalist estimates of the Baluch population and official census figures in the countries concerned. The most far-reaching nationalist claim is an unsubstantiated figure of 30 million suggested by the Khan of Kalat in his 1975 autobiography.[33] Other nationalist writers have presented evidence to support claims of 18 million and 16 million.[34] By contrast, official estimates in Pakistan, Iran, and Afghanistan suggest a Baluch population of at most 3.2 million.

The latest Pakistani census, taken in 1972, did not contain an estimate of the Baluch population as such. It showed a population of 2.428 million in Baluchistan province, and official spokesmen estimated that the Baluch constituted some 55 percent of this figure, or 1.257 million.[35] As for Baluch migrants living outside the province, the 1961 Pakistani census, which was the last one that included linguistic data, listed 1.594 million members of Baluch tribes identified through language, including those living in the Sind and the Punjab (see Figure 2).[36]

Ridiculing these figures, Baluch leaders pointed to the logistical difficulties that have impeded thorough census-taking in mountainous Baluchistan and accused the government of undercounting for political reasons.[37] Moreover, Khair Bux Marri said, "under the prevailing political circumstances, the Baluch have been reluctant to cooperate with anything the government is doing." On the basis of local estimates by tribal leaders, Marri suggested a figure of "at least" 2.2 million Baluch living in Baluchistan province alone, and at least as many living outside of the province.

Whatever the precise extent of the Baluch population in Baluchistan itself, it should be emphasized that nearly as many Baluch live in the Sind and the Punjab. As early as 1891, the British Indian census showed 935,000 Baluch in these two provinces. In 1941, the British data indicated 725,000 in the Sind alone. Chief Justice Mir Khuda Bux Marri cited the 1941 figure in support of his contention that there are 3 million Baluch in the Sind today. Given the threefold increase in the overall population of Sind shown in the 1972 census, Marri argued, there is no reason why a comparable increase should not be assumed for the Baluch. A leading Sindhi politician of Baluch ancestry, Mir Ali Ahmed Talpur, who served as defense minister in the Zia regime, said that Marri's figure might well be low, especially if one takes into account the influx during recent years. However, he distinguished between 1.4 million Baluch who speak Baluchi, more than half of them in Karachi, and some 2 million more who are Baluch by ethnic origin but no longer speak the language. He supported his estimates by pointing to the fact that thirteen of the twenty-seven members elected to the Sind State Assembly in 1970 were Baluch.

The uranium discoveries in the Dera Ghazi Khan district of the Punjab (see Figure 3) have intensified arguments over the proportion of Baluch in the district. Nationalist sources claim that the Baluch hold a majority of 65 percent, while independent estimates suggest a lower figure, some as low as 25 percent. Nevertheless, even if one uses the 25 percent estimate, there appear to be at least 250,000 speakers of Baluchi in Dera Ghazi Khan and neighboring districts of the Punjab adjacent to Baluchistan. Thus, if one assumes a figure of 2 million Baluch in Baluchistan province, 1.4 million in Sind, and 250,000 in the Punjab, the resulting figure for the whole of Pakistan comes to 3.65 million people who identify themselves as Baluch, speak Baluchi, and function politically as part of the Baluch community.

As indicated in chapter six, the discrepancy between official census figures and nationalist claims in Iran is comparable to that in Pakistan. The 1978 official population estimate of 659,297 people in the province of Sistan and Baluchistan includes some 217,000 ethnic Sistanis and excludes many Baluch living in gerrymandered districts attached to other provinces. Shah Bakhsh, leader of the Shah Bakhsh tribe, claimed that there are more than 2 million Baluch scattered throughout Iran. This figure appears grossly exaggerated. However, responses to my inquiries in Iran among Baluch, other Iranians, and foreign observers tended to converge with respect to the location and size of Baluch migration outside Baluchistan, suggesting that the Iranian Baluch number at least one million.* If one assumes a figure of one million in Iran, 3.65 million in

* Many estimates are substantially higher. Lois Beck lists 2 million Baluch in Iran ("Revolutionary Iran and Its Tribal Peoples," *Middle East Research and Information Project Reports*, May 1980, p. 16). Richard Weekes and Stephen Pastner estimate 1.53 million (*Muslim Peoples: A World Ethnographic Survey* [Westport, CT: Greenwood Press, 1978], pp. 64, 510). One of the reasons for the wide discrepancies in these articles lies in the fact that some observers apply the term "Baluch" narrowly to nomadic Baluch tribes in Iran, excluding *shahri* (peasants) in sedentary Baluch settlements and *ghulamzai* (menial ex-slaves) who are an integral part of Baluch society and function together politically with the nomadic tribes. (See Brian Spooner, "Political and Religious Leadership in Persian Baluchistan," [Ph.D. diss., Oxford University, 1967], p. 1.)

Pakistan, 350,000 in the Persian Gulf, 90,000 in Afghanistan, and 13,000 in the Soviet Union, the figure cited in the latest Soviet census, the total Baluch population exceeds 5 million. In the absence of definitive demographic data, I have adopted this illustrative figure to suggest a rough order of magnitude of the population.

The fact that around half of the Baluch population currently lives outside Baluchistan casts a disquieting shadow over the nationalist dream. At best, the establishment of an independent state would be likely to entail large-scale population movements, with all the attendant disruption and hardship. At worst, a new Baluch state could have a serious labor shortage, at least in its early years.

In nationalist propaganda, the Baluch diaspora is attributed wholly to the economic impoverishment of the Baluch homeland. If the Baluch areas were unified and the Baluch constituted a majority, it is argued, Baluchistan would have a government dedicated to Baluch interests for the first time. Such a government, it is said, would rapidly establish industries in which the best jobs were reserved for Baluch, and the new opportunities beckoning in their homeland would draw the migrants back from the Sind, the Punjab, and the Persian Gulf. But would it be that easy? Even if there were Soviet, American, or Arab mentors ready to provide the financial backing needed for rapid industrialization, would Baluch who have become accustomed to life in large urban centers readily return to the remote interior regions of Baluchistan?

Nationalist leaders argue that most of those who have migrated in recent decades would return. One reason cited is that these later migrants have generally been separated from part or all of their families. Another is that there is little social mobility for the Baluch in many of the areas where they have migrated. Doomed to permanent status as a victimized lumpenproletariat, they huddle in Baluch ghettos like those in the Lyari and Kalakot areas of Karachi. There is undoubtedly much truth to both of these arguments. At the same time, some of the more fortunate Baluch migrant laborers have acquired new skills. It is precisely this significant minority of skilled laborers who could contribute most to an independent Baluchistan, but who would, by the same token, have the most to lose by pulling up stakes.

As for the Baluch who migrated more than two or three decades ago, notably those in the rural areas of the Sind, even nationalist leaders do not expect many of them to return to the homeland. Many of these earlier migrants came to the Sind centuries ago. Some of them, such as the Talpurs, established Baluch dynasties that once ruled the Sind. Most of these earlier migrants have melted into Sindhi life and can speak Sindhi. It should be noted, however, that they speak Baluchi at home and function as a tightly knit Baluch ethnic bloc in local politics. They are generally sympathetic to the Baluch nationalist movement, but are less actively involved in it than the more recent migrants in the industrial slums of Karachi.

The dispersion of the Baluch population could pose knotty problems in border areas where Sindhi and Baluch populations mingle. Baluch nationalists envisage the retention of mixed border areas now in Baluchistan, notably in Kachhi, Sibi, Nasirabad, and Las Bela, and the accession of Jacobabad, now in the Sind, to an independent Baluchistan or an autonomous Baluch state affiliated with a redesigned Pakistani federation (see Figure 2).* Since many of these areas are economically oriented to the Sind, however, some Sindhi nationalists would be likely to resist some of these demands. A particular bone of contention could be the Guddur Barrage in the Jacobabad district, which provides water to Sindhi and Baluch farms alike. As experience has shown in contested border areas in other parts of the world, partition plans can be extremely difficult to implement, since the populations concerned are often inextricably intermeshed.

The presence of such a large Baluch population in the Sind has led to intermittent collaboration between Sindhi and Baluch leaders. Mir Ali Ahmed Talpur told me in an August 1978 interview that "if worst should ever come to worst and Pakistan should disintegrate, the Baluch and the Sindhis would be together. They like each other and might well create a federated state of Sind and Baluchistan. But of course, we want Pakistan to survive." Two of Talpur's sons fought with the Baluch People's Liberation Front during the 1973–1977 insurgency. In Baluch eyes, many Sindhis proved to be fair-weather friends during the insurgency. Nevertheless, the idea of a Sindhi-Baluch federation has a strong latent appeal for Baluch and Sindhis alike, especially on economic grounds. With an already existing industrial base and a thriving, established port in Karachi, such a state would be much more viable economically than a separate Baluchistan. Similarly, with the natural resources of Baluchistan, it would be more viable than the independent Sind advocated by Sindhi nationalists.

In early 1981, Ataullah Mengal said that he was "in close touch" with

---

* The Jacobabad and Las Bela districts are the major focal points of controversy. The 1961 Pakistani census showed a Sindhi-speaking majority of 56.42 percent in the Jacobabad district and a Baluchi-speaking minority of 31.51 percent. In Las Bela, 66.58 percent claimed Sindhi as their mother tongue, as against 23.67 percent for Baluchi. The 1972 census did not include language data. (*Census of Pakistan*, v. 3: *West Pakistan* [Karachi: Manager of Publications, 1961], statement 7-A, pp. IV-42, IV-43.) Baluch nationalists claim that many ethnic Baluch in these districts are bilingual.

Sindhi nationalist exiles and that "we have always been very interested in consulting closely with the Sindhis to explore a possible federation." Should such efforts fail, he said, Baluchistan should retain Las Bela, Sibi, Nasirabad, and Kachhi and should acquire Jacobabad, but would not have a "rightful claim" to other areas of Sind claimed by some Baluch zealots. As for the Punjab, Mengal said that Dera Ghazi Khan "clearly" belonged within Baluchistan, recalling that Sher Baz Mazari, the principal Baluch leader there, had long advocated its accession to Baluchistan as part of any linguistic redemarcation of Pakistani provinces.

In addition to the problems posed by the dispersion of so many Baluch outside Baluchistan, the existence of a large Pushtun minority within the province could also complicate the creation of an independent or autonomous Baluch-majority state. The British deliberately split the Pushtun areas and attached some of them to Baluchistan as part of their divide-and-rule policy. Baluch nationalist leaders and a Baluchistan-based Pushtun group, the Pukhtoonkhwa (Pushtun-land) party, share the objective of a linguistic redemarcation of Pakistani provincial boundaries in which Pushtun-majority areas now in Baluchistan would be joined with the Pushtun areas of the adjacent Northwest Frontier Province, while the Baluch-majority areas of Baluchistan would be linked with adjacent Baluch areas of the Sind and the Punjab (see Figure 2). As in the case of the Sind border areas, however, there is a potential for controversy over the disposition of ethnically mixed districts in Baluchistan, notably Zhob, Loralai, Quetta, and eastern Chagai, which have Pushtun majorities but a substantial number of Baluch as well. Some Baluch nationalists claim the eastern portion of Dera Ismail Khan district in the Northwest Frontier Province, which is destined to become a fertile grain-producing area following construction of the projected Chasma Barrage on the Indus. But this demand is not supported by Mengal and other Baluch leaders.

In contrast to the rapport between Baluch and Sindhis that prompted Mir Ali Ahmed Talpur to talk of a Baluch-Sindhi union, the Baluch and Pushtuns have a troubled relationship, marked by a Baluch sense of inferiority in economic competition. The Pushtun tribal system, with its egalitarian ethos, allows more scope for individual enterprise than the hierarchical Baluch system,[38] and many Pushtuns have become prosperous moneylenders, contractors, and farmers. Some of the most productive agricultural areas of Baluchistan are in the northeastern part of the province where Pushtun tribes have increasingly encroached on what were formerly Baluch lands. In general, the Baluch who have gone to the Persian Gulf in recent years have gone—and returned—as laborers. Many enterprising Pushtuns have managed to become minor contractors and have invested their earnings in real estate, especially in Quetta, where Pushtuns now own as much land as the Baluch, if not more.

Although there is strong anti-Punjabi sentiment among the Pushtuns, the sense of alienation from Pakistan and the urge for independent statehood is not as strong among the Pushtuns as among the Baluch for a variety of reasons that I have discussed elsewhere.[39] "The Pushtuns are after a share of the cake," explained a perceptive Sindhi nationalist observer, political scientist Hamida Khurro. "They talk of independence for bargaining purposes. But the Baluch want something more— identity, self-respect, real autonomy." Pakistani leaders, recognizing that the Baluch pose a more serious separatist threat, have deliberately promoted Pushtun strength in Baluchistan as a means of offsetting Baluch power. This determination was illustrated vividly by Bhutto's selection of G. M. Barozai, a Pushtun, as chief minister of Baluchistan following the ouster of Bizenjo and Mengal in 1973.

Even Barozai did not claim that the Pushtuns constitute a majority in the province, suggesting a figure of 40 percent, or roughly one million people, with 55 percent for the Baluch, and 5 percent for Punjabis and others. Bizenjo, however, said that even 40 percent is an inflated figure. He suggested 20 to 25 percent instead, though he observed bitterly that the number of Pushtuns is steadily increasing. Even before the Soviet occupation of Afghanistan, he alleged, Islamabad had actively encouraged Pushtun immigration into Baluchistan. More recently, Bizenjo complained, Pushtun refugees from Afghanistan have been "flooding" the province, many of them wealthy landowners and traders who have immediately begun to compete for local economic and political power.

During 1980 and 1981, the continuing influx of Pushtun refugees into Baluchistan has led to acute Baluch-Pushtun tensions that have erupted in intermittent armed clashes. Against this background, the linguistic redemarcation of Pakistani provinces or the establishment of an independent Baluchistan would undoubtedly provoke serious conflict between the two groups. Pushtun spokesmen express fears that rampaging Baluch would seek to oust Pushtuns from their lands in Quetta and from other lands where Pushtuns have encroached over the years on what were once Baluch preserves. Baluch leaders stress that an autonomous or independent Baluchistan should have a clear Baluch majority and that many Pushtuns who have come in recent years would have to leave in order to make this possible. They envisage "serious discussions" with respect to certain lands recently occupied by Pushtuns. These lands were allegedly vacated by Baluch who lost their flocks during the insurgency and then migrated to the Sind in search of work with the expectation of returning. However, Ataullah Mengal said that "on the whole," Pushtun fears were exaggerated. "We will respect legitimate property rights," he said. "We will work things out in a practical and reasonable way, and we want and expect to have many of our Pushtun neighbors working with us to build Baluchistan. But certainly things cannot go on as they are. The Punjabis are trying to make us a minority in our own homeland."

Tribalism and Nationalism

Let us assume that an independent Baluch-majority state could be established through border adjustments and large-scale migrations and that it could obtain adequate financial support. Even if one makes such favorable assumptions, it does not automatically follow that such a state would prove to be politically stable. Indeed, many skeptical observers, citing the ancient tribal rivalries that divide the Baluch, predict that an independent Baluchistan would promptly collapse into hopeless factionalism. "If a Greater Baluchistan emerges," writes Pakistani author Zahurul Haq, "it will probably be destroyed in no time in a bloody shootout between the chiefs leading the various tribal groups, and nothing like a unified government will surface."[40]

A considerably more positive appraisal of Baluch nationalism is presented in this book. It emphasizes the strength of the historical memories shared by all Baluch and recounts the continuing Baluch search for political identity over the centuries, climaxed by Nasir Khan's eighteenth-century confederacy. It contrasts the obstacles to Baluch political unity in the past with the more favorable opportunities for unification provided by the technology of modern communication and transportation. It shows that the Baluch had never lost their freedom until their conquest by modern Pakistani and Iranian armies and describes the growth of the contemporary Baluch nationalist movement as a response to the unprecedented challenge posed by Punjabi and Persian domination. Above all, it underlines the vitality of the nationalist movement, pointing to the emergence of a broadly accepted leadership that transcends tribal loyalties.

Despite this positive appraisal of Baluch nationalism, it is not my intention to minimize the political problems that would confront the builders of an independent Baluch state. Chapters four and five make clear that the nationalist movement is still in a relatively early stage of development and that its tenuous unity has yet to be seriously tested. As the experience of other nationalist movements has shown, it is easier to unite against a common foe during an independence struggle than it is to consolidate that unity afterward. Moreover, given the lack of education and economic development in Baluchistan, Baluch leaders would clearly have more than their share of the characteristic social and cultural problems that accompany the transformation of fragmented traditional societies into cohesive, modern states.

For Baluch nationalists, the problem of tribalism goes beyond the division of Baluch society into seventeen distinct tribes, each continually jockeying for position in economic and political life. What makes Baluch tribalism potentially troublesome in political terms is the lack of agreement among rival tribal groups over the symbolism to be adopted by the nationalist movement. One group, claiming descent from the ancient Rinds discussed in chapter two, places Mir Chakar Rind on the highest pedestal among nationalist heroes. Another group of tribes, known as Brahuis, regards Nasir Khan as the principal symbol of Baluch nationalism. Still a third group, consisting primarily of tribes linked with the ancient Lasharis, reveres both Mir Chakar and Nasir Khan, while putting forward a few additional heroes of its own.

The smallest of these three groups, the Brahuis, number at most 500,000 of the total Baluch population in Pakistan of some 3.65 million. However, the Brahuis have historically wielded disproportionate influence in Baluch affairs because Nasir Khan and most other rulers of Kalat were Brahuis. Non-Brahui Baluch elements resent what they consider an elitist attitude on the part of the Brahui minority. While grudgingly acknowledging Nasir Khan's role in establishing a unified Baluch state, they blame the failures of the Kalat dynasty as a whole for the present position of the Baluch. Thus, extolling the memory of Mir Chakar Rind, Mohammed Khan Baluch, a Rind, bemoans the strife between the Rinds and the Lasharis that resulted in Brahui control of the Kalat highlands—an "irretrievable national misfortune." With their "narrow and bigoted spirit" and their view of the Kalat state as "a purely Brahui monopoly," he wrote, the Brahuis excluded other Baluch from political life and treated non-Brahui tribes as second-class citizens in their own domain. As an example, Mohammed Khan cited evidence that the Kalat khans gave better rations to their Brahui troops than to other Baluch troops, declaring that Brahui elitism created "a wide political gulf and a national rift between the far-flung Baluch tribes." He alleged that Nasir Khan spoke of Brahuis as "my body" and of other Baluch as his "armor."

Mohammed Khan Baluch showed an ambivalent attitude toward Nasir Khan, describing him as "the best of the line" of the Brahui rulers.[41] But his highest encomiums were reserved for Mir Chakar. By contrast, the late Khan of Kalat, reflecting his Brahui bias, mentioned "the famous Baluch hero, Mir Chakar Rind," in only one short paragraph of his book.[42] Gul Khan Nasir even ridiculed Mir Chakar as a

bandit in one of his works.[43] Mir Khuda Bux Marri attempted to strike
an evenhanded posture, emphasizing the need for Baluch unity and on
the one hand speaking of Nasir Khan as "among the few great Baluch
heroes," while on the other reserving his greatest enthusiasm for Mir
Chakar as an exemplification of Baluch values.[44]

Significantly, the last Khan of Kalat played down the notion of a
separate Brahui identity, charging that Islamabad was seeking to drive a
wedge between Brahuis and other Baluch. He pointedly adopted the
formal title of Mir Ahmed Yar Khan Baluch. In his book *Inside Baluchistan*, the Khan makes only a passing mention of the Brahuis. He
presents himself as a leader of all Baluch and treats the Brahuis as merely
one of the original Baluch tribes that migrated from Aleppo. The Khan's
version of Baluch history is that the Brahuis separated from the rest of
the Baluch tribes by going northeast to Sistan and later migrating into
the Kalat highlands, while the bulk of the Baluch were migrating southward into Makran. Similarly, most leading Baluch nationalist historians,
notably Mir Khuda Bux Marri[45] and Gul Khan Nasir,[46] echo the view that
the Brahuis were among the early Baluch tribes who came from Iran,
stressing the ethnic identity between Brahuis and other Baluch. Even a
Marxist writer who stresses the weaknesses of Baluch nationalism, Aijaz
Ahmed, grants that Gul Khan Nasir has demonstrated "credible ethnic
links" connecting the Brahuis with the rest of the Baluch.[47]

For the most part, the Brahuis have been assimilated into the larger
cultural, social, and political stream of Baluch life and think of themselves as Baluch. Warren W. Swidler, an anthropologist who lived in the
Kalat area, stressed the "many similarities in culture, tradition, and political organization" between tribes that identify themselves as Brahui and
other Baluch.[48] Nina Swidler also found the distinction between Brahui
and other Baluch to be "problematic."[49] To the extent that a distinction
should be made, it is a linguistic distinction, since Brahuis speak a language that contains Dravidian syntactical and lexical elements not found
in Baluchi. However, there is a continuing controversy over whether
Brahui and Baluchi should actually be treated as separate languages.
Brahui enthusiasts emphasize its special characteristics, while Baluch
nationalists point to the fact that Brahui and Baluchi are mutually intelligible and that Brahui has become increasingly indistinguishable from
Baluchi as a result of borrowings.

Mir Khuda Bux Marri attributes the Dravidian influence in Baluchi
to the impact of the Mohenjodaro civilization that flourished between
2500 B.C. and 1500 B.C. in the Indus valley and its environs, including the
Kalat area. Aboriginal Dravidian speakers, he argues, left behind a "lost
language," dating back to the Mohenjodaro period, that was grafted onto

Baluchi when the Brahuis arrived from the west. Marri maintains that only 25 percent of the words in the Brahui language are Dravidian in origin.[50] In terms of vocabulary, it is no doubt accurate to say, as Marri does, that Brahui is merely a variant of Baluchi. However, some authorities dispute his assertion that Dravidian elements were grafted onto a Baluchi substructure, contending that it was the other way around. Syntactically, Brahui should be classified as a Dravidian language, argues Harvard linguist Murray B. Emenau, albeit one that has been "swamped by borrowings from surrounding non-Dravidian languages."[51]

According to linguists, Brahui is gradually converging with Baluchi and will soon lose its separate identity entirely. In the meantime, there is likely to be a continuing element of tension in the cultural arena between Brahui and non-Brahui Baluch intellectuals. Baluch nationalists are attempting to develop a standardized Baluchi language as the vehicle of an ever more widely shared Baluch cultural and political life. By contrast, a small group of Brahui-language enthusiasts is seeking to promote literary activity in Brahui, which now has no written literature, and to obtain governmental recognition of Brahui as a separate language, equal in status with Baluchi and Pushtu. Alvin Moore, a Library of Congress South Asian specialist, reported in 1981 that the future of Brahui "cannot be said to be overly bright" and that "social and political trends" were hastening its demise.[52] Nevertheless, the language issue provoked a brief controversy during the Baluch-controlled National Awami party state regime in Baluchistan. It was partly to deflect Brahui pressures that Bizenjo and Mengal agreed to the designation of Urdu, the Pakistani national language, as the official language of the state government, thus providing a pretext for temporarily setting aside the choice between Baluchi, Brahui, and Pushtu.

One of the most significant indicators of the vitality of Baluch nationalism is likely to be the extent to which the Baluch are able to develop a standardized language rendered in a commonly accepted script. Although a lively literature has developed as an adjunct of the nationalist movement, Baluchi books, magazines, and newspapers reflect a widespread linguistic confusion. As one observer put it, in the absence of a standard Baluchi, "the situation is somewhat analogous to that of English before the crystallization of 'the King's English.' Each author is free to employ the grammatical apparatus, vocabulary, idioms, and pronunciation (and hence spellings) peculiar to his own region."[53]

J. H. Elfenbein, the most authoritative student of the Baluchi language, divides Baluchi into six regional dialects: the Eastern Hill, Rakshani, Sarawani, Kachhi, Lotuni, and Coastal. While there is "no doubt that all dialects are more or less mutually intelligible," Elfenbein stresses, "what differences do exist are deeply rooted" and complicate the development of a standard literary language.[54] In addition to dialectal differences, the situation is further complicated by the use of Brahui and by "classicising" and "purifying" impulses on the part of some elements of the Baluch literati. Writers well versed in Arabic, Persian, or Urdu often use literary words from those languages in an effort to underline their identification with Islamic tradition. Advocates of a "pure" Baluchi often seek to avoid loan words from other languages that are in widespread use and look instead to classical Baluchi literature for Baluchi terms that are unfamiliar to Baluch not schooled in the classical folklore. Despite these obstacles, as the authors of a standard Baluchi-language textbook observed, a "steady, gentle pressure toward standardization" is exerted by the Baluchi Academy in Quetta, by the editors of Baluchi publications, and by Baluchi broadcasts over Radio Karachi and Radio Quetta in Pakistan, Radio Zahedan in Iran, and Radio Kabul in Afghanistan.[55]

The problems of standardization are aggravated by the lack of a universally accepted alphabet for Baluchi. There is a rich and ancient Baluchi folklore that has been handed down orally from generation to generation, but the first attempts to develop a Baluchi script were not made until about 150 years ago. When M. Longworth Dames compiled his definitive anthology of Baluch literature in 1907, he used the Roman alphabet to render Baluchi words, observing that since Baluchi "has never been a literary language, it has no recognized alphabet of its own. The few Baluch who can read or write have usually received their education through the medium of Persian or Urdu and employ the Persian alphabet, as used in those languages, when they attempt to write Baluchi." By 1969, however, when a Baluchi textbook was prepared at McGill University, a distinctive Baluchi alphabet consisting of thirty-seven letters plus diacritics and special symbols, had evolved as an outgrowth of the nationalist movement. The authors of the textbook described it as a modified form of the Persianized Nastaliq style of the Arabic alphabet, which has been adapted to the sounds of Baluchi and contains a number of new letters.[56]

Nastaliq is an elaborate, calligraphic script that does not lend itself readily to use in movable type. For this reason, in part, most Baluchi books and journals must first be copied by a calligrapher and then lithographed. The Nastaliq script is not universally accepted by Baluch writers, and many Baluch nationalist works have been written in Urdu or English. Nevertheless, there are more than 125 books extant in Baluchi, including 42 issued by the Baluchi Academy in Quetta, as well as some 15 monthlies and other periodicals, many of them irregular underground publications such as those mentioned in chapters five and six. Some of these publications contain a linguistic potpourri of Baluchi and Urdu articles appearing side by side.

Baluch nationalists have long advocated the use of Roman letters for Baluchi as a natural accompaniment to the standardization of the Baluchi language and as the best way of spreading a knowledge of Baluchi. The Baluchi Academy has spearheaded this effort, and the 1971–1972 National Awami party regime pushed Romanization during its brief tenure. However, there is considerable division within the ranks of the Baluch on the desirability of using a foreign alphabet for Baluchi, and Baluchi publications continually reflect this controversy.[57] When the Baluch Students Organization–Awami literary magazine published a book on Baluchi literature in 1977, the fact that the book was published in the Nastaliq script provoked a vigorous controversy between readers advocating the Roman alphabet and the editor of the BSO journal.[58]

It should be emphasized that the number of Baluch literate in any language is not more than 300,000 to 450,000,[59] and that Baluch society is still largely nomadic. Would-be Baluch nation-builders thus confront a twofold task. They must overcome the social and cultural divisions within this politicized minority, while seeking to bridge the larger gap, at the same time, between politically sensitized urban centers and the hinterlands. As industrialization slowly displaces nomadic social patterns, class conflicts are also beginning to surface. However, class distinctions are likely to be much less of a problem for nationalist leaders in the foreseeable future than are the tribally based social and cultural conflicts.

As indicated in chapter two, the great majority of Baluch are Sunni Muslims of the Hanafi rite. However, there is a cleavage between the Sunni majority and an estimated 500,000 to 700,000 Zikri Baluch, who live in the coastal Makran area and in Karachi. The Zikris believe in the Messiah Nur Pak, whose teachings supersede those of the Prophet Mohammed himself. This heresy has led to intermittent Sunni repression of the Zikris ever since the sect originated during the fifteenth century. Nasir Khan launched a brutal and sustained crusade against the Zikris, driving most of them from the interior regions of Baluchistan to the coast.[60]

The Zikris have generally been allied with the Baluch nationalist cause in contemporary Pakistani politics, except for a significant segment in Karachi, where Bhutto's People's party mobilized substantial Zikri support. Religious riots broke out between Zikri Baluch and Sunni Baluch in various parts of Makran on several occasions in the late 1970s. Nationalist leaders blamed Pakistani agents for these incidents, but tensions between Zikris and Sunnis, like those between Brahuis and non-Brahuis, could be the cause of occasional headaches for the builders of an independent Baluch state.

In attempting to assess the potential of the independence movement, it would be a mistake to focus narrowly on the social and cultural divisions within Baluch society. It is much easier to perceive such divisions, with their many overt manifestations in everyday life, than to sense the strength of latent nationalist feelings that generally come to the surface only in time of crisis. Yet nationalist sentiment, once activated, can quickly dissolve tribal, religious, and other competing loyalties.

Experience in Baluchistan, as in other parts of the world, has shown that the dynamism of nationalist movements tends to fluctuate in accordance with the intensity of the repression inflicted by their adversaries. Thus, if Zia should continue his "velvet glove" policies toward the Baluch, nationalist leaders could well have considerable difficulty in arousing mass support for a renewed insurgency. Under such circumstances, Islamabad would have a relatively favorable climate for exploiting the internecine conflicts in Baluch ranks. Conversely, if Zia pursued a repressive course, or was goaded into one by the Baluch, nationalist prospects would brighten. Just as the 1973–1977 insurgency galvanized mass political consciousness overnight, so a renewal of hostilities would quickly polarize Baluch political life and solidify nationalist support. As this book has indicated, however, it remains to be seen whether Baluch leaders can create the unified and well-oiled organizational machinery that was so notably lacking in earlier Baluch struggles. In 1981, Mengal and Marri were openly advocating independence for the first time, and serious efforts to forge organizational unity inside and outside Baluchistan were just getting into high gear.

Is Compromise Possible?

Ever since the secession of Bengali East Pakistan in 1971, many observers have blithely compared Baluchistan to Bangladesh, predicting the inevitable emergence of an independent Baluchistan sooner or later. This comparison is valid up to a point, since the degree of psychological alienation from Islamabad now evident in Baluchistan is strikingly reminiscent of the angry climate that was developing in East Pakistan during the late 1960s.[61] On closer examination, however, it is apparent that there are important differences between the two cases.

Although the 1973–1977 insurgency aroused unprecedented political awareness in Baluchistan, Baluch nationalism has not yet acquired the cohesion and momentum that Bengali nationalism had achieved in 1971. Baluch leaders are seeking to build a nationalist movement on the uncertain social and cultural foundations of a fragmented tribal society with a minuscule middle class; low literacy levels; a relatively undeveloped literature with three competing systems of transliteration; a narrow, albeit growing, base of nationalist activists; and a relatively recent tradition of mass participation in political life. By contrast, the Awami League, which led the Bengalis to independence, operated in a relatively homogeneous society with a significant middle class, a well-established cultural and literary life, a vital, standardized language, a broad base of nationalist activists, and a heritage of mass politicization dating back to the struggle against the British Raj. Moreover, the dispersion of the Baluch population poses peculiarly complex and intractable problems for Baluch nationalists. Bengali leaders faced some demographic adjustments in dealing with their Hindu and Bihari Muslim minorities, but these problems were of a lesser magnitude than those presented by the Baluch diaspora.

In military terms, the Bangladesh independence forces were not only protected by the physical separation of East Pakistan from West Pakistan by more than 1,000 miles of Indian territory, but they also received substantial assistance from the Indian army in the critical stages of their struggle. Baluchistan is directly exposed to the adjacent provinces of Pakistan and Iran, and the Baluch had not yet found a foreign mentor in early 1981. To be sure, as earlier chapters have emphasized, it is possible that the Baluch will receive large-scale foreign support at some point in the future, which might well enable them to overcome their handicaps. But in 1981, the prospects for achieving an independent Baluchistan remained uncertain, and slender possibilities thus still existed for political settlements between the Baluch and the Pakistani and Iranian central governments.

It is not my intention to offer specific prescriptive suggestions here concerning the possible terms for such compromise arrangements. Such suggestions would be presumptuous on the part of a foreign observer because they would necessarily involve subjective value judgments. Before concluding this book, however, it is appropriate to assess the prospects for compromise by probing the stated positions of the contending parties in an effort to differentiate between what are hard and fast positions and what are mere negotiating postures. It is my hope that this effort will help to identify the broad areas where there may be some scope for accommodation when—and if—the parties should seek to resolve their differences. My implicit assumption here is that the demands for independence by Ataullah Mengal and Khair Bux Marri cited in chapter four do not completely foreclose negotiations with Islamabad and Teheran.

Reviewing the broad spectrum of Baluch attitudes recounted in these pages, it is clear that continuance of the 1973 Pakistani constitution, in its present form, would not be acceptable to any significant Baluch faction. At the very least, to win Baluch approval, the constitution would have to be amended to incorporate safeguards barring the central government from forcibly ousting an elected provincial government and unilaterally imposing central rule by executive fiat as Bhutto did in 1973.

Ghaus Bux Bizenjo's Pakistan National party made a significant compromise proposal in 1980 that attempted to define the minimum safeguards sought by the Baluch. In a memorandum to the Zia government, the PNP emphasized that the restoration of electoral processes and civilian rule by the military regime would not in itself bring political stability. In addition to demanding constitutional amendments granting "complete national autonomy," the PNP memorandum called for reinforcement of the articles providing for equal representation of the four provinces in the Senate, and a concomitant strengthening of the Senate's powers, as the key to successful federalism in Pakistan. By offsetting the control wielded by the more populous provinces in the lower chamber of the National Assembly, the memorandum said, such a reform would make central intervention acceptable under certain circumstances. It suggested that Islamabad could then be empowered to take over a province if "expressly authorized to do so for a specified and limited purpose, and for a specified and limited period of time" by a two-thirds Senate majority. Previously, Baluch leaders have ruled out central intervention in a province in the absence of a no-confidence motion in the provincial assembly.

In my view, safeguards against arbitrary central government intervention are more critical to the Baluch than the much-discussed issue of the division of powers between Islamabad and the provinces. The principal Baluch leaders have stated their position precisely with respect to the desirable division of powers in a restructured constitutional setup that would allow greater provincial autonomy. The central government would have control over only five spheres: defense, foreign affairs, foreign trade, communications, and currency. All other areas would be controlled by the provincial governments, including the areas on the "concurrent list" in the 1973 constitution, which were previously subject to the joint control of the central and provincial governments. In talking with Baluch leaders, however, I have sensed that there may be room for bargaining over the extent of provincial autonomy if meaningful guarantees against arbitrary central intervention are written into the constitution.

The Baluch are concerned not only with the substance of autonomy but also with the feeling of autonomy. This psychological factor explains why they attach so much importance to the safeguards issue. It also explains their emphasis on the need for a linguistic redemarcation of provincial boundaries that would reduce Pushtun influence in Baluchistan and give the Baluch a clear majority. Clearly, one of the key Baluch preconditions for a political settlement with Islamabad is explicit recognition of a Baluch identity in Pakistani national politics distinct from a multiethnic Baluchistani identity. But it is not clear how much room for bargaining exists concerning the form that such recognition should take.

At present, most Baluch leaders demand that the Baluch be recognized as one of four distinct "nationalities" in Pakistan, a concept which is anathema to many Pakistanis who believe in a monolithic Pakistani nationality. Some Baluch leaders, notably Ghaus Bux Bizenjo, argue that only a voluntary federal union can survive. They link the "four nationalities" concept with a companion demand that the constitution include the right of secession. Thus, as noted in chapter four, Bizenjo proposed a joint declaration with the Tehriq Istiqlal (Movement for Integrity) in 1980 calling for the right of secession in the event that the central government violated rights guaranteed to the provinces in the constitution. Conceivably, Baluch leaders would not insist on the right of secession if enough of their other major demands were met by Islamabad. However, that remains to be seen, since Bizenjo and others contend that a meaningful sense of autonomy requires acknowledgment of the residual right to secede. These Baluch leaders seek to legitimize the secession demand by citing language of the 1940 Lahore Resolution in which the Muslim League had foreshadowed its demand for Pakistan. Envisaging two Muslim states in the subcontinent following the departure of the British, the resolution called for a regrouping of "geographically contiguous... areas in which the Moslems are numerically in a majority, as in the northwestern and eastern zones of India... to constitute independent states *in which the constituent units shall be autonomous and sovereign*" (italics added).[62]

The concept of four coequal nationalities is paralleled by Ataullah Mengal's demand for complete parity for Baluch, Pushtuns, Sindhis, and Punjabis in both chambers of the National Assembly as well as in civil service and military recruitment, irrespective of population disparities. Pointedly withholding support for this position, Bizenjo's PNP has specifically limited its demand for parity in the National Assembly to the upper chamber, which suggests that Mengal's approach to the parity issue may prove to be negotiable. At the same time, all Baluch factions are united in seeking radically upgraded representation in the civil service and the armed forces. The Baluch regard the Pakistani concessions made in this sphere to date as inconsequential.

Turning to an examination of the attitudes of Pakistani leaders, it is important to distinguish between General Zia and like-minded allies, who dismiss the "Baluch problem" and thus the need for compromise, and others in the Pakistani power structure who would like to find a basis for accommodation but regard Baluch demands as extortionate. The gap between Zia and the Baluch is clearly a profound one and is likely to prove unbridgeable. But what if Zia were to be replaced by a more moderate, albeit Punjabi-dominated, regime as the result of another military coup or a successful popular agitation spearheaded by Bhutto's People's party or other opposition groups? Would it make a significant difference? How much room for compromise would exist if one assumed a liberalizing trend in Pakistani politics?

For many non-Baluch Pakistani moderates, Baluch demands for greater representation in the civil service, the armed forces, and the National Assembly would not be too difficult to swallow. Some influential Punjabi lawyers, judges, and bureaucrats have confided to me that they would welcome a Baluch prime minister as a symbol of national unity in the event of a return to civilian rule. Many of these moderates are also cautiously optimistic concerning the possibilities for working out a constitutional settlement that would provide for increased autonomy to the provinces and for safeguards against arbitrary central intervention. With regard to the terms for such a settlement, however, even moderates are greatly disturbed by the extent of Baluch demands for economic autonomy. It is in the economic sphere that a constitutional compromise is likely to be most elusive, regardless of Pakistan's future political coloration.

Economic issues are likely to be peculiarly intractable because the same moderates who respect Western democratic values—and are thus sympathetic to Baluch pleas for greater equity—also tend to be the most avid proponents of economic modernization in Pakistan. These relatively Westernized, development-minded Pakistanis want to see rising living standards in Pakistan as a whole. They are just as disturbed by poverty in the Punjab as by poverty in Baluchistan, and their liberal instincts are just as offended by the ethnocentric attitudes of some Baluch leaders on issues relating to development as by the ethnic arrogance of many Punjabis and other non-Baluch. They favor development programs and policies addressed to the greatest good for the greatest number, which leads them to emphasize the economic interdependence of the different regions of Pakistan. This approach makes them extremely unsympathetic to Baluch demands for exclusive Baluch control over the natural resources that happen to lie beneath the soil of Baluchistan.

The controversy over economic autonomy comes to a focus on two specific issues. One is the Baluch demand for much larger state govern-

ment royalties on natural gas and other resources obtained in the state. The other is the Baluch desire for limitations on the role of non-Baluch entrepreneurs and central government corporations in exploiting the resources of Baluchistan and for the creation instead of state government corporations responsible for resource development. There may be substantial scope for compromise over the terms of royalty payments to Baluchistan, given the disparity cited earlier in this chapter between the 12.5 percent royalty rate received by Baluchistan and the much higher provincial share in some other countries. It might also prove possible to work out "joint arrangements" in various spheres of economic development between Baluchistan, the other provinces, and the central government, as Bizenjo has proposed. But it is unlikely that any Islamabad regime would surrender the residual authority of the central government over the exploitation of natural resources in all parts of Pakistan.

Similarly, in a country subject to increasing population pressures, Baluchistan, with its vast, unpopulated expanses, is likely to attract a continuing flow of settlers from other parts of the country, especially if its water resources are developed. Just as Baluch have been free to go to other parts of Pakistan for work in the absence of employment opportunities in Baluchistan, so non-Baluch are likely to insist on the right to migrate to Baluchistan when and if the pace of economic development there should quicken.

In the interview discussed in the preceding chapter, General Zia emphasized the strategic importance of Baluchistan to Pakistan, especially in the wake of the Soviet occupation of Afghanistan. He sharply rebuffed Baluch demands for the removal of Pakistan Army units from the interior of the province. This attitude is not likely to change under any foreseeable political circumstances in Islamabad. In principle, most Baluch leaders do not challenge the right of the Pakistan Army to operate in Baluchistan, since defense is one of the five powers that would be assigned to the central government under any new constitutional division of authority. In Baluch eyes, however, there is a basic difference between military deployments that are directed toward the defense of Pakistan against a potential Soviet threat and deployments that are primarily intended for the repression of domestic political opponents. Even under a relatively favorable constitutional settlement, Baluch leaders would in all likelihood press for some type of consultative machinery that would give them a voice in the nature and location of military deployments in Baluchistan.

In a conversation with Zia in 1978, I attempted to probe his attitudes concerning the possible creation of new consultative mechanisms that would involve Baluch leaders in economic as well as military decision-

making affecting their areas. He responded that Islamabad already had adequate machinery in the form of elected local councils. Then he volunteered that he did not regard Mengal, Marri, and Bizenjo as the principal leaders of the Baluch "simply because they had won some seats on emotional grounds" in the 1970 elections. One of his aides observed later that Zia could not recognize the claims of the Baluch triumvirate without inviting demands for comparable recognition from other political leaders who won local power in 1970 and have since been swept aside by the military regime.

In the case of Iran, the issues that divide the Baluch from Teheran are strikingly similar to those in Pakistan, though the two cases are different in that there have never been elections in Iranian Baluchistan comparable to the 1970 elections in Pakistani Baluchistan. As a result of the suppression of political activity, there are no leaders in the Iranian Baluch areas who can claim legitimacy comparable to that enjoyed by Mengal, Bizenjo, and Marri, and there has never been a public dialogue on the terms for a constitutional settlement comparable to the intense debate that took place both before and after the 1970 Pakistani elections. The two cases also differ in that the Baluch pose the most serious organized threat to the stability of Pakistan, while in Iran, it is the Kurds who have waged the most determined military struggle against successive Teheran regimes. If there is a Baluch independence struggle, it is likely to be led by the relatively developed Baluch nationalist movement in Pakistan rather than by the disorganized, newly emerging nationalist forces in Iran, though the Iranian Baluch would undoubtedly enter the fray.

In Pakistan and Iran alike, it is evident that the prospects for compromise settlements with the Baluch are inseparably linked with the overall course of political developments in the two countries. It is unlikely that special arrangements for autonomy would be made with the Baluch in the absence of larger processes of constitutional reform resulting from basic political upheavals in Islamabad or Teheran or both. By the same token, should compromise efforts fail, it is unlikely that the Baluch would launch an independence struggle on their own without some expectation that other disaffected minorities would eventually follow suit or, at the very least, start diversionary military actions in support of their cause. Finally, as we shall see in the next chapter, the Baluch are unlikely to embark on a new guerrilla struggle unless they are confident of substantial foreign assistance and believe that regional political trends make the odds for success favorable.

The Soviet occupation of Afghanistan has provoked a growing debate over Soviet intentions in Baluchistan. Many analysts argue that it is only a matter of time until Moscow annexes the Baluch areas to a Greater Afghanistan or unleashes a Soviet-supported Baluch guerrilla struggle for independence. Pointing to the traditional Russian interest in the warm-water ports, discussed in chapter one, these analysts depict the Soviet move into Afghanistan as part of an inexorable southward thrust toward the Indian Ocean, the Arabian Sea, and the Persian Gulf oil fields.[1] Some of these observers also place great emphasis on projections of a serious Soviet-bloc petroleum shortage. Since Moscow will soon be competing with the West for a major share of Persian Gulf oil, they argue, Soviet interest in military facilities along the Baluchistan coast near the Strait of Hormuz is likely to grow in direct proportion to the increasing Soviet stake in Middle East petroleum resources.[2]

Disputing this assessment, other observers have offered a variety of explanations for the Soviet move into Afghanistan that do not necessarily point to further Soviet expansionism. George Kennan and some European specialists have interpreted the Soviet occupation as a defensive response to the rise of Islamic fundamentalism in neighboring countries.[3] My own interpretation has emphasized the accidental emergence of a national-communist leader in Kabul, Hafizullah Amin, who was increasingly regarded in Soviet eyes as a potential Tito.[4]

On the issue of Soviet-bloc energy prospects, many observers argue that predictions of a Soviet-bloc shortage are exaggerated.[5] Similarly, on military issues, experts differ with respect to the strategic importance of the Baluchistan coast. Some contend that a Soviet attempt to block tanker traffic in the Strait of Hormuz could trigger a global war in which control of the strait, as such, would become a marginal factor. While Gwadar and other Baluch ports would be useful to Moscow, it is said, their development would involve disproportionately costly, multibillion-dollar outlays in order to deal with desilting and other technical problems. Proponents of this view add that Moscow is not likely to make enormous investments at Gwadar and Chah Bahar as long as it has the use of Aden. In any event, according to one military analyst, Baluchistan is too far

their criticisms of superpower imperialism, but they take a relatively
an enigma to the Russians. They do not exempt the Soviet Union from
are outspoken and freewheeling personalities who must be something of
As the interviews in chapter four reveal, the principal Baluch leaders
prosecuting a Baluch insurgency and in governing an independent state.
non-Communist nationalists would be inherently unreliable allies both in
directly with its own forces if the going got rough. Yet in Soviet doctrine,
successful insurgency. Moscow might well be called upon to intervene
sustained financial, technical, and logistical help, in order to conduct a
nationalist movement would need massive military aid, reinforced by
frontation with the United States? Although far from negligible, the
costs and risks of a military adventure there, including a possible con-
base in Baluchistan, would the Soviet Union be prepared to incur the
in the foreseeable future. Given the lack of a Communist organizational
ily through non-Communist groups if it were to promote independence
whole, this analysis makes clear that Moscow would have to work primar-
non-Communist nationalist elements in Baluch political life. Taken as a
point to the implications of this failure, discussing the dominant role of
either the Pakistani or Iranian Baluch areas. Chapters three through six
accordingly, to develop strong, Soviet-oriented Communist parties in
nationalist goal of an independent Greater Baluchistan and has failed,
Chapter seven shows that Moscow has explicitly opposed the Baluch
the ambivalence of the Soviet attitude toward Baluch nationalism.

warning of possible Soviet intervention, this study sharply underscores
issue as a target of opportunity for Moscow. At the same time, while
The evidence presented here emphasizes the volatility of the Baluch
Southwest Asia and enhances the danger of further Soviet adventurism.
nationalist movement enlarges the options now open to the USSR in
into Afghanistan, it is clear that the existence of a significant Baluch
Regardless of how one interprets the reasons for the Soviet move

confront Soviet and American policymakers.
thus to help clarify the nature of the opportunities and constraints that
to add a new dimension to analysis of the prospects in Southwest Asia and
dynamic political phenomenon in its own right, this book has attempted
tentions in Baluchistan. Rather, by focusing on Baluch nationalism as a
military and economic factors that figure in the debate over Soviet in-
Soviet occupation of Afghanistan or to assess the full range of specialized
It is not within the scope of this study to analyze the reasons for the

oil fields.[6]
visions rather than infantry forces if it should ever attempt to seize the
useful invasion route, and Moscow would be likely to use airborne di-
from the oil installations at the head of the Persian Gulf to serve as a

positive view of the Soviet record with respect to the Baluch themselves and speak hopefully of the Russians as potential liberators. They condemn the United States for its military assistance to the Punjabi- and Persian-dominated governments in Islamabad and Teheran and for its "reactionary" policies in the Third World. But, they keep the door open for American and other non-Communist support, while making clear that they regard the USSR as the most likely source of military assistance.

What the Baluch leaders appear to have in mind, in the case of the Russians, is an agreement to provide military facilities or bases in exchange for unfettered internal control over an independent Baluchistan and enough economic help to make independence viable. Such an arrangement would be a high-stakes gamble for both parties. For the nationalist leaders, there would be an ever present danger that the Russians would use their military presence to build up a Communist movement, subvert the non-Communist forces, and make Baluchistan a Soviet satellite or annex it to a Soviet-controlled Afghanistan. For the Russians, the risk would be that the nationalists would turn to other sources of foreign support and would eventually oust the Soviet military presence. However, if the Russians are able to establish their control over Afghanistan, they might well feel emboldened to gamble in Baluchistan. In Soviet eyes, the risks involved in working through non-Communist leaders might be offset by the critical fact that these leaders were confirmed as the accredited spokesmen for Baluch aspirations in the 1970 Pakistani elections. A Soviet-sponsored independent Baluchistan headed collectively by Mengal, Marri, and Bizenjo would have an aura of legitimacy that might well enable Moscow to win widespread international recognition of such a new state.

In early 1981, the Soviet Union was intensifying its efforts to build up Communist networks in the Baluch areas, but Moscow continued to stop short of supporting Baluch independence. Apart from the lack of a Communist organizational base, there are other factors that explain this cautious Soviet posture. The most important of these is Moscow's overall assessment of short-term political prospects in Islamabad and Teheran. Soviet strategists appear to believe that a reasonable chance still exists to replace the Zia dictatorship in Pakistan and the Islamic fundamentalist government in Iran with more compliant regimes. Moreover, while political instability is growing in both of these multiethnic countries, Soviet planners are not persuaded that either of them has reached the breaking point and could be readily dismembered. In particular, Soviet analysts question whether Communist strength is solid enough in the other ethnic minority regions of Pakistan and Iran to ensure coordinated support for a Baluch insurgency in at least some of these regions.

Soviet sponsorship of an independent Baluchistan would not be likely to occur in isolation but rather as the first step in a larger strategy of regional Balkanization designed to set up a new constellation of Soviet satrapies in place of the existing Pakistani and Iranian states. At a minimum, Moscow would be likely to link a major move in Baluchistan with parallel action in the Sind.

In the case of Baluchistan, Soviet policymakers recognize that although Baluch nationalism is boiling, it is still at a relatively low boil. So long as it remains at a low boil, the USSR is likely to seek maximum flexibility in pursuing its broader diplomatic and political objectives in the region, especially if the prospects for increasing Soviet influence in Islamabad and Teheran appear favorable. Conversely, in a climate of growing Baluch discontent, the Soviet Union would be tempted to follow an adventurist course. The temptation would be enhanced if Moscow confronts an entrenched anti-Soviet theocracy in Teheran and if it writes off its hopes for detaching Islamabad from its military ties to Peking and Washington. Moscow can afford to bide its time in deciding whether to play the Baluch card so long as there is no movement toward political settlements between the Baluch and the central governments of Pakistan and Iran. Should Baluch leaders reach an accommodation with either Islamabad or Teheran, or both, the Baluch issue would no longer be very tempting for Moscow, since it would be difficult for the Soviet Union to organize an effective insurgency and to legitimize an independent Baluch regime in the absence of strong Baluch nationalist support.

Some observers maintain that a decisive factor deterring a Soviet adventure in Baluchistan is the likelihood that Moscow will be bogged down in Afghanistan for some time to come. Here one should think twice, though, for military realities could well compel Moscow to relieve pressure on the Afghan front by activating an insurgency in Baluchistan. Just as Soviet hopes for winning greater influence in Islamabad and Teheran deter Moscow from encouraging a Baluch insurgency, so its desire to punish Pakistan and Iran for providing sanctuaries and assistance to the Afghan resistance forces could prompt Soviet retaliatory action in the Baluch areas. In the case of Pakistan, Moscow is already using increasingly explicit threats of intervention in Baluchistan to dissuade Islamabad from serving as a conduit for Western military aid to the Afghan resistance and from upgrading its military links with Washington and Peking.

Taking into account the many factors that affect Moscow's calculations, it would be premature to assume that Soviet intervention in Baluchistan is inevitable and to base American policy on that assumption. On the contrary, American policymakers should recognize that the Soviet approach to the Baluch issue is likely to be influenced to a significant extent by the nature of the evolving American role in Pakistan and Iran. There is still a chance to avert a superpower confrontation over Baluchistan through restraint on both sides; and by the same token, there is a growing danger that pre-emptive moves by one side or the other could set in motion an uncontrollable chain reaction of challenge and response.

In shaping its policies in Southwest Asia, the United States, like the Soviet Union, must weigh a number of considerations that are beyond the scope of this book. The Baluch issue is only one of the factors conditioning American policy decisions, but it is a pivotal one because Baluchistan is so conspicuously vulnerable to Soviet political and military pressures. The impact of Baluch nationalism on Soviet and American policy options is not symmetrical. The USSR can manipulate the Baluch issue flexibly in accordance with changing circumstances. Soviet interests would be well served whether Moscow uses the threat of Baluch separatism to make Islamabad and Teheran more malleable or carves up Pakistan and Iran into smaller satrapies. For the United States, by contrast, the Baluch issue is a complicating factor, seriously inhibiting and circumscribing the choices open to American policymakers.

The issue of whether and how to aid the Afghan resistance illustrates the impact of the Baluch issue on U.S. policy options. It would be dangerously myopic for American strategists to view the Afghan struggle in isolation. Prudence dictates that they should weigh carefully the grave risks that would be incurred if Moscow were to make good on its threat to retaliate in Baluchistan. American officials should take clearly into account Islamabad's political isolation in the Baluch areas and the difficulties that would be involved in helping to defend this area in the face of pervasive local opposition. At the same time, the vulnerability of Baluchistan underlines the desirability of finding a solution to the Afghan crisis that would bring about the withdrawal of Soviet forces. The purpose of American policy in Afghanistan should not be merely to raise the costs of the Soviet presence or, as Chinese deputy premier Deng Xiao-ping has urged, to "tie them down" until the inevitable third world war.[7] Rather, the United States should explore exhaustively and persistently the possibilities for a diplomatic-*cum*-political settlement. As I have argued elsewhere,[8] the search for such a settlement need not preclude limited external military assistance that would help to keep the resistance alive and to bolster its bargaining power. But the Baluch issue makes military aid to the Afghan resistance a risky gamble and reinforces the other factors that point to the need for an Afghan policy focused on diplomacy rather than military confrontation.

The Baluch problem should also be taken into account in formulating military and economic assistance policies in Pakistan. For example, if the United States were to obtain the use of Pakistani territory for anti-Soviet intelligence monitoring in return for military aid, as it did from 1958 to 1966, there would be a significant danger of Soviet retaliation in Baluchistan and the Northwest Frontier Province. Similarly, an agreement providing for American military access to Pakistani ports and airfields would be viewed as provocative by Moscow and could lead to Soviet pressures in Pakistani border areas.

As for providing military equipment and weaponry to Islamabad, the debate over this multifaceted issue has focused largely on whether Pakistan would be likely to deploy such weaponry on the Afghan or the Indian border; on the pros and cons of using Pakistani forces as surrogates in shoring up Persian Gulf regimes; on the domestic controversy within Pakistan over ties with Washington; and on whether strengthening the armed forces would adversely affect the prospects for the democratization of Pakistani political life. Little attention has been paid to the Baluch factor. In deciding upon the scope and character of any military assistance to Pakistan, however, American officials should be clearly aware that much of such assistance would probably find its way to garrisons in Baluchistan.

Washington should not minimize the risks and costs that would be involved in helping Islamabad to suppress a renewed Baluch insurgency, even in the unlikely event that the Baluch were to embark on a military adventure without Soviet or other foreign backing. At first glance, it might appear feasible and indeed desirable under such circumstances to obtain a quick fix by providing assistance that would enable Islamabad to crush the Baluch before the Russians had a chance to intervene. On closer examination, however, this option becomes less attractive. As the account of the 1973–1977 insurgency in chapter three makes clear, there would be little or no likelihood of winning a conclusive victory over the Baluch in short order. Protracted hostilities would mean a steadily growing danger of direct or indirect Soviet involvement. Moscow could calibrate such involvement in a series of gradations short of overt participation by Soviet forces or advisers. Moreover, experience in many countries shows that popular support for guerrilla movements is generally intensified by counterinsurgency programs, which often include air attacks on civilians and other indiscriminate applications of military force. American military assistance could well add to the current polarization of political forces in Baluchistan and would thus help to create a favorable environment for Soviet intervention.

Large-scale American military inputs would accelerate the present tendency in Islamabad to view the Baluch problem in military terms. Yet as this book shows, the differences between the Baluch and Islamabad are basically political in character and are likely to be resolved only through major constitutional reforms. To the extent that external powers can have an impact on the domestic policies pursued by Islamabad, they should seek to further a liberalization of political life based on a devolution of power and resources to the provinces. In the absence of such political settlements with the Baluch and other ethnic minorities, there is a danger that any foreign weaponry supplied to Islamabad for counterinsurgency activity would be used not against Soviet-supported subversion but against dissident elements among the Baluch and other ethnic minorities who are fighting for greater autonomy within Pakistan. That is precisely what happened during the 1973–1977 Baluch insurgency against the Bhutto regime.

To some extent, the United States has shown sensitivity to the Baluch problem by seeking to earmark economic aid to Pakistan for use in the Baluch areas and other undeveloped regions of the country. However, in the absence of constitutional reforms giving Baluch nationalists a voice in economic development decisions, the political benefits of such aid for Islamabad are likely to be minimal, especially if it is addressed primarily to building a militarily focused infrastructure of roads and airfields.

While seeking to encourage political reforms, the United States should face the fact that the Baluch issue may well prove to be intractable, posing increasingly complex policy dilemmas during the years ahead. So long as hope persists for political settlements with the Baluch in Pakistan and Iran, the basic U.S. commitment to the territorial integrity of these two countries will provide a clear framework for the discussion of policy options. Some will contend, as I do, that a devolution of power offers the best hope for preserving Pakistani and Iranian unity. Others will be guided by the Punjabi-Persian argument that too much regional autonomy would only set the stage for secession. Regardless of which view prevails, the American objective will continue to be the preservation of the territorial integrity of Pakistan and Iran.

But what if Baluch leaders should abandon their hopes for constitutional settlements, set up a government-in-exile, and rekindle their insurgency with help from the Soviet Union, India, Arab countries, or some combination of foreign sources? Would the United States then invoke its 1959 security agreement with Pakistan, offering to help Islamabad and Teheran in crushing the Baluch militarily, or would Washington give its support to Baluch independence in order to pre-empt or offset Baluch reliance on Moscow?

Support for Baluch independence would conflict directly with ex-

plicit American commitments to the territorial integrity of Pakistan and
Iran and is thus regarded as unimaginable by most American officials,
especially in the context of the Reagan administration's effort to solidify
ties with Islamabad. Significantly, however, the possibility of American
support for an independent Baluchistan is treated with the utmost seri-
ousness by many Baluch, Pakistani, and Iranian leaders. Despite its commitment to the integrity of Pakistan, these leaders point out, the Nixon
administration acceded to the creation of Bangladesh, albeit at the eleventh hour.

Baluch leaders predict that Pakistan will continue to crumble inter-
nally, eventually compelling Washington to reassess its commitment to
the perpetuation of the Pakistani state in its present form. Iranian leaders, for their part, fear that Washington and its Arab allies will never
become reconciled to the Islamic revolution in Iran and will attempt to
use the Baluch movement as leverage against Teheran. This suspicion is
not surprising against the background of American support for the
Kurdish revolt as a weapon against Iraq. In Iranian eyes, the Pentagon,
hoping to resurrect the military bases along the Strait of Hormuz that
were being developed by the Shah, might well support an independent
Baluchistan as a means for obtaining these bases or at least denying them
to Moscow. Islamabad, too, believes that Washington and Moscow would
like to strengthen their Persian Gulf military presence by acquiring bases
in Baluchistan. But Punjabi leaders have a special nightmare of their own
in which India is cast as the evil genius behind the Baluch movement and
Moscow or Washington or both decide to join with New Delhi in liqui-
dating Pakistan.

Some American leaders, notably former president Richard Nixon
and former secretary of state Henry Kissinger, have made no secret of
their belief that the Punjabis are justified in their fears of an Indo-Soviet
dismemberment strategy. Nixon and Kissinger have charged that New
Delhi would have invaded what was then West Pakistan during the final
stages of the Bangladesh war but for American intervention.[9] No solid
evidence has been presented to substantiate this charge, which has generally been discounted, coming as it did amid a heated U.S. political
controversy over the Nixon administration's pro-Pakistan "tilt." Nevertheless, the possibility of future Indian support for separatist movements
in Pakistan cannot be entirely ruled out, especially in the event of a major
Sino-American military build-up in Pakistan.

In Indian eyes, Islamabad wants to use the Afghan crisis as a means
of bolstering its power position vis-à-vis New Delhi, just as it used the cold
war for the same purpose when it entered into its earlier, ill-fated alliance
with Washington in the fifties. Moreover, India sees the specter of a new

American-Pakistani alignment as part of a larger challenge embracing China. Given Peking's long-standing role as a major military supplier to Islamabad, the American decision in 1980 to extend limited military assistance to China aroused profound concern in New Delhi. Defense Secretary Harold Brown's ill-considered joint declaration with Chinese leaders that Peking and Washington share "common strategic objectives" in South Asia[10] attracted little attention in the United States. In India, however, it was viewed with alarm as the harbinger of a concerted Sino-American-Pakistani effort to block the further expansion of Indian power and influence in the South Asian region.

It should be remembered that Indian attitudes concerning the existence of Pakistan continue to be somewhat ambivalent. On the one hand, many Indian leaders stress privately that a viable Pakistan is desirable as a buffer against Soviet influence and that a Balkanization of Pakistan could turn South Asia into a battleground of contending foreign interests. Pointing to Hindu-Muslim tensions in India, these leaders say that the absorption of additional Muslims would impose a grave strain on the Indian political structure. On the other hand, the partition of 1947 left deep wounds in the Hindu psyche. For most of India's Hindu majority, it was deeply exasperating that a Muslim state should be created in part of the motherland depicted in the ancient Hindu scriptures. Partition was accepted as an unavoidable expedient, but it was assumed that the new Muslim state would be short-lived and that India could "win back the seceding children to its lap."[11] At worst, it was felt that Pakistan would eventually settle down as a deferential junior partner within an Indian sphere of influence.

Islamabad's alignment with Washington during the early cold war decades constituted an explicit challenge to New Delhi's regional aspirations and thus reinforced the underlying ambivalence in Indian attitudes concerning the acceptability of a Pakistani state. During the seventies, the reduction in Pakistani power resulting from the secession of Bangladesh, coupled with Pakistan's tentative moves toward a non-aligned foreign policy, led to a moderation of Indo-Pakistani tensions for a brief interlude. But Indian attitudes toward Islamabad have changed in the aftermath of the Soviet occupation of Afghanistan. Many Indian leaders now talk in terms of the "strategic unity" of the South Asian subcontinent and would like to have friendly ties with an economically and politically stable Pakistan. As these leaders view such a relationship, however, Pakistan would necessarily have a subordinate position and would not seek to alter substantially the existing military balance between New Delhi and Islamabad. In the wake of the Afghan crisis, New Delhi sees a danger that Pakistan will once again be able to utilize external support to achieve a disproportionately powerful diplomatic and military posture. This anxiety tends to neutralize Indian fears of a possible expansion of Soviet influence in South Asia.

One of the most significant barometers of the shifting climate of Indo-Pakistani relations in past decades has been Indian policy toward the manipulation of the non-Punjabi minorities in Pakistan. During periods of tension, India has intermittently provided support to Baluch, Sindhi, and Pushtun separatists as a means of putting pressure on Pakistan. Since 1974, as Pakistani leaders acknowledge, New Delhi has refrained from such tactics as part of its post-Bangladesh effort to stabilize relations with Islamabad. However, were the United States, China, and Pakistan to forge substantially expanded military ties, there are likely to be renewed pressures in India for efforts to destabilize Pakistan. Such sentiment has already started to grow as a result of Pakistani preparations for a nuclear explosion and would be intensified if Islamabad were to receive large-scale foreign support for its conventional forces side by side with its efforts to develop a nuclear capability.

The danger of a Balkanization of Pakistan would clearly be accentuated by a Soviet-American confrontation there and by the concomitant growth of tensions between Islamabad and New Delhi. For this reason, American strategists should tread very warily in Southwest Asia. American policies should be damage-limiting rather than risk-inviting. They should not be governed solely by immediate U.S. objectives in the Persian Gulf or Afghanistan or Pakistan, but should rest on a broader recognition of the interdependence of long-term American interests in the entire region reaching from India through Iran.

With respect to the Baluch issue, the American goal should be to forestall the necessity for a choice between the Scylla of supporting repressive counterinsurgency programs and the Charybdis of supporting Baluch independence. In the final analysis, however, it is the Punjabis, the Persians, and the Baluch who will define the choices that confront the superpowers, and these choices could well prove to be extremely unpalatable to Washington. Recognizing the limits of American power in Islamabad and Teheran, the United States should begin, even now, to consider what the nature and range of its interests and options would be in the event that Pakistan or Iran or both should prove incapable of resolving their peculiarly stubborn federal problems.

If the will for compromise on the part of the indigenous actors is strong enough, the Soviet Union is not likely to find the Baluch issue a very easy one to manipulate. If there is little hope of compromise, no amount of American leverage is likely to succeed in pushing the parties to the bargaining table. Fortunately, in both Pakistan and Iran, the avenues toward a meaningful dialogue have not yet been completely closed off. But the possibility of national disintegration is increasing in both countries, opening up new horizons of opportunity for Moscow in Southwest Asia and deepening U.S. dilemmas.

Notes

Chapter One

1. Marvin and Bernard Kalb, *Kissinger* (Boston: Little, Brown, 1974), pp. 63–64.

2. "Issues and Answers," American Broadcasting Company, 30 December 1979.

3. See chapter nine for an explanation of this estimate, which is higher than official census figures in the countries concerned but lower than Baluch nationalist estimates.

4. Estimates of casualties suffered during the 1973–1977 insurgency are based primarily on interviews with twenty-three Pakistani military officers and defense officials; thirty-five residents of Baluchistan, many of them non-Baluch, who did not participate directly in the fighting, and sixty-five Baluch combatants and members of their families, most of them interviewed in the Kalat-i-Gilzai and other guerrilla camps in southern Afghanistan, described in chapters three and five. The insurgency is discussed at length in chapter three and in my article "After the Afghan Coup: Nightmare in Baluchistan," *Foreign Policy* 32 (1978).

5. For example, see Ainslie T. Embree, "Pakistan's Imperial Legacy," in *Pakistan's Western Borderlands,* ed. Ainslie T. Embree (Durham, NC: Carolina Academic Press, 1977).

Chapter Two

1. M. Longworth Dames, *Popular Poetry of the Baloches,* vol. 1 (London: Royal Asiatic Society, 1907), p. 45. See also J. H. Elfenbein, *The Baluchi Language: A Dialectology with Text,* Royal Asiatic Society Monographs, vol. 27 (London, 1966), pp. 41–45.

2. This estimate refers to literacy in all languages among Baluch in Pakistan, Iran, and the Persian Gulf. Robert G. Wirsing found that the highest literacy rate in eight of the nine districts in Pakistani Baluchistan was 7.7 percent ("South Asia: The Baluch Frontier Tribes of Pakistan," in *Protection of Ethnic Minorities: Comparative Perspectives,* ed. Robert G. Wirsing [New York: Pergamon, forthcoming], p. 18). Alvin Moore, South Asia specialist of the Library of Congress, estimated that there were 132,000 literates in Baluchi in 1981 ("Publishing in Pushto, Baluchi and Brahui, Part 2," in *South Asia: Library Notes and Queries* [Chicago: South Asia Reference Center, University of Chicago Library, March 1980], p. 3). *The Census of Pakistan,* vol. 3 (Karachi: Manager of Publications, 1961), p. IV-94, reported 87,000 literates in Baluchistan province. The 1972 census did not contain comparable tables.

3. John C. Griffiths, *Afghanistan* (London: Pall Mall, 1967), p. 52.
4. Sardar Mohammed Khan Baluch, *History of the Baluch Race and Baluchistan*, rev. ed. (Quetta: Gosha-e-Adab, 1977), pp. 5, 16–18, 22–25.
5. Ma'n Shana al-Ajli Al-Hakkami, *Balushistan Diyal Al-Arab* [Baluchistan: Land of the Arabs] (Bahrain: 1979), an Arab work citing Baluch sources. See also Mir Ahmed Yar Khan Baluch, *Inside Baluchistan* (Karachi: Royal Book Co., 1975) for the text of the Khan of Kalat's memorandum to the 1946 British Cabinet Mission, which states (p. 262) that the ruling family of Kalat is of Arab origin, having emigrated originally from Oman to Makran and thence northward.
6. Mir Khuda Bux Bijarani Marri Baloch, *Searchlight on Baloches and Baluchistan* (Karachi: Royal Book Co., 1974), pp. 12–14. See also Mir Gul Khan Nasir, *Tarikh-e-Baluchistan* [History of Baluchistan] (Quetta: Qaumi Ghar, 1952); Malik Mohammad Saeed, *Baluchistan Maqable Tarikh* [Baluchistan in Prehistory] (Quetta: Baluchi Academy, 1971); Abdur Rahim Sabir, *Baluchistan ki Vadiyun men* [In the Valleys of Baluchistan] (Karachi: Baluchi Adabi Board, 1962); Shams Uzzuha, *Hamara Baluchistan* [Our Baluchistan] (Quetta: Bolan Book Corp., 1972); Kamil ul Qadri, *Qadim Baluchistan* [Ancient Baluchistan] (Quetta: Bolan Book Corp., 1971); Nur Ahmad Khan Faridi, *Baluch Qaum au us ki Tarikh* [History of the Baluch Nation] (Multan, Pakistan: Qasr ul Adab, 1968); and Mir Muhammad Husain 'Anqa' Baluc, *Inquilabi Baluci Tarikh* [Ancient History of the Baluch Nation] (Quetta: Gosha-e-Adab, 1974).
7. Mir Khuda Bux Bijarani Marri Baloch, *Searchlight on Baloches.*
8. J. H. Elfenbein, "Baluchi," in *Encyclopedia of Islam* (Leiden: E. J. Brill, 1960), p. 1006. See also Elfenbein, *The Baluchi Language*, esp. pp. 41–45; and Richard N. Frye, "Remarks on Baluchi History," *Central Asiatic Journal* 4, no. 1 (1961): 49. See also an unpublished study by Jozef Adamik, "The Origins and Dialect Differentiation of Balochi" (1979). Mr. Adamik is a former student in the Department of Near Eastern Languages and Civilizations, Harvard University.
9. M. Longworth Dames, *The Baloch Race: A Historical and Ethnological Sketch* (London: Royal Asiatic Society, 1904), p. 43.
10. Ibid., p. 44.
11. Mir Khuda Bux Bijarani Marri Baloch, *Searchlight on Baloches*, p. 62.
12. Sardar Mohammed Khan Baluch, *History of the Baluch Race*, p. 48.
13. Mir Khuda Bux Bijarani Marri Baloch, *Searchlight on Baloches*, p. 61. For other examples of Baluch popular ballads, see also Dames, *Popular Poetry*, pp. 43–46; Elfenbein, *The Baluchi Language*, pp. 43ff.; and M.A.R. Barker and Aqil Khan Mengal, *A Course in Baluchi*, vol. 2 (Montreal: Institute of Islamic Studies, McGill University, 1969), esp. Unit 29, pp. 263–273.
14. Mir Ahmed Yar Khan Baluch, *Inside Baluchistan*, p. 84.
15. Nina Bailey Swidler, "The Political Structure of a Tribal Federation: The Brahui of Baluchistan" (Ph.D. diss., Columbia University, 1969).
16. Mir Ahmed Yar Khan Baluch, *Inside Baluchistan*, p. 85.
17. Sardar Mohammed Khan Baluch, *History of the Baluch Race*, p. 86.
18. The definitive Persian account of Dost Mohammed's defeat was written by the general who waged Reza Shah's successful campaign to subdue Baluchistan: Gen. Amanullah Jahanbani, *Amaliyat-i Qushun dar Baluchistan* [Army Activities in Baluchistan] (Teheran: 1957). See also Sir Henry T. Holland, "A Meeting with Dost Mohammed," *Asiatic Review* 30, no. 112 (1936): 694ff. For examples of Baluch nationalist adulation of Dost Mohammed, see Mohammed Akbar Baluch, *Baluch Qaum Apni Tarikh ke Aineh men* [The Baluch Nation and Its

History] (Quetta: Bolan Book Corp., 1975), and a cover story in the defunct Baluchi monthly *Baluchi Dunya* [Baluch World] (Karachi), February 1972.

19. Sir Henry Pottinger, *Travels in Belochistan and Sinde* (London: Longman, Hurst, Rees, Orme and Brown, 1816), p. 285.

20. J. H. Elfenbein, *The Baluchi Language*, pp. 42–43.

21. Barker and Mengal, *A Course in Baluchi*, p. 400.

22. Brian Spooner, "Tribal Ideal and Political Reality in a Cultural Borderland: Ethnohistorical Problems in Baluchistan" (Paper presented at the Ethnohistory Workshop, University of Pennsylvania, 10 April 1978), p. 8.

23. Ibid., p. 15.

24. Ibid., p. 16.

Chapter Three

1. Mir Ahmed Yar Khan Baluch, *Inside Baluchistan*, (Karachi: Royal Book Company, 1975), pp. 110–114.

2. Stephen Philip Cohen, "Security Decision-Making in Pakistan" (Report prepared for the Office of External Research, U.S. Department of State, September 1980), p. 41.

3. Karim Baluch, "The Democratic Struggle in Baluchistan," *Siyasat* no. 3 (London, 1975): 3.

4. Inayatullah Baloch, "Afghanistan-Pashtunistan-Baluchistan," *Aussen Politik* no. 3 (English ed.; Hamburg, 1980): 300. See also a pioneering study of this period by the same author, "The Emergence of Baluch Nationalism: 1931–47," *Pakistan Progressive* nos. 3–4 (New York, December 1980).

5. Mir Ahmed Yar Khan Baluch, *Inside Baluchistan*, p. 294.

6. Ibid., pp. 255–296. See esp. pp. 261, 268.

7. "Baluchistan" (a Note issued by the Information Ministry of the Pakistan Government, 2 May 1980) cites studies recounting the role of the gathering on June 29, 1947. Of eight participants mentioned in the Note, three were Baluch. See also Wayne Wilcox, *Pakistan: The Consolidation of a Nation* (New York: Columbia University Press, 1963), pp. 75–76, for an account of the accession issue drawing on Pakistani and British sources.

8. Inayatullah Baloch, "The Emergence of Baluch Nationalism," p. 19.

9. *Baluch Qaum Ke Tarikh-Ke Chand Parishan Dafter Auraq* [A Few Pages from the Official Records of the History of the Baluch Nation], comp. Malik Allah Bakhsh, Protocol Minister (Quetta: Islamiyyah Press, 20 September 1957), p. 17. This publication contains the major speeches made in the September and December Assembly sessions. For further elaboration of the Khan's position on the 1947 accession issue, see also *Mukhtasir Tarikh-Qaum-e-Baluch Wa Khawaneen-e-Baluch* [Short History of the Baluch Nation and the Baluch Khans], written under the orders and instructions of Mir Ahmed Yar Khan Baluch, Khan-I-Azam of Kalat (Quetta: Islamiyyah Press, 1970); and Mir Ahmed Yar Khan Baluch, *Baluch Qaum Ke Nam Khan-e-Baluch Ka Paigham* [Message from the Khan of the Baluch to the Baluch Nation] (Karachi: Litho Art Press, 1972).

10. Ibid., p. 43.

11. Mir Ahmed Yar Khan Baluch, *Inside Baluchistan*, pp. 180–190. See also Wilcox, *Pakistan*, p. 206; Herbert Feldman, *Revolution in Pakistan* (London: Ox-

ford University Press, 1967), pp. 42–43; Karim Baluch, "Democratic Struggle in Baluchistan," p. 5; and Sylvia A. Matheson, *The Tigers of Baluchistan* (London: Oxford University Press, 1967). Mrs. Matheson said in an interview in Teheran in 1978 that the blocking-out of certain portions of page 186 of her book included a description of the bombing of the Khan's palace by the Pakistan Air Force and a skeptical reference to the charge of a conspiracy with Afghanistan.

12. For a perceptive study of center-state tensions during the short-lived Baluch National Awami party regime in Baluchistan, see Philip Jones, "Center-Province Relations in Pakistan: The Case of Bhutto and the Regionalists" (Paper delivered at the 32nd Annual Convention of the Association for Asian Studies, Washington, DC, 23 March 1980). See also Robert G. Wirsing, ed., *Protection of Ethnic Minorities: Comparative Perspectives* (New York: Pergamon, forthcoming). The Pakistan government's view of the events leading up to the 1973 insurgency can be found in *White Paper on Baluchistan* (Rawalpindi: Government of Pakistan, 19 October 1974) and in the concluding address in the Pakistan Supreme Court by Yahya Bakhtiar in *Government's Reference on NAP's Dissolution* (Rawalpindi, 8–17 September 1975).

13. "List of Incidents Showing Firing Cases in Baluchistan from February 22, 1973 to December 31, 1975," Annexure G-5, pp. 108–113, and "Details of Firing and Other Acts of Sabotage/Terrorism in Baluchistan during 1974–75," Annexure G-3, pp. 99–103, in *State (Through Secretary, Minister of Interior)* v. *Abdul Wali Khan and Others*, a Complaint filed by the Government of Pakistan, Islamabad, before the Special Court, Hyderabad, 15 April 1976 (Notification F 44 (1)/76-A of 20 February 1976). See also the Supplementary Complaint filed before the Special Court. For a Pakistan Army officer's view of the insurgency, see Brigadier Muhammad Usman Hasan, *Baluchistan: Mazi, Hal Aur Mustaqbil* [Baluchistan: Past, Present and Future] (Karachi: Indus Publications, 1976), pp. 113–116. Among the few accounts of the insurgency published by the Western press were "Pakistan's Civil War," *Manchester Guardian*, 24 January 1975; and Alexander Dastarac and Robert Dersen, "Baluchistan: The Forgotten War," *Le Monde Diplomatique*, August 1976.

Chapter Four

1. Robert N. Pehrson, *The Social Organization of the Marri Baluch*, Viking Fund Publications in Anthropology, no. 43 (New York: Wenner Gren Foundation for Anthropological Research, 1966), p. 20.

2. "Bizenjo's Statement," *Imroze* (Lahore), 29 August 1978, p. 1. See also "Bijenjo and Nationalities," *Pakistan Times* (Lahore), 28 August 1978, p. 1; Salamat Ali, "Shaking the Foundations," *Far Eastern Economic Review*, 15 September 1978, pp. 24–25; and Mir Ghaus Bux Bizenjo, "The Basics of Our Politics," *Viewpoint* (Lahore), 28 August 1978, pp. 7–8.

3. Mir Ghaus Bux Bizenjo, "The Problems of Pakistan," *Pakistan Times*, 8 February 1978. See also a Punjabi rejoinder in a letter from Lt. Col. Rafi Nasim, *Pakistan Times*, 16 February 1978.

4. "Hum Apne Wattan Baluchistan Ko Azad Dekhna Chahte Hain" [We Want to See Our Country Baluchistan Free], *Nedae Baluchistan* [Voice of Baluchistan] 1, no. 4 (London), February 1981, pp. 2–4. See also a letter from Mengal in the January 1981 issue of *Nedae Baluchistan*.

Chapter Five

1. *Strategy for Liberation: The War in Baluchistan* (Paris: Baluchistan People's Liberation Front, 1976), p. 8.
2. *Jabal* (Bulletin of the Baluchistan People's Liberation Front), December 1976, p. 1. The London Group, which edited *Jabal*, used the name *Baluchistan People's Liberation Front*, reflecting their desire to play down the group's ethnic identity and emphasize its character as a Marxist-Leninist organization championing a cause related to leftist objectives throughout Pakistan. However, Sher Mohammed Marri and Mir Hazar said this was an "error" and that the proper nomenclature is the Baluch People's Liberation Front. This dispute exemplified the tensions between the London Group and other Front leaders that led to the defection of some London Group adherents in 1981.
3. *Jabal*, February 1977, p. 10A.
4. *Jabal*, February 1978, p. 2.
5. "Talib Ilm Tanzeem Aur Harawal Party May Farq Karna Lazimee Hay" [It Is a Must to Differentiate between Student Organization and the Vanguard Party], Excerpts from a report of the BSO-Awami National Council, 4th sess., in *Pakistan Forum* (Karachi), September 1978, p. 10.
6. "Mazakarat Aur Aam Maafi Ka Nushk" [Negotiation and the General Amnesty], *Pajjar,* January-February 1978, p. 2. See also the references to Sher Mohammed Marri in Nargis Latif, "BSO (Awami) on Student Politics," *Viewpoint* (Lahore), 10 January 1979, p. 13. For a useful summary of BSO activities and policies, see the special issue of *Baluchi Dunya* [Baluch World], October 1972, on the BSO, esp. the lead article, "Baluch Talaba Ka Ittehod Zindabod" [Long Live the Unity of Baluch Students], pp. 5–8.
7. See the transcript of "Panorama," (BBC Transmission 1925(2), 31 January 1980), p. 10, in which Kurd is interviewed by correspondent Tom Mangold.
8. "What PNP Stands For," *Viewpoint* (Lahore), 19 August 1979, p. 7. See also "A National Party Is Born," *Viewpoint,* 10 June 1979, p. 10.

Chapter Six

1. Sir Olaf Caroe, *Wells of Power: The Oil Fields of Southwestern Asia,* History and Politics of Oil Series (1951; reprint ed., Westport, CT: Hyperion Press, 1976).
2. Philip C. Salzman, "Adaptation and Change among the Yarahmadzai Baluch" (Ph.D. diss., University of Chicago, 1972), pp. 266–268. For an excellent overview of tribal society in Iranian Baluchistan, see Brian Spooner, "Political and Religious Leadership in Persian Baluchistan," (Ph.D. diss., Oxford University, 1967) and "Politics, Kinship and Ecology in Southeast Persia," *Ethnology* 8, no. 2 (1969). See also Philip C. Salzman, "The Proto-State in Iranian Baluchistan," in *Origins of the State: The Anthropology of Political Evolution,* ed. R. Cohen and E. Service (Philadelphia: ISHI, 1978); "Adaptation and Political Organization in Iranian Baluchistan," *Ethnology* 10, no. 4 (1971); and "Continuity and Change in Baluchi Tribal Leadership," *International Journal of Middle East Studies* 4, no. 4 (1973).
3. *Sistan va Baluchistan: Mutala'at Bar Nameh Tavaso'i Iqtisadi va Ijtimai'l* [Sistan and Baluchistan: Studies in Economic and Social Development] (Zahedan:

Planning Office, Sistan and Baluchistan, 1976), Table 3-A. For earlier official census figures relating to the Baluch, see *Census Report* (Teheran: Iranian Statistical Center, 1968) and Zabibullah Nasih, *Introduction to the Culture and Civilization of Iran,* vol. 8 (Teheran: Kitab Khanae Ibnsina, 1965), which cites a figure of 271,584 Baluch in Iran in 1930.

4. C. L. Sulzberger, "Belief in Crude Reality," *New York Times,* 22 April 1973.

5. *Middle East Monitor,* 1 June 1973. See also "Pakistani Leader Ends Stay in Iran," *New York Times,* 15 May 1973.

6. "The Shah on War and Peace," *Newsweek,* 14 November 1977. p. 70.

7. *Natije Amaar Giri Edareh Kohl Amouzesh Va Parvaresh Ostan, Sistan Va Baluchistan Dar Sall Tahsili 2536–2537* [The Results of the Statistics Done by the Department of Education, Provinces of Sistan and Baluchistan, in the Educational Year 1977–1978] (Zahedan: Department of Education, Provinces of Sistan and Baluchistan, 1978), Table 19.

8. Ibid., Tables 1, 7, 3, 12.

9. "U. S. Aides Slain in Ambush in Iran," *New York Times,* 26 March 1957.

10. "Pakistanis Press Iran Killer Hunt," *New York Times,* 11 April 1957. See also "U. S. Halts Aid in Southeast Iran," *New York Times,* 2 April 1957.

11. "Iranian Troops Seek Seized U. S. Woman," *New York Times,* 29 March 1957.

12. Jean Viennot, "Baluchistan: A New Bangladesh?" *Le Monde Diplomatique,* November 1973.

13. For example, see repeated references to Dad Shah in Mohammed Akbar Baluch, *Baluch Qaum Apni Tarikh ke Aineh Men* [The Baluch Nation and Its History] (Quetta: Bolan Book Corp., 1975).

14. *Baluchistan: Introduction and Liberation Struggle* (Baluchistan Liberation Front, n.d.), p. 12. This pamphlet, issued clandestinely and bearing no name of a publisher or printer, was obtained in Teheran in December 1972 by Philip Salzman, professor of Anthropology at McGill University, Montreal. The author is grateful to Professor Salzman for making it available.

15. Ibid., p. 18.

16. For a description of Baluch links with the Arabs in the mid-sixties, see "Arab Support for Baluchistan," *Foreign Report* (London, Economist Newspaper Limited), 14 February 1973, p. 5.

17. Sepehr Zabih, *The Communist Movement in Iran* (Berkeley: University of California Press, 1966), pp. 180–183.

18. "Political Program of the Democratic Party of Baluchistan," in Mahmoud Panahiyan, *Farhang Gughraphia-e-Milli Baluchistan Iran* [Culture and Geography of the Baluch Nation in Iran] (Baghdad: 1971), pp. 8, 11, 15–19. This program was ratified at the first and only conference of the Democratic party of Baluchistan (Iranian), 20–23 February 1972, according to K. B. Nizamani.

19. *Baluchistan: Introduction and Liberation Struggle,* p. 17.

20. Kianuri's interview in *Nepszabadsag* (Budapest) was reported in *Foreign Broadcast Information Service Daily Report (Iran),* 22 January 1980, pp. 12–13.

21. Brian Spooner, "Religion and Society Today: An Anthropological Perspective," in *Iran Faces the Seventies,* ed. E. Yar-Shater (New York: Praeger, 1971). See also Spooner, "Political and Religous Leadership in Persian Baluchistan," p. 446–448; and Philip C. Salzman, "Islam and Authority in Tribal Iran: A Comparative Comment," *Muslim World* (Hartford Seminary Foundation) 1975, no. 3, pp. 186–192.

22. Interview in *Ayandegan* (Teheran), 22 July 1979, trans. in *Review of Iranian Political Economy and History* 4, no. 1 (1980): 75.

23. See "Baluchi Movement Congratulates Revolution," *Foreign Broadcast Information Service Daily Report (Iran)*, 12 February 1979, p. R-32; and "Khomeini Sends Envoy to Sistan-Baluchistan," *FBIS Daily Report (Iran)*, 2 April 1979, p. R-13.

24. "Sunni Leader in Baluchistan," *FBIS Daily Report (Iran)* 28 March 1979, p. R-6.

25. *Review of Iranian Political Economy and History* 4, no. 1 (1980): 75–77.

26. *Makran* 1, no. 1 (Teheran, 1979): 2.

27. Ibid., p. 1.

28. "America Mesr Iraq Arabistan va Ordon Barai Ejade Eghteshash va Tajzeye Iran de Tavafuq Rasedand" [America, Egypt, Iraq, Arabistan, and Saudi Arabia Have Reached Agreement for Creating Disturbances and Dividing Up Iran), *Kayhan* (Teheran), 29 January 1981. See also Radio Teheran commentary in Arabic, reported in *FBIS Daily Report (Iran)* 2 February 1981, p. I-16.

29. Najib Al-Rayyes, "Balushistan: Thawrah Tabhath An Sha'ir" [Baluchistan: A Revolution in Search of a Poet], *Al-Mostakbal* [The Future] (Paris), 29 September 1979, p. 15.

30. "Tahridan Ala Urubat Balushistan" [Calling for the Arabization of Baluchistan], *Al-Mostakbal*, 2 February 1980, p. 10.

31. Ibid., p. 12.

32. Ma'n Shana al-Ajli Al-Hakkami, *Balushistan Diyal Al-Arab* [Baluchistan: Land of the Arabs] (Bahrain: 1979), p. 7.

33. Ibid., p. 35.

34. Sally Quinn, "The Arabs in London: The Merchant," *Washington Post*, 18 July 1977.

Chapter Seven

1. "Draft Program of Action of the Communist Party of India," *International Press Correspondence*, 18 December 1930, cited in "The Communist Party of India," U. S. Office of Strategic Services, Research and Analysis Branch, Report no. 2681 (August 1945).

2. G. Adhikari, *Pakistan and Indian National Unity*, (Bombay: People's Publishing House, 1944), p. 8. See a discussion of the Congress-Communist debate over this issue in Selig S. Harrison, *India: The Most Dangerous Decades* (Princeton: Princeton University Press, 1960), pp. 150–156.

3. Memorandum of the Communist party of India to the British Cabinet Mission, mimeographed, (15 April 1946). See related sources cited in Harrison, *India*, p. 154.

4. Gene D. Overstreet and Marshall Windmiller, *Communism in India* (Berkeley: University of California Press, 1958), p. 81.

5. "Questions and Answers: Nationalities and the Right of Secession," *Crossroads* (New Delhi), 6 September 1953, p. 10.

6. Yuri V. Gankovsky, *Narody Pakistane: Etnicheskaia Istoriia* [The Peoples of Pakistan: An Ethnic History] (Moscow: Nauka Publishing House, 1964), p. 225. An English edition was brought out by the same publisher in 1971.)

7. Ibid., p. 208.

8. M. G. Pikulin, *Beludzhei: Istoriia i Ekonimiia* [The Baluch: History and Economy] (Moscow: Nauka Publishing House, 1959).

9. M. G. Pikulin, "K Voprosy o Natsional'noi Konsolidatsii Beludzhei Pakistanskogo Beludzhanistana" [On the Question of the National Consolidation of the Baluch of Pakistan], *Izvestiia Akademii Nauk UzSSR* [News of the Academy of Sciences of the Uzbek SSR], 1960, no. 4, p. 20.

10. Yuri V. Gankovsky, *Natsional'nyi Vopros i Natsional'nye Dvizheniia v Pakistane* [The National Question and National Movements in Pakistan] (1967; reprint ed., Moscow: Nauka Publishing House, 1977), pp. 206, 250.

11. Beknazar Ibragimov, *Beludzhei Pakistane* [The Baluch of Pakistan] (Moscow: Nauka Publishing House, 1973), p. 4.

12. Ibid., p. 94.

13. Ibid., p. 210.

14. M. S. Lazarev, "K Natsional'noi Situatsii na Sovremennom Vostoke" [On the National Situation in the Contemporary Orient] in *Natsional'nye Problemy Sovremennogo Vostoka* [National Problems in the Contemporary Orient] (Moscow: Institute of Oriental Studies, 1977), p. 50.

15. "Pakistan's So-Called Left," *People's Front* (London), February 1979, p. 3.

16. Aijaz Ahmed, "The National Question in Baluchistan," in *Focus on Baluchistan and the Pushtun Question,* ed. Feroz Ahmad (Lahore: People's Publishing House, 1975), pp. 30–31. The article first appeared in *Pakistan Forum* (June 1973).

17. "Strategy Document: Struggle for Independent National Democracy in Pakistan," mimeographed (1 May 1976), pp. 44–45.

18. " 'Free' Elections in Afghanistan," *People's Front,* April 1980, p. 1.

19. David Housego, "Baluchis Bitter At Army Occupation," *Financial Times* (London), 5 February 1980.

20. Han Xu, "Peaceful Coexistence in the Asia-Pacific Region," in *Day after Tomorrow in the Pacific Region, 1981* (New York: Worldview Magazine and the Asia Society, 1981), p. 27.

21. Interview with the author.

22. *People's Front* first advocated independence in April 1979 (see "Our Aim: National Freedom," 19 April 1979, p. 1).

23. Inayatullah Baloch, "Afghanistan-Pashtunistan-Baluchistan," *Aussen Politik* 3 (English ed.; Hamburg, 1980): 291–292.

24. Eden Naby, "The Iranian Frontier Nationalities: The Kurds, the Assyrians, the Baluchis, and the Turkmens," in *Soviet Asian Ethnic Frontiers,* ed. William O. McCagg, Jr., and Brian D. Silver (New York: Pergamon, 1979), p. 105.

25. "For the Oppressed Peoples of Afghanistan," Program of the People's Democratic party of Afghanistan, *Khalq* (Kabul), 11 April 1966.

26. *Basic Lines of Revolutionary Duties of the Government of the Democratic Republic of Afghanistan,* Broadcast by Prime Minister Nur Mohammed Taraki (Kabul: Democratic Republic of Afghanistan, 9 May 1978), p. 33.

27. Ibid., p. 34.

28. "H. Amin's Address to Charmang and Bajaur People," *Kabul Times,* 5 August 1979.

29. "H. Amin: This Is a Revolution Which Handed Power From One Strata to the Other," *Kabul Times,* 21 August 1979.

30. "Spongers, Oppressors Have No Power Now in Afghanistan," *Kabul Times,* 20 September 1979.

31. "Babrak Karmal Greets Afghan Nation," *Kabul New Times,* 1 January 1980.
32. "An Honest Leader: Press Conference," *Kabul New Times,* 8 January 1980.
33. "Unbreakable Links with Our Brothers," *Kabul New Times,* 17 January 1980.
34. "U. S. Arming Pakistan," *Kabul New Times,* 20 February 1980.

Chapter Eight

1. Robert G. Wirsing, "South Asia: The Baluch Frontier Tribes of Pakistan," in *Protection of Ethnic Minorities: Comparative Perspectives,* ed. Robert G. Wirsing (New York: Pergamon, forthcoming), p. 25.
2. In the Supreme Court of Pakistan (Rawalpindi), *Constitutional Petition No. One-R of 1977,* Begum Nusrat Bhutto v. Chief of Army Staff, etc., p., 18. See also pp. 33, 47, 104. See also In the Supreme Court of Pakistan, *Criminal Appeal No. 11 of 1978,* The State v. Zulfiqar Ali Bhutto, pp. 23–28.
3. Selig S. Harrison, *India: The Most Dangerous Decades* (Princeton: Princeton University Press, 1960).

Chapter Nine

1. Alex Beam, "Polisario War in the Sahara," *Nation,* 21 January 1978, p. 43. See also "Shifting Sands," *Time,* 3 September 1979, p. 31.
2. Shahid Javed Burki, *Pakistan under Bhutto* (New York: St. Martin's, 1980), Table 5.1, p. 94.
3. See chapter two, note 2.
4. Robert G. Wirsing, "South Asia: The Baluch Frontier Tribes of Pakistan," in *Protection of Ethnic Minorities: Comparative Perspectives,* ed. Robert G. Wirsing (New York: Pergamon, forthcoming), p. 18.
5. "Baluchistan," mimeographed (A Note issued by the Information Ministry of the Pakistan Government, 2 May 1980), pp. 3–4. See also *The New Face of Baluchistan* (Islamabad: Pakistan Publications, May 1980).
6. Letter to Harrison from Khalid Ali, Press Counselor, Embassy of Pakistan (Washington, DC), 2 February 1981, citing Article 160 of the Pakistani constitution.
7. Letter to Harrison from Khalid Ali, 19 December 1980, citing a notification in the *Gazette of Pakistan,* 9 June 1975. See also Lukin Robinson, "Equalization and the Price of Oil," *Canadian Forum* (Ottawa), October 1980.
8. Mir Khuda Bux Bijarani Marri Baloch, *Searchlights on Baloches and Balochistan* (Karachi: Royal Book Co., 1974), pp. 269–271.
9. "Production of Barytes in Baluchistan," *Jabal,* November 1977, p. 3.
10. "Baluchistan ki Mulazemataun se Baluchaun ki Mahrumi" [The Baluch Are Deprived of Jobs in Baluchistan], *Nedae Baluchistan* 1, no. 1 (London, 1980): 1. See also "Baluchistan: Turbulent Fragment," *Time,* 15 January 1979, p. 33.
11. "Baluchistan," (Information Ministry), p. 11.
12. Stephen Philip Cohen, "Security Decision-Making in Pakistan," (Report

prepared for the Office of External Research, U.S. Department of State, September 1980), p. 37.

13. "A Note on the Resource Development Corporation's Saindak Porphyry Copper Deposits, Chagai District, Baluchistan" (U.S. Embassy, Rawalpindi, 1978). See also "Riches on a Troubled Border," *Far Eastern Economic Review*, 21 March 1980, p. 86.

14. *White Paper on Baluchistan*, (Rawalpindi: Government of Pakistan, 19 October 1974), p. 31.

15. "Baluchistan" (Information Ministry), p. 10.

16. *Achievements of the People's Government, 1972–76: Baluchistan* (Islamabad: Ministry of Information and Broadcasting, 1976), pp. 6–7.

17. *White Paper on Baluchistan*, p. 33. See also "Pledges Made in 1970 Fulfilled," *Pakistan Times* (Karachi), 25 January 1977.

18. "Baluchistan" (Information Ministry), p. 5.

19. "Imperialism, Oil and the Baluchistan Revolution," *Jabal*, July 1977, p. 6.

20. Charles C. Yahr, "The Economic Development Potential of the Baluchistan States of Pakistan" (Ph.D. diss., University of Illinois, 1956), pp. 201–202.

21. "Mineral Development," *Dawn* (Karachi), 9 January 1978, p. 6. See also "Search for Mineral Wealth On," *Pakistan Affairs* (Pakistan Embassy, Washington, DC), 10 April 1978, p. 3.

22. "Abundant Promise in New Oil and Gas Finds," *Financial Times* (London), 11 August 1978, Pakistan Supplement, pp. 13–14.

23. "Oil Prospecting Soon," *Pakistan Times*, 3 November 1977.

24. "Golden Triangle Seen," *Dawn*, 22 December 1976.

25. Letter to Harrison from J. C. Van Wagner, Resident Manager, Amoco Far East Exploration Company (Singapore), 26 July 1978. Mr. Van Wagner served as Amoco's resident manager in Pakistan from 1973 to 1977.

26. "Imperialism, Oil and the Baluchistan Revolution," p. 7.

27. Mir Ahmed Yar Khan Baluch, *Inside Baluchistan* (Karachi: Royal Book Co. 1975), p. 42.

28. "Imperialism, Oil and the Baluchistan Revolution," p. 5.

29. Societa Generale per Progettazioni, Consulenze e Partecipazioni (Italconsult), "Economic and Social Development Plan for the Southeastern Region" (Project 37, Buildings Materials Research, Rome, May 1962), esp. pp. 3, 6, 9, 17, 28, 219.

30. M. B. Pithawalla, *The Problem of Baluchistan: Development and Conservation of Water Resources, Soils and Natural Vegetation* (Karachi: Ministry of Economic Affairs, 1952), esp. pp. 17, 48, 55, 90.

31. Mir Khuda Bux Bijarani Marri Baloch, *Searchlight on Baloches*, p. 303.

32. The Baluch settlers in East Asia are discussed in Walter T. Brown, "A Pre-Colonial History of Bagamoyo (Tanzania)" (Ph.D. diss., Boston University, 1971), pp. 256–266.

33. Mir Ahmed Yar Khan Baluch, *Inside Baluchistan*, p. 207.

34. Sardar Mohammed Khan Baluch, *History of the Baluch Race and Baluchistan*, rev. ed. (Quetta: Gosha-e-Adab, 1977), Prologue; and Mir Khuda Bux Bijarani Marri Baloch, *Searchlight on Baloches*, pp. 15–24.

35. Interview with Chief Minister G. M. Barozai of Baluchistan province, 3 February 1977. Data relating to the 1972 census was provided by the Information Ministry, Government of Pakistan.

36. *Census of Pakistan*, vol. 3, *West Pakistan, Tables and Report, Population, 1961* (Karachi: Ministry of Home and Kashmir Affairs), Statement 7-B.
37. For example, Mir Khuda Bux Bijarani Marri Baloch, *Searchlight on Baloches*, p. 16.
38. Frederik Barth, "Ethnic Processes on the Pathan-Baluch Boundary," in *Indo-Iranica*, ed. G. Renard (Wiesbaden: Harrassowitz, 1964).
39. Selig S. Harrison, "After the Afghan Coup: Nightmare in Baluchistan," *Foreign Policy* 32 (1978): 153.
40. Letter to Harrison, 20 January 1981.
41. Sardar Mohammed Khan Baluch, *History of the Bâluch Race*, pp. 124–127.
42. Mir Ahmed Yar Khan Baluch, *Inside Baluchistan*, pp. 66, 71.
43. Gul Khan Nasir, *Tarikh-e-Baluchistan* [History of Baluchistan] (Quetta: Quami Ghar, 1952), p. 112.
44. Mir Khuda Bux Bijarani Marri Baloch, *Searchlight on Baloches*, p. 239.
45. Ibid., p. 110.
46. Mir Gul Khan Nasir, *Tarikh-e-Baluchistan* [History of Baluchistan] (Quetta: Qaumi Ghar, 1952), p. 11.
47. Feroz Ahmad, *Focus on Baluchistan and Pushtoon Question* (Lahore: People's Publishing House, 1975), p. 16.
48. Warren W. Swidler, "Technology and Social Structure in Baluchistan, West Pakistan" (Ph.D. diss., Columbia University, 1968), p. 29.
49. Nina Bailey Swidler, "Brahui Political Organization and the National State," in *Pakistan's Western Borderlands*, ed. Ainslie T. Embree (Durham, NC: Carolina Academy Press, 1977), p. 112. See also Nina Bailey Swidler, "The Political Structure of a Tribal Federation: The Brahui of Baluchistan" (Ph.D. diss., Columbia University, 1969), p. 29.
50. Mir Khuda Bux Bijarani Marri Baloch, *Searchlight on Baloches*, pp. 110, 226.
51. Murray B. Emeneau, *Brahui and Dravidian Comparative Grammar* (Berkeley and Los Angeles: University of California Press, 1962), and "Linguistic Desiderata in Baluchistan," in *Indo-Iranica*, ed. G. Renard (Wiesbaden: Harrassowitz, 1964), pp. 73–77.
52. Alvin Moore, Jr., "Publishing in Pushto, Baluchi, Brahui, and Other Minor Languages of Pakistan, Part 3," *South Asia: Library Notes and Queries* (Chicago: South Asia Reference Center, University of Chicago Library, June 1980), p. 3.
53. M.A.R. Barker and Aqil Khan Mengal, *A Course in Baluchi*, vol. 2 (Montreal: Institute of Islamic Studies, McGill University, 1969), p. 7.
54. J. H. Elfenbein, *The Baluchi Language: A Dialectology with Text*, Royal Asiatic Society Monographs, vol. 27, (London, 1966), pp. 3, 10.
55. Barker and Mengal, *A Course in Baluchi*, p. 8. However, Baluchi publications continually carry complaints that Radio Karachi, Radio Quetta, and Radio Teheran do not use Baluchi often enough. For example, see "Baluchi Zaben Se Imtiazi Suluk Kun?" [Why Is There Discrimination against the Baluchi Language?], *Baluchi Dunya* [Baluch World] (Karachi), December 1971, p. 33–34.
56. M. Longworth Dames, *Popular Poetry of the Baloches*, vol. 2 (London: Royal Asiatic Society, 1907), p. 201. Barker and Mengal in *A Course in Baluchi*, p. 1, describe the Baluchi alphabet. The author is indebted to Richard N. Frye for a clarification of the relationship between Baluchi and the Arabic alphabet.

57. For example, see "A Plea for the Use of the Roman Script," *Baluchi Dunya*, November 1971, p. 14; and A. S. Sorbazi, "Baluch Ka Rasm Ul Khat Kia Ho" [What Script Should Be Used for Baluchi?], *Baluchi Dunya*, January 1973. See also *Jabal*, May-June 1978, p. 3.

58. See letters from advocates of the Roman script in *Labzank* [Treasure of Language], June 1977, pp. 78–79.

59. See chapter two, note 2.

60. Stephen Pastner, "A Nudge from the Hand of God," *Natural History*, March 1978, pp. 32–34. See also Pastner, "Power and Pirs among the Pakistani Baluch," *Journal of Asian and African Studies* 13, nos. 3–4 (1978): 231–243; and Stephen and Carroll McC. Pastner, "Secular and Sacred Leadership among the Pakistani Baluch" (Paper prepared for a U.S. Department of State Conference on Baluchistan, 10 March 1980). For an account of alleged Pakistani government efforts to exploit differences between Zikris and other Baluch, see "Baluchistan Main Fir Qa Warana Fasadat Karane Key Sazish" [Conspiracy to Instigate Sectarian Riots in Baluchistan], *Pajjar*, May-June 1978, p. 3.

61. For an analysis of this climate two years before the secession of Bangladesh, see Selig S. Harrison, "East Pakistanis Resent Army Takeover," a two-part series from Dacca, *Washington Post*, 30 March and 1 April 1969.

62. Cited in Zulfiqar Ali Bhutto, "Pakistan Builds Anew," *Foreign Affairs* 51, no. 3 (1973): 545. See also Mohammed Iqbal's 1930 proposal for a "loose federation of all India" in Sir Reginald Coupland, *India: A Restatement* (London: Oxford University Press, 1945), p. 189.

Chapter Ten

1. For example, see Richard Pipes, "Soviet Global Strategy," *Commentary*, April 1980, pp. 31–39; and Sol W. Sanders, "Moscow's Next Target in Its March Southward," *Business Week*, 21 January 1980, p. 51.

2. Herbert E. Meyer in "Why We Should Worry about the Soviet Energy Crunch," *Fortune*, 25 February 1980, pp. 82–88, presents the view that the Soviet bloc will have a growing energy shortage.

3. See Kennan's testimony on 27 February 1980 in *U.S. Security Interests and Policies in Southwest Asia*, Hearings before the Committee on Foreign Relations, U.S. Senate, 96th Cong., 2nd sess., pp. 87–120.

4. Selig S. Harrison, "Dateline Afghanistan: Exit Through Finland?" *Foreign Policy* 41 (1980-81): 163–187.

5. Marshall Goldman in "Is There a Russian Energy Crisis?" *Atlantic*, September 1980, pp. 55–64, disputes projections of a Soviet-bloc energy shortage.

6. Edward N. Luttwak in "After Afghanistan, What?" *Commentary*, April 1980, pp. 43–44, argues that its low population density makes Baluchistan more advantageous as a Soviet invasion route than a route farther west originating from bases in the Caucasus. But he concludes that an airborne attack on the oil fields would be more likely than a land invasion. See also Vernon V. Aspaturian, "Moscow's Afghan Gamble," *New Leader*, 28 January 1980, pp. 7–13; and David Lynn Price, "Moscow and the Persian Gulf," *Problems of Communism*, March-April 1979.

7. "Deng: A Third World War Is Inevitable," *Washington Post*, 1 September 1980.

8. Harrison, "Dateline Afghanistan," pp. 180-181.

9. For a perceptive account of the Nixon-Kissinger policy toward India and Pakistan, see William J. Barnds, "India, Pakistan and American Realpolitik," *Christianity and Crisis,* 12 June 1972. See also Joseph Alsop, "U.S. Role in South Asia," *Washington Post,* 14 January 1972.

10. Transcript of a Press Conference by U.S. Secretary of Defense Harold Brown (Beijing: 9 January 1980), p. 1.

11. *Congress Bulletin* (New Delhi), All-India Congress Committee, 10 July 1947.

Index

Afghanistan: and Baluch guerrillas, 39, 50, 51, 81; as buffer state to British Indian empire, 19; Communist movement in, 80, 81, 82, 142–148; Durand line, 19, 143, 144, 146; Greater, 143; and Kalat revolt, 26; and Liberation Front, 80–83; Parcham regime, 82; Soviet occupation, 1, 51, 59, 121, 137, 195, 196, 203; U.S. and, 199. *See also* Baluch, Afghan; Soviet Union

Agriculture, Baluchistan, 8, 9

Ahmad, Feroz, 144–45

Ahmadzai tribe, 15

Ahmed, Aijaz, 135

Ahmed Shah, 105

Al-Hakkami, Ma'n Shana al-Ajli, 121–23, 124

Al-Khalifa dynasty, 123

Al-Mohammed, Sheikh Mohammed Bin Hassan, 123, 124, 125, 140

Al-Rayyes, Riyad Najib, 121

American Smelting and Refining Company (ASARCO), 166, 170

Amin, Hafizullah, 87, 140, 195; on Greater Afghanistan, 143–45; Soviet removal of, 146

Amoco, petroleum operations in Baluchistan, 172–73

Amouzegar, Jamshid, and economic development of Iranian Baluchistan, 99–100, 167

Anjuman-e-Ittehad-e-Baluchistan. *See* Organization for the Unity of Baluchistan

Arabian Sea, 1, 2, 195

Arabs: and independent Baluchistan, 106–07, 121–22, 125

Arafat, Yasser, 106, 120

Arya, Khalidad, 117

ASARCO. *See* American Smelting and Refining Company

Awami League, 88

Awami Tehriq. *See* People's League

Ayub Khan, 27; imposition of One Unit plan, 43, 45; and Khair Bux Marri, 45, 46; and Muslim League, 153

Bahrain sheikhdom, 123, 125

Bajpai, Shankar, 43

Bakhsh, Shah, 107, 112, 177

Bakhtiar, Shahpour, 199

Baloch, Inayatullah, 24, 26n, 141

Baluch, Hamid, 87

Baluch, Khair Jan, 74, 75, 81; Communist associations, 138; guerrilla activity, 86

Baluch, Mohammed Khan, 17, 183

Baluch, Rahim Bux, 86

Baluch: cultural heritage, 11–12; early efforts at political unification, 12, 15–19; origins, 10–11

Baluch, Afghan, 82; number of, 178; Pushtuns versus, 89, 142–47, 158, 180–82

Baluch, Iranian: different views on independence, 111–12; employment discrimination against, 103; expanded educational facilities, 101–03; gerrymandering to reduce political force of, 96; migration of, 96; military control over, 94–95; number of, 177; oil boom effect on, 100–01; tribal differences in reaction to Shah, 110; and U.S., 119–20

Baluch, Pakistani: employment discrimination against, 164; fight for regional autonomy, 3; number of, 177–78; politicization, 4; Pushtuns